# wolf
# nation

# wolf
# nation

## THE LIFE, DEATH, AND RETURN
## OF WILD AMERICAN WOLVES

brenda peterson

A Merloyd Lawrence Book
DA CAPO PRESS

FOR THE WOLF AND THE WILD—

ALWAYS IN OUR WORLD

# CONTENTS

# PROLOGUE: THE BIG, GOOD WOLF

When I was growing up in the Sierra Nevada in a small US Forest Service cabin, wild animals lived alongside us. Even though there hadn't been wild wolves hunting in our California forest for almost a hundred years, their spirits still haunted their native woods. I listened to every yip-yip of a coyote to see if that sharp, staccato song would be answered by the soaring, plaintive howl of a returning wolf.

In the vast Plumas National Forest, I grew up on the sweet, lean meat of the game my father often brought home to feed his family. Predator-prey relationships shaped our wildlife management and hunting culture. I learned to love what was wild and would never belong to me, what was not a pet or daily companion but wary, hidden away, untouchable. I loved most what was not tamed or domesticated. I learned about the wolves' power, their generosity, their fiercely tender protection of those in their care. I wanted to grow up to be a wild wolf.

I hoped that one day a wolf might return to my birth forest, perhaps even in my lifetime. That hope was finally fulfilled in 2012 when a lone wolf, OR7—called Journey—returned to the Plumas Forest to become the first wolf in California since 1924. Journey reclaimed his rightful habitat after leaving his original family and traveling over twelve hundred miles alone. His story has helped to grow public acceptance and even celebration of the wild wolf in America. Such stories need to be told to balance our unnatural history of prejudice against wolves, for our American character is reflected in the history of how we treat wolves.

Wolves are both the most misunderstood and maligned of animals and at the same time among the most majestic and mysterious of all our fellow creatures. We still hunt them, and they hunt us by haunting our imaginations. Science alone will not restore them to their rightful habitat. We need new stories of the wolf-human bond, a new history that embraces wolves not as enemies but as mirrors, allies, and good neighbors.

*Wolf Nation* is a narrative of restoration science often trumped by political shenanigans, of generational prejudice yielding to new ways of living with wild wolves. Here are stories of wolves followed as passionately as rock stars, wolves as tragic heroes and picaresque, even playful characters, trying to endure against great odds. Although they are fascinating research subjects, they are also individuals with names, histories, family trees, and emerging generations. *Wolf Nation* is their story, as well as my own, and that of the people who devote their lives to wolf recovery.

The story of wild wolves in America is a chronicle of war and love, a history of hatred and redemption. Why do we need wild wolves? Because they help us heal our natural world, because humans and wolves have always belonged together. We are top predators, partners, fellow survivors.

*Brenda Peterson*
Seattle, Washington
2017

*Wolves enliven the northern mountains, forests, and tundra like no other creature, helping to enrich our stay on the planet simply by their presence as other highly advanced societies in our midst.*

—Gordon Haber, "Wolf Family Values"

# part one

# WHAT WE ALMOST LOST

# 1. AN HISTORIC RAGE

A bumper sticker on a battered Montana pick-up shows a sketch of a wolf and exhorts, "Smoke a Pack a Day." A mustached man with a wide-brimmed cowboy hat holds up a protest sign: "Wolves are Illegal Immigrants." A huge brightly colored billboard in Eastern Washington with paintings of elk, deer, cattle, dogs, and a smiling little girl on a swing asks, "The Wolf— Who's Next on the Menu?" An Idaho Anti-Wolf Coalition leader clad in camouflage gear warns that "wolves are terrorists on the order of Osama bin Laden."

Search the Internet for "war against the wolf," and there are photo galleries of grinning bounty hunters, "wolfers," proudly posing on a porch in front of a rack of twenty wolf skins hanging down from metal hooks. Surrounding one live wolf roped around the neck, there are five men on horseback, ready to ride off in all directions—and tear the wolf to pieces. In another photo an entire family of black wolves lie in a snowy meadow, a bloody circle. Most revealing of all is an image of a gang of hunters with rifles and white KKK-style masks over their faces as they triumphantly drape a dead wolf in a huge American flag.

Why is there still such fury against an animal that has been hunted almost to extinction in this country? The historic rage against sharing control of prey and territory has its roots in both European and American history—and in the hunting culture that still dominates every wildlife policy.

To the early European settlers the wild wolf—like the mysterious and vast wilderness itself—was not a precious partner of the New

3

World to be preserved. Along with native peoples, wolves were another impediment to western expansion—enemies to be subdued and excluded. Chickasaw author Linda Hogan writes eloquently about her people's traditionally balanced relationship with predators: "From the men's cave comes the howling of wolves. I think that these are the songs of lives struggling against extinction, even translated through human voices, they are here inside the earth, inside the human body, the captive, contained animals."

Early American colonies continued the Old World persecution of wolves. To Europeans the wolf was the enemy, like the Big Bad Wolf tales told in the seventeenth-century French court, a metaphor for predatory men who might prey upon aristocratic daughters. Wolves are the villains in "The Three Little Pigs," Russia's "Peter and the Wolf," and in many Grimm and Aesop's fairy tales. Sadly these associations and myths were not left behind in Old Europe.

European settlers rarely fenced in their sheep or cows; livestock wandered about, easy prey for wolves and other predators. In the 1630s Massachusetts Bay and Virginia instituted wolf bounties, and many other colonies followed suit. In a gesture of dominion over both nature and Native Americans, Virginia demanded that local tribes kill a yearly wolf quota and turn in the hides as tribute.

In his groundbreaking anthology *War Against the Wolf: America's Campaign to Exterminate the Wolf*, Yellowstone wolf researcher Rick McIntyre chronicles this history of hatred and decimation. "What the colonists tried to do in their local area—the extermination of all wolves—became the policy of our emerging nation. Destruction of predators became a heritage passed on for generation after generation."

McIntyre points out that humans haven't always felt so threatened and hostile to wolves. Early hunter-gatherer cultures coexisted with wolves in what one wolf biologist, Ed Bangs, now calls "brothers in the hunt." An NPR story, "Who Let the Dogs In? We Did, About 30,000 Years Ago," notes that "there may have been a faithful Fido walking with a human before the end of the last Ice Age (and before agriculture)."

Researchers have for centuries assumed that today's gray wolf was the genetic ancestor of the modern dog. But genetic studies reported in the 2015 *Scientific American* article "From Wolf to Dog" reveal the surprising news that "an extinct type of wolf gave rise to the dog before the agricultural revolution began around 12,000 years ago." That means the current-day gray wolf is a "sister taxa, descended from an unknown ancestor that has since gone extinct." The article documents studies of dogs and wolves, where both species are bottle fed, hand raised, and trained to obey simple commands. The conclusion: "Despite having lived and worked with the scientists for seven years, the wolves retained an independence of mind and behavior that is most un-doglike." Even raised by people, wolves "lack such respect for human authority."

So *Canis lupus*, the wild wolf, evolved independently from our domesticated dogs, and this independence is perhaps what triggers our intolerance, even outrage. One definition of the word "wild" is "self-willed." Wolves are certainly self-willed and do not obey our commands, even if we raise them by hand. A dog respects our authority, our "*No!*," and, even on the hunt, must stop short of a canine instinct to kill: a well-trained hunting dog will wait for the hunter to retrieve a fox or pheasant for himself. *Canis lupus'* willfulness has worked against their survival.

As our nomadic ancestors settled into agriculture, hunter-gatherers no longer had to wander in far-ranging packs to feed their families. We could, as the Bible seemed to ordain, "be fruitful and multiply" into growing and settled populations. After depleting the Old World of wild animals like wolves and destroying old-growth forests, the European settlers migrated to a New World and simply repeated their profligate and unsustainable use of the natural world. Bountiful game, like the vast Great Plains bison, was hunted almost to extinction as settlers expanded their range. When the bison disappeared, the wolf "brothers in the hunt" had much less prey. They were forced out of the wilderness and closer to our farms and ranches. Wolves had little regard for our fences. They were out of our control and therefore rivals to be destroyed, just like any animal or peoples who got in the way of Manifest Destiny.

McIntyre tells the story of visiting an Alaskan Inupiat village called Shaktoolik along the Bering Strait in 1993 to talk about predators with tribal high school students. When he showed them

historic slides of thousands of wolves killed by strychnine poisoning, the Native students were shocked and troubled. This was a
tribe in which hunting was a way of life. But Inupiat hunters were
accustomed to killing wolves only if they attacked local reindeer
herds.

One of the teenage boys asked McIntyre, "Why did they want to
kill off *all* the wolves?"

McIntyre realized that the Native boy was unaware of the massive government wolf extermination programs in the lower forty-
eight states. "The concept of attempting to destroy all the members of a wildlife species was completely alien to them," he writes.
The boy walked away shaking his head in dissatisfaction. "None of
it related to the reality of his world, a Native American world of
traditions, ethics, and morals that set limits on what humanity can
do to fellow forms of life."

In the nineteenth century European settlers claimed huge
swaths of government-given free land—*if* they agreed to farm it.
Farmers and wealthy ranchers, "stockmen," were given priority
in government policies on private and public lands. In *The Great
American Wolf* Bruce Hampton writes that in 1906, "the U.S. Forest
Service acquiesced to the stockowners and enlisted the help of the
Bureau of Biological Survey to clear cattle ranges of gray wolves. In
other words, the Bureau became a wolf-extermination unit."

A 1907 Department of Agriculture bulletin echoes this wolf-
control zeal as it addresses "the best methods for destroying these
pests," citing wolf predation on cattle ranges and loss of game on
forest lands. The goal of the bulletin was "to put in the hands of
every hunter, trapper, forest ranger, and ranchman directions
for trapping, poisoning, and hunting wolves and finding the dens
of the young. . . . Prime wolf skins are worth from $4 to $6 each,
enough to induce trappers and enterprising ranch boys to make an
effort to secure them."

One of the most efficient ways to destroy wolves was "denning,"
or killing the pups while still in the den. One pup would be saved
and chained to a tree to call the parents and wolf pack for help.
Then the government trappers would gun down the entire family. When the trappers used poisoned carcasses to bait wolves, the

collateral damage included bears, ravens, foxes, and eagles who fed on what the wolves left behind. The bounty hunts and government wolf-eradication programs that began in the nineteenth century continued until as late as 1965, offering $20 to $50 per wolf. Today the historic reluctance to share our habitat with other top predators is still very much alive.

Even in a twenty-first century of enlightened science, with recognition of the balancing roles that predators play in our ecosystems, this prejudice thrives. When I grew up in a national forest there was no concept of the forest as wild and complex, an interconnected biosphere, complete in itself, without serving our human needs. The mandate for forest and wildlife managers was "multiple use," with an emphasis on human utility. And many in the hunting culture I was raised in viewed wolves as "pests" or competition or sometimes just trophies.

I GREW UP WITH HUNTERS. They fed me. Like wolves, they also kept the deer and elk populations from overgrazing the high meadows so the forests and streams were healthier. And hunters told hilarious stories around the campfire while we devoured their barbequed bounty. I still have deep respect for skilled hunters who have a keen knowledge of nature, who can track, patiently wait, and sustainably hunt for their family, like my father. He taught us that wild animals like deer and elk died so that we might live. And of this sacrifice we must be mindful.

"Think about how hard it was to hunt this supper and who you're eating," my father would say. Or, as we munched on sausage cookies made from moose meat or venison, "Nothing wasted."

We used *all* parts of the animal, so that a big elk might also be ground into stew meat or sliced into thin salami. The elk head and horns went on the wall to watch us more earnestly than any babysitter. Every Christmas Eve we made our own moccasins for the New Year out of whatever Father had tanned. In my childhood forest we recognized ourselves as intricately linked to the food chain and the fate of the forest. We knew, for example, that a forest fire meant that at the end of the line we'd suffer too. We'd have buck stew instead of venison steak, and the meat would be stringy, withered tasting. Because in the animal kingdom, as it seemed with humans, only the lean and shrewd survived losing their forests.

Unlike my family, wolf packs have not survived losing their forests. When I was born, wild wolves were nearly all eradicated in America's lower forty-eight states. After the relentless, systematic, and successful official extermination of wolves in the United States, only a few hundred of the original 2 million wolves still survived, mostly in the upper Midwest and Alaska.

The hunter bias is still reflected in today's many states' agencies outdated names—Fish and Game Boards instead of Fish and Wildlife Service. The US Forest Service falls under the authority of the Department of Agriculture—as if our public lands and wilderness areas are only for livestock, and wildlife exists as our private game preserve. Or as if our forests are simply tree farms for timber.

In America's wildlife agencies predator control often falls within the same governmental department as wildlife protection, creating a clear conflict of interest. For example, Wildlife Services, an often under-the-radar agency, still kills millions of wild animals every year, though it was once part of the Fish and Wildlife Service charged with the exact opposite mandate: enforcing the Endangered Species Act. On its website Wildlife Services' official mission is "to resolve wildlife conflicts to allow people and wildlife to coexist." But the reality is devastating: a 2013 *New York Times* editorial called for a congressional investigation of Wildlife Services, pointing out, "since 2000, some two million dead animals. Coyotes, beavers, mountain lions, black bears and innumerable birds." The article concludes, "The agency's real mission? To make life safer for livestock and game species. . . . Wildlife Services' lethal damage is broad and secretive."

More recently the USDA reported that Wildlife Services had "killed at least 3.2 million wild animals in 2015 alone—many of which were large predators. 1,681,283 of that total were animals native to the United States." Coyotes (69,905) were widely targeted, but also 384 gray wolves, 284 cougars, 480 black bears, 731 bobcats, 3,045 foxes, 20,334 prairie dogs, 21,557 beavers, and even 17 domestic dogs. Birds took the greatest hit, with hundreds of thousands of starlings, red-winged blackbirds, and cowbirds—species that travel with livestock—all killed in this one year by Wildlife Services. This is especially bad news for the 47 million bird watchers in the United States, about 20 percent of the population. Contrast this agency's "take" with the fact that Americans who view and value wildlife is increasing: Fish and Wildlife Services in 2011 reported 71.9 million wildlife watchers, including 13.7 million hunters (4.3 percent of the 318.9 million Americans) and 33.1 million anglers. In the United States hunters are mostly male and 94 percent are white, 3 percent African American, and 0.5 percent Asian.

"Wildlife Services is one of the most opaque and least accountable agencies," protested Oregon congressman Peter DeFazio. "They are a world unto themselves. And that's a world we are not allowed to see into."

The tab that taxpayers paid for in 2014 for Wildlife Services to destroy all those wild animals was $1 billion. An award-winning investigative documentary, Exposed, by Brooks Fahy of predatordefense.org blows the whistle on this "barbaric, wasteful, and misnamed agency within the USDA and exposes the government's secret war on wildlife on the taxpayer's dime." The film interviews former Wildlife Services trappers who have the courage to protest the carnage they were being asked to commit and keep secret.

One former Wildlife Services trapper explained that the Wyoming Department of Agriculture was using poisons that had been banned since the 1970s to sell to predator control boards and ranchers. In a troubling echo of this revelation, a former special agent for US Fish and Wildlife Law Enforcement, Doug McKenna, said of his investigations, "It always seemed the words 'eagles, coyotes, and wolves' led us to poisons, and led us to Wildlife Services."

In a particularly harrowing story from the film, Rex Shaddox, a former Wildlife Services trapper who participated in the Wyoming sting operation that helped expose some of his agency's animal abuse, narrates the turning point that led him to blow the whistle on Wildlife Services. He talks about the agency's disregard for posting any poison notices, even along trails, leaving poisons exposed for "tree huggers and environmentalists to come in, take pictures, and mess with our units." This is not only dangerous for animals but also for people, who might stumble on the M44 cyanide poison ejectors. If triggered, the poison can lead to permanent brain damage and paralysis in all species.

These often-hidden toxins also poisoned, maimed, and killed people's pets. When domestic dogs were found dead, Shaddox says, the Wildlife Services officials were ordered to "get rid of the dog's collars, bury the dogs, and never report their deaths—that was standard practice. So that's what we did."

Everything changed for Shaddox one morning when he was ordered to report to the city dump in Uvalde, Texas City. There he found other Wildlife Services trappers, his district supervisor, and the Animal Control officer from Uvalde. There was also a truckload of domestic dogs who were to be used to test the sodium cyanide pills often used to eradicate wolves. The pills were expired and supposed to be buried as toxic waste. Though it is illegal for the Wildlife Services to use sodium cyanide on domestic dogs, the Wildlife Services supervisor held down the dogs, and one at a time, force-fed them sodium cyanide pills.

"Within seconds," Shaddox recalls, "the dogs would start whining, dropping down in their hind quarters, hemorrhaging from their nose and mouth, eyes rolling back . . . in a lot of pain." Then the Wildlife Services supervisor would pop open the nitrate antidote under the dog's nose to revive the dogs and bring them back to life. That same dog would again be forcibly dosed with the sodium cyanide capsule, go through the same horrible pain, and finally be kicked in the side and rolled off into the garbage of the city dump. "And the dogs just lay down there," Shaddox finished with a shake of his head, "hollering and whining until they died."

Shaddox got into a heated argument with his supervisor over the treatment of those dogs at the city dump. Shortly after his protests Shaddox quit Wildlife Services.

"Predator management in the U.S. primarily means flying helicopters, setting cyanide ejectors, hiding traps, and using ambush and sniper tactics to slay animals," writes federal and university researcher John A. Shivik in his book, *Predator Paradox: Ending the War with Wolves, Bears, Cougars, and Coyotes.* "Modern predator management looks like a war not only with predators, but one with nature itself." Since the 1914 federal appropriation, the war against wildlife, says Shivik, is "the longest war carried out by the U.S. government. . . . The death toll is tremendous: 84,584 wolves, coyotes, bears, and lions were terminated by the Department of Agriculture and Wildlife Services, in 2011 alone. At 365, wolf deaths amounted to exactly one wolf a day for the year."

*One wolf killed every day for a year.* And in that same year the federal government delisted wolves, declaring them fully recovered and sustainable populations. This 2011 federal delisting was not based on sound science. In fact, many of the government's own scientists in a peer-reviewed 2014 panel protested this political decision; in an independent and unanimous decision the panel determined that the delisting proposal was premature and not based on "the best available science."

Since federal delisting and the return of wolf management to the states, over four thousand wolves have been legally killed in five states. In Idaho, which is America's ground zero for state-sanctioned wolf hunting, the battle has been particularly bloody. And yet even among government-hired wolf trappers there are those who, like the Wildlife Services whistle-blowers, promote a more ecological and humane approach to wolf management.

Wolf trapper turned wolf advocate Carter Niemeyer, author of the lively memoir *Wolfer*, tells the story of leaving Wildlife Services after twenty-six years in 1999 to move to Idaho and work on wolf recovery issues for the US Fish and Wildlife Service. Instead of killing wolves, Niemeyer began teaching biologists how to shoot running wolves with tranquilizer darts from helicopters for relocation. Often caught in the crossfire between antiwolf ranchers and prowolf advocates, Niemeyer's decades of trapping and studying wolves lent him more informed knowledge of wild wolves than most in this polarized debate.

"From the moment I arrived in Idaho," writes Niemeyer, "I felt like I was in a war zone." Wolf advocates were suspicious and insistent that he, a former trapper, wouldn't be fair minded when it came to wolf recovery. On the other side, Niemeyer documents how the antiwolfers, with their "Idaho wolf hysteria" and "tedious, fire-and-brimstone style" scare tactics, triggered a statewide Anti-Wolf Coalition that had great influence on local politicians. Its founder, Ron Gillet, and his antiwolf "brand of evangelism" tried and failed to gather enough signatures for a ballot initiative to "get rid of wolves once and for all."

After trying to talk with such furious ranchers, Niemeyer concluded, "It wasn't the wolves that made me more inclined to be on the wolf's side, it was the macho swagger of people like this." It reminded Niemeyer of the wildlife official, Ed Bangs, who commented about our wolf battles: "Wolves have nothing to do with reality." Meaning that our human passion plays around wolf politics are not grounded in the reality of wolves in the wild. Hate them as terrorists or love them as noble remnants of the wild, the real lives of wolves are often overlooked in our own struggles for dominion and management. "My principal goal in Idaho was wolf recovery," Neimeyer says, "but I was having the most trouble with people."

In Idaho, as in many states, the antiwolf voices were a minority, but they received a disproportionately high degree of media, political, and governmental attention. Niemeyer could "count on one hand the number of folks with real wolf trouble." Because "most wolf issues happened on public land," Niemeyer argues, for ranchers "losing livestock to predators should be an accepted cost of doing business." But Niemeyer concludes, "Maybe livestock interests are too powerful. Or maybe most people are just unaware that the system still operates as though the West is still being settled."

A 2011 report from the Department of Agriculture documented that only 0.2 percent of all livestock losses that year were due to wolf predation. Compare this with over 50 percent of livestock deaths due to calving/birthing complications, respiratory issues, and bad weather. Yet the livestock industry still demands the US government manage wildlife to benefit humans over any ecological needs. Contrary to statements by the hunting lobby, new research shows that wolves are *not* really fierce competition for game animals. In the Bitterroot Valley researchers discovered that wolves are responsible for only 5 percent of elk predation.

Other ranchers and hunters are taking a different tack when it comes to wolves. Their voices are often unheard, but they are powerful. In a special 2014 "Hunter's Edition," the National Wolf Watcher Coalition published many letters advocating for wolf recovery. Hunters across the country explained why they oppose wolf hunting. A hunting family from Pennsylvania submitted a photo of their sign, "REAL HUNTERS DON'T KILL WOLVES." They write, "Hunting wolves is wrong and immoral . . . my family was brought up to respect life." In New York a hunter believes, "the wolf encounter provides a connection. Such reverence both ways is impossible to experience in a predatory relationship."

Slowly the earlier centuries' prejudices, regressive fears, and single-minded priorities are evolving as new generations consider the whole ecosystem. This means awareness not just of what humans need but also what the forest, the streams, and the wildlife need to thrive. Those who most successfully balance the ecosystem are not human hunters; they are the self-regulating predators, like wolves. With a single breeding pair in each family, wolves self-limit their offspring according to available food prey and climate conditions. Humans might consider modeling their appetites on that of the wild wolf. Wolves do not destroy an entire species or habitat as a way to defend their territory—there are limits to their hunting. Wolf parents pass down hunting skills to their young, comparable to what the Boone and Crockett Club, one of America's oldest conservation organizations, calls "Fair Chase Ethics." These guidelines advise their hunter members to "Behave in a way that will bring no dishonor to either the hunter, the hunted, or the environment." Instead of more generations of wolf control, we need more self-control.

As my hunter friends often remind me, "The wolf is a *good* hunter."

## 2. "WHO SPEAKS FOR WOLF?"

There have always been voices raised in defense of wolves. In their creation stories Native Americans included the wolf and regarded them as First People. Clans named themselves after wolves and modeled this great hunter's skills. They were Wolf People. The Lakota tribe recognized the Buffalo Wolf, *Sung'manitu-tanka Oyate*, or "Wolf Nation," as another sovereign tribe that also claimed the Great Plains as its territory. That wolf bond was strong in the famous Lakota Sioux warrior, Crazy Horse.

Many indigenous peoples—from the Hopi and Navajos of the Southwest to the southern Cherokee and Seminole, the northeast Penobscot and Algonquian to the midwestern Chippewa tribes—believed the wolf was a spiritual guide and ally. Here in the Far Northwest both the Makah and Quileute tribes with whom I've worked regard wolves as their own ancestors. The late Quileute elder Fred Woodruff explained his tribe's creation story: "Our tribe originally descended from wolves. We believe they are our relatives and are always welcome in our land."

On one of my visits to the Quileute reservation in LaPush, Washington, Woodruff's daughter, a talented Native artist, presented me with a wolf carving painted with the stylized red and black totemic design. Her father said thoughtfully, "We learned from the wolf how to survive and how to be more human. How to honor our elders, to protect and provide for our families—and we learned from wolves the loyalty you need to really belong to a tribe."

Native peoples talk much about "soul loss," and shamans often don wolf skins to do their spiritual work from within the animal as they cross over into other worlds. There they call upon the wolf's power to summon back lost or sick souls. The Shoshone tribe believes that the wolf can heal a person who is suffering soul loss. Wolf medicine confers the power to call our wandering spirits back. We risk soul and habitat loss when we destroy the wild wolf, who helps us bring our shared lands back to life.

One of the most far-sighted and still ecologically true tales of the wild wolf is a traditional Oneida story passed down for thousands of years to the late Paula Underwood (Turtle Woman Singing). She translated the original oral history into English as "Who Speaks for Wolf?" This story is an example of the growing body of ancient and modern Native Science being reclaimed by researchers. The Oneida tribe, part of the Iroquois Confederacy, live in New York and Pennsylvania. The story begins with a familiar dilemma: "LONG AGO / Our people grew in number so that where we were / was no longer enough."

The tribe considered moving to a new territory. As in any council decision there was always someone "to whom Wolf was brother." This tribal member "was so much Wolf's brother / that he would sing their song to them / and they would answer him." Taking the point of view of the animals who shared their homes, the tribe could then always heed the Iroquois admonition that we must make all our decisions with the next seven generations in mind. Those future generations include wolves.

But in this choice about where to move their tribe, they did not consider the Wolf Brother's counsel; instead, the tribe decided to resettle their tribe deep into wolf territory. The council said, "Surely the Wolf could make way for us / as we sometimes make way for Wolf." The tribe's new home was generous, with thriving forests, abundant game, and clear, cool streams. But as they settled, the hunters noticed that the squirrels and deer they'd hunted and slung up into trees for safekeeping would soon disappear. At first the hunters figured that sharing some of their hunt with wolves was "an appropriate exchange." But this feeding of the wild wolves was not a good idea because "WE HAD NO WISH TO TAME WOLF." To live in this land some of the hunters had to be always on alert to drive away the wolves, "AND WOLF WAS SOON HIS OLD UNTAMED SELF."

But this combative way of living with wolves did not please the people. The tribe now considered a task that would require much energy over many years: "to hunt down this Wolf People / until they were no more."

THEY SAW, TOO
That such a task would change the People:
they would become Wolf Killers
A People who took life only to sustain their own
Would become a People who took life
rather than move a little
IT DID NOT SEEM TO THEM
THAT THEY WANTED TO BECOME SUCH A PEOPLE

The Oneida tribe concluded that they had learned an unforgettable lesson: "Wolf Brother's vision / was sharper than our own." Never again would the tribe's elders make a decision based on only their human needs. "LET US NOW LEARN TO CONSIDER WOLF!" So for thousands of years this wisdom was passed down:

TELL ME NOW MY BROTHERS
tell me now my sisters
WHO SPEAKS FOR WOLF?

BY 1856 most wolves had been hunted into extinction in the eastern states. Henry David Thoreau, author of *On Walden Pond*, was one of the very first writers to speak on behalf of the vanquished wolves, "the nobler animals." Writing in his journal, Thoreau mourned living in a natural world stripped of top predators that was "tamed, and, as it were emasculated," so now "lamentably incomplete." He asked, "Is it not a maimed and imperfect nature that I am conversant with? As if I were to study a tribe of Indians that had lost all its warriors. I listen to a concert in which so many parts are wanting."

Ironically, some of the most poignant stories of wolves in the nineteenth and twentieth centuries, when wolves were being so relentlessly killed, are told by wolf hunters. British-born Ernest Thompson Seton, who later founded the Boy Scouts of America, worked as a young man trapping wolves. His best-selling animal stories were often devoted to wolves, especially the true story of "Lobo: The King of Currumpaw," published in 1898 in *Wild Animals I Have Known*. The love story of the magnificent "King" Lobo and his delicate mate, Blanca, has all the catharsis—the pity and fear— of Aristotle's *Poetics*. And for Seton, Lobo and Blanca's tale would change his life's course.

In the vast, sometimes hallucinatory New Mexican mesas, Lobo, Blanca, and their small family pack reigned—and were recognized—as fierce wolf royalty. Powerful, cunning, passionately loyal, Lobo led his family on a five-year triumph over cattlemen, sometimes killing a cow a day. Such were Lobo's sensory skills at scenting metal hidden along well-traveled trails or strychnine-laced bait—even when soaked in cow's blood—that no one could trap him. With each inventive trap set for him, Lobo learned how to deny the trap its lethal due. Lobo shrugged off the thousand-dollar wolf bounty on his head the way a wolf's dense wolf fur easily sheds falling snow.

This majestic wolf scorned all his hunters. When Seton took his turn at trapping Lobo, all his inventions—scentless poisons, metal-fanged traps buried deep in the heads of dead cows—again failed. For months Seton hunted. But then Seton had an insight into Lobo's true character, not just his habits or wily behaviors. Intuiting Lobo's fatal flaw, Seton finally asked: What did Lobo care most about in this world? His family and, most of all, his mate, Blanca. How to manipulate that devotion into self-destruction?

Seton noted that King Lobo allowed his mate to run in front of him, taking the lead. If any of the other formidable wolves in his family dared try this insurrection, Lobo would have disciplined them with a bared fang, one terrifyingly guttural growl, or even a blood fight. But Blanca often trotted ahead of her mate, taking the forward position that is always the riskiest in any pack. Like a soldier walking ahead of his patrol scouting for danger, Blanca's authority was no challenge to Lobo. (It would be another century before wolf researchers recognized that a female could also be the leader of a family or share alpha status alongside her mate.) Seton figured that Blanca or one of the smaller wolves might be tricked by a trap buried inside a cow's head. So he placed this type of beef-head trap away from the poisoned bait that Lobo immediately focused on as fatal. As always, Lobo led his family away from the danger. But Blanca, a smaller wolf, strayed to investigate the cow's head, as most wolves do any dead animal. Slam! The trap snapped shut on her delicate legs.

Seton found Blanca galloping in terror, the fifty-pound trap dragging her down, the horns of the beef head snagging on branches and brambles as she ran. Finally she fell, exhausted and vulnerable. "She was the handsomest wolf I had ever seen," Seton wrote. Her blazing white fur, eyes wide, teeth gnashing, now useless. Blanca let out a desperate howl. Lobo answered. Then Blanca turned to face her destroyers. Old-West style, Seton and several cowboys on horseback circled the beautiful white wolf. Each tossed a lasso over her neck. Seton writes, "Then followed the inevitable tragedy, the idea of which I shrank from afterward more than at the time."

Straining their horses, the men rode off fast in different directions, their ropes strangling Blanca "until blood burst from her mouth, her eyes glazed, her limbs stiffened and then fell limp." A brutal, torturous way to die—for any animal or human. Why not a simple gunshot to the heart? As the wolf hunters rode home, they were followed by the haunting howls of Lobo for his lost mate. Lobo's cries were "sadder than I could possibly have believed," Seton writes. "Even the stolid cowboys noticed it, and they said they had 'never heard a wolf carry on like that before.'"

Lobo's end after losing Blanca was inevitable. His grief, Seton notes, made him "reckless." Love was Lobo's tragic flaw. Did the mighty wolf simply allow himself to get trapped in 4 of the 150 steel traps that Seton set out for him? As Seton dragged Blanca's body along the trail, the intimate scent of his beloved mate drew and doomed Lobo. The loyal wolf followed the scent of his lost mate, just as he'd followed Blanca when she ran strong and confident far ahead of him. Soon the several traps sprung and seized Lobo. For two days and nights he struggled against those piercing metal teeth, just as deadly as any other challenger he'd ever faced.

By the time Seton found him Lobo had lost his struggle with the wolf traps. Exhausted and blood-soaked, Lobo summoned up enough energy and pride to lunge at his hunter. "Each trap was a dead drag of over three hundred pounds," Seton wrote, "and in their relentless fourfold grasp, with great steel jaws on every foot, and the heavy logs and chains all entangled together, he was absolutely powerless." Lobo let out one plaintive howl for his family. No answer.

Instead of strangling Lobo with his lasso as he had Blanca or shooting him, Seton lashed the wolf's jaws shut and removed the traps. Then he heaved him onto his horse and slowly brought his massive trophy into town. There he tried to feed Lobo and observe him more closely. The wild wolf refused to meet Seton's eyes or acknowledge his existence—or power. Lobo gazed past anything human to the "great rolling mesas . . . his passing kingdom, where his famous band was now scattered." Lobo also refused food. Seton believed the wolf was dying of "a broken-heart." The next morning he discovered Lobo dead, "in his position of calm repose." Seton and a cowboy unchained Lobo and laid him beside Blanca. "There, you *would* come to her," the cowboy spoke to Lobo respectfully. "Now, you are together again."

Lobo's death profoundly changed Seton. Seton evolved from wolf killer to wolf champion. His books were read by millions and gave him a voice to protect wild animals. Seton helped create the first national parks in North America; as founder of Boy Scouts of America, he inspired generations to learn wilderness skills and respect nature and other animals. "Ever since Lobo," Seton writes, "my sincerest wish has been to impress upon people that each of our native wild creatures is in itself a precious heritage that we have no right to destroy or put beyond the reach of our children." Lobo's pelt is still on display in the Earnest Thompson Seton Memorial Library and Museum near Cimarron, New Mexico.

In his "Note to the Reader" in *Wild Animals I Have Known,* Seton sounds his lifelong note of remorse over Lobo's death: "The life of a wild animal *always has a tragic end.*" He hopes that readers still find "a moral as old as Scripture—we and the beast are kin." Certainly Lobo and Blanca's tragedy reminds us what researchers have finally documented in best-selling books such as bio-ethicist Marc Bekoff's *The Emotional Life of Animals*: animals have deeply emotional lives, complex family dramas, and stories that mirror our own. Those who observe wolves closely often comment on the drama both within wolf families and around their existence. Power struggles, devotion, fear, gratitude, self-sacrifice, generosity, betrayal—watch wolves in the wild and recognize how familiar their family dramas are to ours.

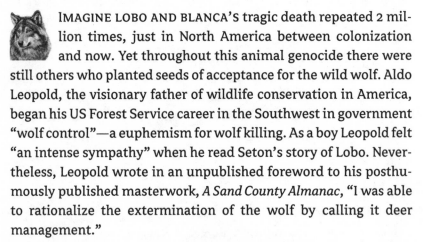 IMAGINE LOBO AND BLANCA'S tragic death repeated 2 million times, just in North America between colonization and now. Yet throughout this animal genocide there were still others who planted seeds of acceptance for the wild wolf. Aldo Leopold, the visionary father of wildlife conservation in America, began his US Forest Service career in the Southwest in government "wolf control"—a euphemism for wolf killing. As a boy Leopold felt "an intense sympathy" when he read Seton's story of Lobo. Nevertheless, Leopold wrote in an unpublished foreword to his posthumously published masterwork, *A Sand County Almanac*, "I was able to rationalize the extermination of the wolf by calling it deer management."

In 1909 young Leopold graduated from the Yale School of Forestry and landed a job with the US Forest Service in Arizona on the Apache National Forest. In those days the US Forest Service would kill any wolves within rifle range, and forest service employees managed national forests and public lands with "game production" most in mind.

In a 1915 editorial, "The Varmint Question," Leopold urged a "more satisfactory bounty law" against wolves and other top predators. He helped forge a powerful antiwolf alliance between the government's Biological Survey agency, cattlemen, hunters, and sportsmen that still exists today. So intense was the young Leopold's zeal to wipe out wolves that by 1920 he could proudly report in "The Game Situation in the Southwest" that in New Mexico they had officially reduced wolves from three hundred to just thirty. This extermination took only three years. Leopold concluded that the Biological Survey "is making splendid progress in eradication work. . . . It is going to take patience and money to catch the last wolf or lion in New Mexico. But the last one must be caught before the job can be fully successful."

Leopold's evolution from zealous wolf killer to astute wolf advocate is a great conversion story. An avid student of history as well as nature, Leopold well understood their intimate connection. An essay, "The Historical Sense of Being in the Writings of Aldo Leopold," notes "Leopold often touched on topics like history and wilderness that he felt had the potential to affect human character." Certainly Leopold's character was shaped both by his early years on the Mississippi River in what was then a fairly wild Burlington, Iowa, and by his early work as a predator-control agent with the US Forest Service.

Over the decades Leopold worked in and out of the US Forest Service. In 1922 he had the foresight to propose that New Mexico's Gila National Forest be designated a wilderness area. In 1935 Leopold left government service to become a professor of game management at University of Wisconsin. Leaving the US Forest Service for an academic career made it possible for Leopold to see beyond the government's antiwolf agenda of wildlife management. He would soon found the Wilderness Society.

It was a matriarchal wolf who startled Leopold into a new relationship with wildlife. In the unpublished foreword to *Sand County Almanac* Leopold reflected upon his younger self: "I was young then, and full of trigger-itch." Remorsefully he wrote, "my sin against the wolves caught up with me. . . . I had . . . played the role of accessory in an ecological murder."

Leopold's epiphany was vivid, heartbreaking. He poignantly recounts the moment in his signature essay, "Thinking Like a Mountain." Leopold imagines the wild wolf from the point of view of the mountain. Instead of asking what the cowman or the hunter believes about the wolf, Leopold wonders: What does the deer, the coyote, and the mountain perceive when the wolf howls her haunting song? Then he tells this story: One day Leopold and some friends are lunching on a high rim-rock, the jagged pastel perch that defines the Southwest. Below them they believe they see a deer paddling across the river. The animal emerges from the fast water, shakes herself dry on shore. Surprisingly she's a mother wolf, happily greeting her six grown pups.

Anyone who has ever witnessed a wolf parent play with their pups knows the fond abandon, the affectionate nuzzles, the faux fights and feints that one day will determine family structure, loyalty, and responsibility. Today video and visits to national parks or sanctuaries have given us the privilege of witnessing a wolf family romping together as if we—or the mountain—had never lost them.

But Leopold and his fellow hunters have "never heard of passing up a chance to kill a wolf." They take aim. The mountain echoes with the ricochet of their rifles. The family scatters, one pup dragging his leg and disappearing. The mother wolf, wounded, lays on the ground. Does she look up at the rim rock in shock at so many snipers? Or does she, like King Lobo and so many wolves before her, simply stare flatly in full knowledge of her fate? As the men scramble down to the riverbank perhaps she focuses on the solace of rushing water, the rustle nearby of any pups who might have survived her. What is left of her family may have howled out for each other. Or perhaps they hushed and kept a wary silence, as wolves always do when humans come near.

The wounded wolf looks up at Leopold as he leans over her to catch the "fierce green fire dying in her eyes." In that eye-to-eye with the wolf the man is changed forever. He recognizes "something new to me in those eyes—something known only to her and to the mountain." What does the mother wolf see in this young man's eyes at the moment of her death? The man will never again kill another of her kind. Her death will become legend—a rallying cry for those who work to save wolves for new generations.

Anyone who has sat vigil with the dying knows that in an instant—when the eyes fiercely focus, then fix, then extinguish their light—that last sight can last a lifetime. The old mother wolf's green eyes may have haunted Leopold for as long as he lived. She transmitted to him another way of seeing his and *her* world. After her death, when Leopold considered "the newly wolfless mountain" as "state after state extirpate its wolves," he realized the wild without wolves meant defoliation by "deer herd, dead of its own too-much." Leopold at last fathomed that "just as a deer herd lives in mortal fear of its wolves, so does a mountain live in mortal fear of its deer." When humans destroy wild wolves, it is because we "have not learned to think like a mountain. Hence we have dust-bowls, and rivers, washing the future into the sea." Like the deer, humans have not yet learned the lessons of our own "over-much." Left unchecked without predators like the wolf, the deer overgraze and basically eat themselves out of their habitat. The wild wolf is their balance—and ours.

Leopold's story of this dying wolf was later published only in 1949—the same year Leopold died. She lives on, just as does Leopold's "Thinking Like a Mountain." The "green fire" in the old wolf's eyes had transformed and tempered Leopold from antagonist to hero of what would come to be called "ecology." Or of what Leopold himself termed as "the land ethic." This new and more communal way of seeing the land and other animals possessed Leopold; his philosophy was "the end result of a life journey."

One of the most important lines Leopold ever wrote is this: "For one species to mourn the death of another is a new thing under the sun." We mourn those we know and love. As we tell and listen to more stories of wolves we have known—like Seton's King Lobo or Leopold's mother wolf—we recognize wolves as kin to us. Finally, we might even ponder the world from the wolf's perspective—to "see the world truly," as the Hopi Indians, First People's of the Southwest, have always taught.

GROWING UP in the Forest Service, I had witnessed first-hand the tensions between Aldo Leopold's legacy of ecology and the more utilitarian, pragmatic conservation of Gifford Pinchot. Leopold, Pinchot, and Sierra Club founder and author John Muir—these were the icons of nineteenth- and twentieth-century conservation. Leopold was Pinchot's pupil at his mentor's family-founded Yale Forest School. After Pinchot became the first chief of the US Forest Service, he hired his former pupil, and Leopold began his Forest Service tenure. Pinchot was passionate about conserving forests and natural resources for the future. Under his guidance and with help from his friend, President Theodore Roosevelt, millions of acres of wilderness were set aside for wilderness.

Controversy about how to best manage those national forests led to a split between mentor Pinchot and his protégé, Leopold. Pinchot was the progressive but "ever practical idealist" whose forest ethics focused on "Wise Use," or the "efficient, utilitarian-based management and development of the nation's public and private forestlands." In the 1930s Leopold began to reject Pinchot's environmental pragmatism in favor of his own belief that the land was alive and animals were part of a community that included *but did not just exist for* human use. These tensions were not only played out between Pinchot and Leopold but also between conservationists across the nation.

An article Pinchot published in 1908 compared North America to a family farm: "On the way in which we decide to handle this great possession hangs the welfare of those who come after us." I often heard forest service employees talking about managing the forests for "multiple use" or with "the twin virtues of beauty and utility" in mind. Think of Pinchot as *utility* and Leopold as *beauty*—there you have the tense balancing act between what are now called conservationists and environmentalists.

The environmental movement of the 1960s and 1970s marked a time of upheaval and change in our national forests. In 1978 my father was appointed chief of the US Forest Service and I had recently left my editorial job at the *New Yorker* magazine to live and work a ramshackle farm my mother had inherited near Boulder, Colorado. While working as fiction editor at *Rocky Mountain Magazine*, I also commuted to the Southwest, where I worked as a writer-in-residence at Arizona State University. It was in these vast deserts— where Seton and Leopold had their own *Canis lupus* encounters and epiphanies—that I often traveled deep into Native lands of the Hopi and Navajo.

One day I got lost on the Navajo reservation and wandered into a dilapidated trading post. I stumbled from the relentless sun into the trading post, looking for more water. Perhaps it was dehydration or sun stroke, but once inside the shack my head was throbbing painfully. The closer I came to one glass counter, the more intense the headache. I thought I might faint, and the world seemed to tilt. For balance I leaned against the glass case of inexpensive trinkets— earrings, bracelets with cheap turquoise chips, bead strands frayed and broken.

When I placed my hands on the cool glass I felt an almost gravitational pull. "Something's . . . here . . ." I stammered.

A Navajo woman in a purple velvet blouse and strands of silver wound around her neck and wrists walked over to the case. With some surprise, she studied me closely.

"Yes," she said after some time in her rich, low voice. "Something *is* here."

She reached under the shabby trinket tray and lifted up an astonishing necklace of spider-web turquoise, a huge 1921 silver dollar, delicate coral fish, dimes pounded into rounded beads, teeth carved of antler bones. It was a museum-quality medicine necklace. What was it doing buried under faded velvet and cheap trinkets in a trading post that seemed lost in time?

Holding the extraordinary necklace, the Navajo woman said simply, "It is awake."

I had a dim memory of someone once showing me animal teeth he'd found in the forest. "Are those . . . ?"

"Wolf teeth," the Navajo woman finished firmly. "Wolves used to live here with us." Sighing and with obvious regret, she held the necklace out to me. "It is wide awake again . . . you must take it."

I dared not touch the necklace she offered. I felt too young to be even in the presence of such sacred medicine. I didn't recognize it as a traditional Skin-walker necklace that Navajos used to ward off evil spirits, but I did sense its power. If I had known its frightening shape-shifter traditions and darkly authoritative magic, I might have turned and quickly fled that trading post.

"My father made this many years ago, " the woman explained. "To protect someone . . . but he never came back from the war. So my father told me, 'Hide this medicine, until someone recognizes it is here.'"

She reached out and laid the necklace in my hand. I fingered the impressive and still-sharp wolf fangs, darkened by age and decay, the roots deep.

"*Lobo*," the woman breathed.

I recognized the word: Mexican gray wolf, long hunted into extinction in the Southwest. Holding the necklace, I felt no sense of ownership or possession or that it belonged with me. I did not possess this Skin-walker wolf necklace. It possessed itself—and now me. At last my headache vanished. I felt clear-eyed and somehow steady, though still afraid of this beautiful and useful medicine necklace. What did it want with me?

"It has its own work to do," the woman stepped away, refusing to take the necklace from my outstretched hands. She added with a meaningful look. "Maybe you will need the protection."

# part two
# WOLF WARS

# 3. WOLF TEETH ON AN AIRPLANE WING

Arriving at the Anchorage airport for a 1993 Wolf Summit, I was startled by a towering stuffed polar bear, fangs forever frozen in greeting. The Alaska Board of Game had passed a plan that winter to return to aerial shooting of wolves—a practice that had been banned for years. This would reverse the Airborne Hunting Act of 1971 that prohibited any shooting or harassing an animal from aircraft. Alaska's Governor Walter Hickel proposed to exploit a loophole in the act to allow airborne hunting to "protect wildlife." His Board of Game had just voted to return to lethal wolf control that winter when the snow was deep so the wolves would easily be sighted and shot. However, the international outcry against this aerial wolf hunt prompted Governor Hickel to call media, wildlife managers, hunters, and wolf advocates to a February Wolf Summit in the hope of forestalling a threatened tourism boycott that would cost the state $85 million.

Hundreds of men in camouflage arrived at the airport as if dressed for hunting and winter kill, not a Wolf Summit. These men in bright orange-clad vests also donned wolf-skin hats, gloves, and pelts—trophies of their wolf hunts. In this snow-draped land of the midnight sunshine, the sun did not rise and set in any semblance of what I recognized as daytime and night. On the shuttle to Fairbanks I noticed that bullet holes riddled every road sign. We passed a bull moose roadkill being efficiently flensed by a passerby. The sight wasn't troubling, as I'd watched my father and his hunting buddies efficiently strip the skin off a deer. Yet as the days passed I noticed that everyone in Alaska seemed so well prepared to kill—expectant, even anticipatory. This culture of killing would overshadow the Wolf Summit.

After retiring from eight years as chief of the US Forest Service, my father would also be attending the summit in his new job as executive vice president of the International Association of Fish and Wildlife Agencies. In this position he often advocated before Congress for stronger wildlife preservation and habitat, stressing that "more than 90% of the funds that states have for wildlife comes directly from anglers and hunters, which means that less than 10% of state fish and wildlife agency funding is for the conservation of 86% of our nation's non-game wildlife species."

It is still a mystery to me why my father had invited me to accompany him at this raucous official showdown between hunters and environmentalists arguing over aerial wolf control. No doubt he invited me because of my article "Primal Howls—Wolves, Wild Women, and Wild Men—If That Wild Animal Dies Out, So Will the Wild in Humans," written as a commentary on Governor Hickel's proposed aerial wolf control and published in the *Seattle Times* that fall of 1992.

I was attending the Wolf Summit as a journalist, deeply troubled by the fact that Hickel had recently declared, "You can't just let nature run wild!" Alaska and Minnesota were the only states in America where wolves were not endangered, with the Alaska wolf population estimated at seven thousand. But Alaska's Board of Game was determined to resume aerial wolf hunting to increase caribou populations for hunters, both subsistence and sportsmen. Several of my friends, who were also hunters, fervently believed that wildlife managers should never again take up the practice of shooting radio-collared wolves from airplanes, nor should recreational hunters be licensed to hunt from helicopters, chasing wolves down until they were utterly exhausted, then land and shoot them—they did not see this as an ethical hunt.

At about that time *Women Who Run with the Wolves* by Clarissa Pinkola Estes was urging women not to be tame but to claim the wild in their inner lives. "The word *wild* here is not used in its modern pejorative sense," Pinkola Estes notes, "meaning out of control, but in its original sense, which means to live a natural life, one in which the *criatura*, creature, has innate integrity and healthy boundaries."

In my article I had pointed out that her book didn't go far enough to help the wolves as much as it did women. At a publishing convention I'd seen women proudly don the book's swag—baseball caps that proclaimed, "*Not* Tame!"—and was troubled that we were claiming the wolf only as an archetype, a story to tell ourselves, while taking no real action to help the real animal survive. This disconnect between our worship of the wild wolf and our lack of protection for them in our shared habitat has always disturbed me. If we reclaim the wild wolf in our collective psyche without taking action to preserve the actual wolf in our wilderness areas, we will miss an opportunity to mend the broken treaties between our species. It's another example of how we often use animals only for our own psychological needs.

 THE INTENSE COLD was not as deep as the frosty stares following us as we traipsed through the snow banks to the ice rink where the Wolf Summit was held. Picketers with red-splashed signs proclaimed, "Eco-Nazis Go Home!" and "Iraq—Want Some Wolves?" A man with an entire wolf pelt draped around his shoulders held a homemade poster: "Environmentalists Kiss My Alaskan Ass!" Boos and hisses were the soundtrack for those of us summit attendees plodding through the snow. There were a few cheers and opposing signs: "Wolf Hunt Is Bad Science" and "Dead Wolves Kill Tourism." But the majority of the protesters outside—and inside on the bleachers encircling the rink—were packed with antiwolf voices. Thundering boots on the bleachers completely drowned out anyone who spoke for the wolf.

"It's a circus, not a summit!" one of the Game Board members commented as we all took our assigned seats. The board member was a veterinarian, fervently in favor of wolf hunts.

There were 120 participating biologists, wildlife managers, and journalists attending this Summit—and 1,000 observers. Often I had to stomp my own hiking boots because the press tables were pitched directly *on* the ice rink, which was covered by a thin tarp. We joked that they'd put the press "on ice" in the hope we might leave off covering the summit to seek warmth for frozen feet.

The mood at the Wolf Summit was surly, the deck already stacked. A burly fellow dressed in a wolf-skin parka and buckskin pants told me that the state had already bought many more wolf traps. "This summit is just the governor's shill game . . . a publicity stunt for media folks like you who believe you have any say in what Alaskans want for Alaskans."

Every year Alaska's Department of Fish and Game oversaw the killing of one thousand wolves, most of it by legal trapping, hunting, and snares. Although more than 80 percent of Alaskans weren't licensed hunters and although wildlife viewers contributed one and a half times more to the state's economy than hunters and trappers, their voices are most often drowned out by antiwolf advocates. In 1993 66 percent of Alaskans were actually opposed to aerial shooting of wolves.

At the Wolf Summit catcalls and baritone boos from encircling bleachers of the ice rink rang louder than voices from Defenders of Wildlife, Greenpeace, the National Audubon Society, or Alaska Wildlife Alliance—those who spoke up for the value of the wolf in wilderness. Standing ovations and cheers rose up whenever anyone vilified the wolf as no more than "vermin" or "nuisance animals" or "rats in a dump." Hunters' groups had already applauded the Board of Game's controversial decision to return to aerial wolf hunts. The director of the Alaska Outdoor Council, Randy Smith, said that it would take too long to build up moose and caribou game populations if wolves weren't killed. "These animals are being managed for the benefit of man," he declared. "And that's the way it should be."

Enthusiastically echoing this hunter agenda, the director of the Alaska Division of Wildlife Conservation, David Kelleyhouse, told the *New York Times* that the state had already outfitted 25 wolves with radio collars, so aerial hunters could easily track and shoot as many as 475 other wolves from helicopters. Kellyhouse promised that this would be a significant boon for game hunters in reducing the wolf population by 80 percent. He predicted that aerial shooting would kill 300 to 400 wolves each year for the next five years. This wolf hunt would "create a wildlife spectacle on a par with the major migrations in East Africa." The spectacle he predicted was massive herds of caribou and moose, Dall sheep and grizzlies, all stampeding across or grazing along the Alaskan tundra—a hunter's paradise.

Every time a speaker, whether scientist or wolf advocate, presented any case against aerial wolf hunting, the bleachers erupted with boos and hisses. I glanced around the ice rink, feeling as skittish as a deer. These hunters were not what I was used to—those whose wry jokes, acceptance, and sharing their wild game nourished me. At the Wolf Summit it was a hunter's eye that considered the wolf—and that eye was trained on wolves as if through a rifle's scope.

There were a few hunters at the summit who actually spoke out against aerial wolf hunting. Local Fairbanks trapper Sean McGuire said he'd lived in the bush and witnessed the land-and-shoot hunters firsthand. "I've voted to stop them," he said. "They'd come in the spring, when the days were sixteen to eighteen hours long. I'd be working trap lines, and hunters in planes would be chasing the wolves until the pack dropped in exhaustion. Then the planes would land, and the guys would get out and blow the wolves away. I'm not opposed to hunting," he concluded. "But I am opposed to that."

On the Wolf Summit program there were only four women out of the thirty invited speakers. I counted that men outnumbered women by nine to one. Even at sporting events like football games the gender ratio would have been more balanced. There were a few more women at the press table but almost no female wildlife managers. A woman who worked for the state handed me a packet of clippings on recent studies on wolf predation in Alaska.

"Wolves are not the determining factor in stabilizing ungulate populations here," she said sotto voce. "Humans are. We have overfished, overhunted, and overkilled. The scary thing is that we really don't know what we're doing. Now we're trying to fix our dwindling game populations by killing other top predators like wolves."

This courageous woman would continue to send me clippings as I wrote my articles about the Wolf Summit. She raised important issues: the only reason wolves still existed in Alaska, she said, was their "inaccessibility." Once officials trapped and placed radio collars on wolves, that inaccessibility was removed. Collared and tracked, wolves were already being controlled and managed, even in the most remote wild areas.

Another speaker at the Wolf Summit who was troubled by radio collars already on wolves in many wilderness areas was wildlife biologist Renee Askins of the Wolf Fund. Often called the "Jane Goodall of wolves," Askins had been working for over a decade to reintroduce wild wolves to Yellowstone National Park.

Askins had the courage to call out Alaska on its "holocaust" against the wild wolf. "Here in Alaska," Askins declared, raising her voice above the considerable din, "the wolves are making their last stand." The bleachers exploded in furious protests as Askins added, "The wolf is a signal that, although embattled, wilderness still exists . . . it is vital to us all."

In a later interview for her book, *Shadow Mountain: A Memoir of Wolves, Wilderness, and a Woman,* Askins would question the continued use of telemetry collars on wolves in terms of our "addiction to controlling our environment. Once you start controlling something," she said, "you lose the gift of reciprocity."

Askins would show the same bravery while giving testimony before Congress three years later as she worked tirelessly to help return wild wolves to Yellowstone. She told the House Committee on Resources that emotions, not facts, had controlled the wolf debate. Wolf recovery was "fundamentally an expression of a culture in transition," she said. "The story of this conflict is the story of how we view ourselves in relation to animals, whether we can replace the assumption of 'dominion' that has been so destructive to us and the natural world with a worldview that recognizes that we live in a state of reciprocity with the birds and the beasts—that we are not only the product of nature but also part of it."

After her speech at the Wolf Summit I interviewed Askins out of sight, under the bleachers. Not quite hidden, we were still surrounded by the milling and outraged orange antiwolf crowd. I took notes as we talked but did not dare hold a tape recorder up to Askins.

In the chaos of the Wolf Summit I was fighting off real fear. I recalled the Defenders of Wildlife speaker telling a riotous crowd: "What makes the deer so fast? The wolf's tooth." I remembered that the deer's spine has evolved its delicate notches to exactly fit the wolf's fangs. Deer don't survive being knocked unconscious. As prey animals, they've learned how to die quickly.

"Ever feel like a prey animal?" I joked with Askins.

Askins glanced around and said softly, "Remember, these hunters are terrified of us—that's why they're so angry. We wolf advocates are a real threat to their way of life, their dominion."

Looking around the ice rink at the multitude of fur-clad men, I knew Askins was right. This was just one state, albeit a vast territory. But below us there was a lower-forty-eight intent on wolf recovery and on having their say on public lands.

"Maybe this summit is a last stand for hunters," I said.

This Alaskan Wolf Summit was a collision—a violent clash of cultures. Each side was in each other's crosshairs. I actually expected a gunshot to ring out when controversial Denali Park wolf researcher Dr. Gordon Haber took the podium. Haber's field work with wolves was extensive; he'd been studying wolves in Alaska since 1966. No one in Alaska had more field experience with wolves than Haber. He was an old-fashioned, live-in-the-field scientist who preferred direct experience with his study animal. A believer in hard data, he never anthropomorphized wolves; he simply knew them from decades of close observation. He followed the wolves by snowshoe, sometimes sitting in a blind, watching their complex social dynamics for days at a time. In his book, *Among Wolves*, one of the most riveting images is a black-and-white photo: the shadow of Haber's small bush plane hovers over the Toklat wolf family as they travel single-file through the snow. Over his forty-three-year career Haber studied generations of wolf families; his long-term research was vital for wolf recovery.

Haber's research would reveal that wolves play on the average of every thirty minutes. Their communication skills, like howling, are profound and practical. Haber documented that "wolf family social ties are unsurpassed, even among humans" and that "wolves have traveled hundreds of miles to return to their families . . . that each individual has its own personality, and their ability to express emotions becomes obvious after one watches the same individuals for even a short time." Monogamous, loyal to their families, wolves have many adaptive behaviors and traditions passed on through generations. Haber concluded that wolves "can be considered a culture."

The year before the Wolf Summit Haber had told *Alaska* magazine that a wolf was never just one animal but always an extended family "all acting as one to survive." He pointed out that most wolf biologists used a "superficial, numbers-based" view when figuring out a healthy wolf population. That was how they could justify killing 30 to 40 percent of the wolf population every year and expecting the wolves to thrive. Haber vehemently disagreed. "The problem is," he explained, "wolves have complex societies. It takes a long time, at least several generations, for a family group to reach its societal cruising speed."

What Haber understood in 1992 about the complexities of wolf families has since been repeatedly proven by other wolf biologists. But at the 1993 Wolf Summit Haber's data was dismissed. Haber often compared wolf groups to human families. He did not like the term "pack" because it was pejorative and a false caricature of the wolf as a vicious killing machine. The close parallels Haber drew between human and wolf families did not make him friends with state or federal wildlife officials. At the summit Haber met Friends of the Animals director Priscilla Feral, who funded some of his later wolf research. This association with an international animal rights group made Alaska wildlife managers suspicious that outsiders were controlling Haber. Haber was described as "brash, unconventional, and extremely confrontational." It's ironic that Haber was also called a "lone wolf" himself, as his long career was devoted to the close social family bonds in wolves.

Alaskan filmmaker Joel Bennet, who served over a decade on the Board of Game, was one of Gordon Haber's friends. He portrayed Haber as "dedicated. He doesn't let up." Bennet noted that Haber was tireless in his campaigns to protect the Denali wolves from trapping and hunting. The Game Board "knew he was a credible scientist who could show up at these conferences around the world and cause trouble for them."

Soon after the Wolf Summit Haber would cause huge international trouble for Alaska's Board of Game when he went into the field with an Anchorage newspaper photographer and reporter. They discovered several wolves trapped in snares the Department of Fish and Game had set out. One of the wolves had chewed off his own leg. State officials rarely showed graphic photographs of all the wolves killed or skinned. This video of the Department of Fish and Game employee's botched trapping of the wolf aired on national television and sparked such furor that Alaska quickly—and temporarily—suspended its wolf-control programs. A new democratic governor, Tony Knowles, would advocate for only nonlethal management of wolves.

When I met Gordon Haber at the Wolf Summit I was impressed with his no-nonsense approach to the wolf debate. What others perceived as a brusque manner I felt was due to his sense of urgency and frustration. He made several quips about the summit as the governor's publicity stunt before Alaska would probably revert to its wolf-hunting ways. Haber seemed both bemused and disgusted with the event. His weathered face showed his decades of living outdoors. His deep-set eyes, encircled by dark rings, grooves of concentration in his forehead, and his perpetual frown revealed the toll the endless wolf politics took on him. In typical impatient style, Haber told the *New York Times* that Alaska's decision to return to aerial wolf hunting was "bad biology all around, almost insulting from a scientific standpoint. They are making a very dumb mistake."

When he spoke at the Wolf Summit few of the state and even federal wildlife officials even considered Haber's research. Fewer still seemed to grasp their own bias toward protecting hunters at the cost of the rest of the public, let alone of a balanced ecology. Among wolf biologists Gordon Haber was definitely in the minority at the Wolf Summit and throughout his four decades of research. His fearless and single-minded persistence made him often seem as much a pest to Alaska wildlife officials as the wolves themselves. Not only did Haber show up at every Board of Game meeting; he also appeared at cocktail parties thrown by Alaska's most successful wolf hunter, a surgeon appropriately named Jack Frost. Calling himself a "mechanical hawk," Frost tracked wolves in his plane, relentlessly chasing them down until the wolves could barely walk. Then he would land and shoot them. It must have been chilling for Haber at Frost's parties to observe wolf pelts "hanging every three feet on bannisters" and wolf trophies "everywhere in Frost's house." But, ever the researcher, Haber's inside information about Jack Frost's aerial wolf hunts would help prove a case against the surgeon. In 1991 Frost finally pled guilty to illegal wolf hunting. Some of the most incriminating evidence were transcripts of Frost's radio transmissions from his plane.

"The damn thing jumped up and bit my wing," one of the transcripts recorded. A wolf that Frost had gunned down left his teeth marks on his airplane wing. "He wasn't completely dead," the transcript said. "We'll go back later."

Several times when Haber spoke at the Wolf Summit he was interrupted by men jumping up from the bleachers and swearing to shoot him. Someone even threatened an old-fashioned tar-and-feathering. Firmly, the gruff Haber continued his talk, barely a glance at the bleachers. With his graphs and charts he disproved the myth that wolves kill indiscriminately; instead, wolves were careful and subtle in their attacks on game animals, killing moose in only 5 percent of all hunts. That hardly made them a competitor for human hunters. Wolves did not kill more than they could eat. In winter wolves depended most on scavenging winter-killed animals, which made up three-fourths of their diet.

Haber was followed by the drone of wildlife officials, with their Orwellian doublespeak. No antiwolf speakers ever mentioned the word "kill"—the euphemisms were "lethal control," "sustainable yield," "harvesting the wolves," or "caribou calf crops." As I dutifully took notes, I felt dispirited. It struck me that when we talk about other animals, our language clearly shows our bias: if we celebrate wolves, we call them "noble" or "kindred" or "fellow creatures." If we want to eradicate them, we must reduce them to quantifiable farming terms like "harvest" or "crop."

Gordon Haber noted this reductive bias: "What leaves me shaking my head the most about all these predator control programs is the missing sense of wonder," he wrote. "Listening to biologists . . . I am always struck by how blandly and matter-of-factly they talk about killing wolves. They seem to think being 'objective' in ignoring items like behavior and sentience is the mark of a good wildlife scientist. How sad and revolting that professionals entrusted with the management of these fascinating, important creatures view them in such shallow ways. . . . We are the ultimate losers from all this wolf killing."

# 4. A TAXIDERMIST'S DREAM

After a day at the Wolf Summit my father invited me to join him and other wildlife officials at a Fairbanks bar. That night was a scene that has always stayed with me, and it reveals the hunting traditions in wildlife management that still dominate today. In the rustic bar I was surrounded by jovial wildlife officials—the same men who had fiercely taken the Wolf Summit podium to argue in favor of aerial wolf hunts. The camaraderie reminded me of my father's hunting buddies and my southern grandfather's dictum to all his grandsons: "I'll teach you to hunt, shoot—and vote the Republican ticket."

In the smoke-filled bar my father introduced me to the table of six men as simply his daughter. Without my press badge I could enjoy the banter among the guys as my father told one of his hunting stories, which I'd heard a hundred times. I was beginning to relax for the first time here in Alaska—and was also finally warm, parking myself nearest the robust fireplace. But soon the undercurrent of wolf-control conversation led to talk of how to convince the state and federal powers-that-be that renewed aerial wolf control was needed to assure higher populations of game for hunters. The Hunt Club atmosphere, the smoky backroom, the teasing cronyism and entitlement reminded me of a private game club where members played poker with other species. Wolves and other predators were always the top losers. After all, wolves didn't buy hunting licenses to fund Fish and Game Boards.

I forced myself to remain quiet, gazing up at a bar adorned with so many elk, moose, and caribou antlers that it looked like a taxidermist's dream workshop. But I found myself privately riffing on the word "game"—that our English language had named wildlife after a sport, a hunt. In our very words we'd clearly betrayed the bias that other animals were to be played with, won or lost.

One of the wildlife managers, outfitted for the Far North in a Filson plaid hunting jacket and Russian fox fur hat, frowned as the talk turned to wolf advocates. "They just don't get it," he sighed with exasperation. "Hunters are the wolves' best friends up here. We don't want to kill all the wolves, like ranchers down in the lower forty-eight. We want wolves here in Alaska."

"Yeah, without trapping and hunting regulations . . . oversight . . . wolves would be hunted illegally and poached into extinction," a man added as he raised his beer in a quick toast to the gathered guys. "Without management, there would be no wolves left at all in Alaska."

"Or elk or caribou or deer, for that matter," a slim man in down-bib overalls and an impressive red beard noted drily.

His words reminded me of a chilling fact about the first centuries of hunting in this country in Elizabeth Marshall Thompson's *Hidden Life of Deer*: "By the middle of the nineteenth century, remorseless, nationwide, year-round hunting had all but eliminated every kind of deer, from the moose in the North to the mule deer and the elk in the West to the whitetails in the East. Only the caribou remained, too far north to be available to most hunters." It was the game biologists and government officials—like those sitting at this Fairbanks bar table—who finally began to conserve and manage deer. "No other mammal in the world has been so heavily managed," Thomas concludes.

The problem now was that the managers' traditional bias toward hunters often inflated wolf population statistics and deflated game prey populations, as Gordon Haber had pointed out at the summit. These prejudicial stats justified bounty hunts, wiping out entire wolf families in the unproven hope for more game. Now the deer in many states were out of control, overgrazing.

When talk turned to caribou "crops" and wolf hunt "quotas," I tried to imagine a future in which this roundtable was evenly balanced by nonconsumptive wildlife voices. What might happen if top predators were actually managed for everyone and the environment, not just hunters? But like the Game Boards, very few other points of view were represented here. In fact, I'd just learned at this summit from an ex-Game Board member that in the 1990s Game Board appointees were required to hold a hunting license—a rule that obviously excluded nonhunters from finding a seat at the table on any wolf-control discussions.

At our bar table a trim, muscular man with a Jack London mustache now added with a shake of his head, "Those wolf people don't know wolves . . . not the real animals."

Another man nodded in agreement. "Wolves don't just cull the sick and elderly in a caribou herd," he said. "I've seen wolves kill an entire sheep herd, much more than they could eat. Wolves also kill just for sport."

"Like us," someone admitted. And everyone laughed and pounded the table so hard that it shuddered.

"You know, the way that Wolf Fund gal talks," remarked a hefty guy in a white wolf-skin cap, "you'd think she believed wolves had souls or something!" In the scoffing that followed I couldn't help but reach into my down parka for my Navajo wolf necklace. If I'd had the courage to speak up, if I didn't want to expose myself as a spy, I would have said, "Well, Eskimos and other Native Americans certainly believe animals have souls—and yet they still hunt them to survive. It's mutual respect."

But then I remembered how shocked I'd been during the summit when a Native Alaskan man, arriving by snowmobile, had received a standing ovation from the bleachers as he'd raised his fist and shouted, "Alaska for Alaskans! These wolves belong to us!"

Fingering the necklace beads like a rosary, I glanced up at the red EXIT sign near the pool tables and calculated how fleetly I could disappear, like a deer from a hunter's scope. Just the past winter I'd tried to give the wolf necklace for safekeeping to a Cherokee friend of mine who was a curator of Native American Art at the Smithsonian Institute.

"How did you come by this medicine?" she asked gravely.

I told her the story, and she listened attentively.

"Navajos are more ambivalent about wolves than your tribes in the Pacific Northwest," she explained. "Navajos believe there are real wolves who are good and part of nature. But there are also witches who disguise themselves as wolves." Now she did fix me with a sober expression. "You never know who you're dealing with. This wolf medicine necklace with its real teeth can protect someone from those Skin-walkers."

She carefully handed the wolf necklace back to my reluctant hands. Touching my shoulder as if in benediction or direction, she advised, "This wolf medicine has some work to do—and just maybe so do you."

Although I was silent in that Fairbanks bar surrounded by wildlife managers, I would not be silent when I reported on what I'd witnessed at the Wolf Summit. As just a daughter, a woman, I was not recognized here as a stakeholder in any discussion of wildlife. But I was a witness—a wolf in sheep's clothing.

On the final morning of the Wolf Summit there was a small earthquake in Fairbanks. The aftershocks made the ice rink often tremble beneath our frigid feet. I decided to brave the riotous but much warmer bleachers with some of my wolf-advocate friends rather than take my place at the press table.

"What we do here at this Wolf Summit isn't just about Alaska and its wolves. The whole world is watching us," one of the summit speakers concluded and the crowd quieted down. "In the end, in the future, it will not be all the programs we put into place as wildlife officials that determine the fate of wild wolves." He paused and adjusted his glasses. "What will determine how wolves and all wildlife in this country are managed is public perception."

This Wolf Summit prediction would prove true over the next decades as more humane and nonconsumptive voices would join the very public conversation about how to manage our shared wilderness and wildlife. As the US Humane Society recently noted, "Ultimately, the public will drag the wildlife departments along with them as they demand that the system change for the benefit of the non-hunting majority, and most importantly, for the animals themselves."

The very last afternoon of the Wolf Summit I took a field trip with a Far North friend of mine, Alaskan poet Peggy Shumaker, in her tiny but intrepid truck. She drove us through ice-rutted switchback roads way up into the expansive Brooks Mountain Range. The brief Alaskan sunlight had given way to a rather rugged-looking moon. According to the *Farmer's Almanac*, this fading New Year's moon was called a Wolf Moon. Below us, crossing a frozen valley, was a vast herd of caribou. I couldn't hear the hooves crunching in the deep snow below us, but I was awestruck by the pulsing, headlong movement. With my binoculars I could make out the blur below of their thick tan and buff fur, the syncopated stride of powerful legs. We felt a faint rumble as the elk herd trotted together in a slow-motion stampede. Their jagged, curved antlers, like bone antennae, were raised high as they scented the chill wind for wolves.

Were wolves also watching this slow wave of prey below us—the throbbing heat of fur and bodies so tightly packed together for protection? Perhaps a starving wolf family was poised nearby and calculating the risks of tackling any caribou straggler in such a huge herd. How much stamina to chase and take one down? Worth the risk of life and family?

"Amazing," I murmured. My breath haloed the air with a quick warmth.

"It's good to get up here," Peggy nodded with a faint smile, her face blister red and chapped with the cold. "You can see a lot farther." Her poem "Caribou" describes what she saw.

Hoof—
> one hoof
>> enters powder, sinks
>>> through fresh snow
>> touches,
>>> breaks
>>>> the light crust
>>>> pushing deeper

to hard pack. Haunch deep.
> Only then

can she
    move on.

The change we
    need so delicate
        so crucial

it might be
    silent, it might
        be this quiet
            step, breath

"We can see what the wolf sees," I said, regarding the herd below with narrowed eyes like a predator. Here in the Brooks Range it was the wolves who were aerial hunters.

Our own aerial view of the caribou throng was like that of a small bush plane—the kind Jack Frost had used in his illegal hunts when a wounded wolf leapt up and left teeth marks on his wing. Or like government planes that Fish and Game officials would employ to harass—then land and shoot wolves—for the next two decades. From this same perspective Gordon Haber had flown over the Denali wolf families—a guardian shadow. Wolves often recognized his bush plane, howling as Haber circled them, making his notes, taking endless photos. The wolves never ran away from Gordon Haber's plane. The year after the Wolf Summit Haber said in an interview that each time he flew over to study a wolf family, "I wondered if it would be the last time. I knew they would start disappearing right before my eyes."

WOLVES ARE STILL DISAPPEARING in Alaska. Republican governors in Alaska have escalated wolf hunting after Democratic governor Tony Knowles's two terms (1994–2002) had somewhat curtailed it. A brief ban on aerial wolf hunting voted in by a public initiative in 1996 was overridden by a Republican state legislature. Official and public aerial wolf control by wildlife officials returned under nine years of Republican governors determined to revamp the Game Board and increase lethal wolf control—even though 70 percent of Alaskans oppose it. Under Governor Sarah Palin wolves were shot from helicopters and wolf dens were gassed to kill pups, and in 2007 her office "offered 180 volunteer pilots and aerial hunters a $150 cash prize for turning in the legs of freshly killed wolves."

Over twelve hundred wolves were still killed each year in Alaska from bounty hunts, snares, and continued aerial shooting. This widespread and lethal wolf-control method continued, despite mounting evidence that such aerial gunning was *not* actually increasing caribou or game populations as predicted by wildlife managers. "The lack of accurate population estimates has led to over-harvest of wolves," one report concluded. "State wildlife managers have failed to provide adequate justification for their controversial programs." In the summer of 2016 the Obama administration's USFW banned aerial hunting of wolves on the 76 million acres of Alaska wildlife refuges—for the first time in decades "handing hunters, the National Rifle Association and the state's own Board of Game a huge defeat." But the new rule still allows wolf hunting in Alaska's sixteen wildlife refuges, just not the longtime "intensive predator management" of aerial hunts.

As of 2015 Alaska's wolves were classified as big game and as furbearers and open to trapping with snares and shooting by anyone with a license. In 2015 the Denali Park wolves—once so admired and protected by Gordon Haber—were now at a "historic low." Denali used to be one of the most likely places in the world to witness wolves in the wild, but in 2001 the Board of Game had removed a no-kill buffer around Denali Park, allowing for an average of four or five wolves killed along the boundary every year. Conservation biologist Richard Steiner points out that "most of the killing of Denali wolves is conducted by just one or two trappers or hunters for sport, not subsistence purposes." Denali tourism brings in $500 million yearly to Alaska, but the chances of seeing wolves in the park has dramatically decreased. In a 17,640-square-kilometer area of Denali National Park in 2015 there was the lowest-ever recorded density of wolves—just fifty-one wolves in thirteen packs. This is "the lowest number since wildlife biologists began counting them 30 years ago."

Depending upon the governor, the wolves have had short-term reprieves and long-term attacks. In 2014 state wildlife officials gunned down the entire radio-collared Lost Creek pack—eleven wolves killed in a single day, which wiped out twenty years of research. The National Park Service biologist who had studied the Lost Creek pack, John Burch, said about Alaska, "There's no negotiations anymore. They kill almost all the wolves they can find. These last two winters, they've pretty well gotten most of them."

In the summer of 2016 the watchdog group Public Employees for Environmental Responsibility (PEER) reported that "the state of Alaska has gunned down so many radio-collared wolves outside the Yukon-Charley Rivers National Park that the National Park Service has dropped a 23-year study of the predators." Losing so many radio-collared wolves meant that scientists could no longer track wolf populations and observe dens. The report notes that "intensive management"—state-sanctioned aerial hunting of wolves by Alaska's Department of Fish and Game—has killed ninety wolves, including all twenty-four members of the Seventymile pack. Alaska maintains that such lethal management is necessary to protect rural subsistence hunters. But caribou calf survival in Alaska has not increased. "We are aware of no other instance in which a state has so extensively compromised the ecological integrity of a federal conservation area," PEER board member Richard Steiner said. "The State of Alaska is foolishly, almost vindictively, squelching a generation of invaluable scientific inquiry into predator-prey dynamics." Park superintendent Greg Dudgeon adds that Alaska's lethal management has resulted in a wolf population that has drastically changed "from a self-sustaining population to one reliant on immigration of wolves from outside the area . . . the wolves are no longer in a natural state."

The National Park Service has petitioned the Board of Game sixty times since 2001 to "exempt hunting practices that unfairly manipulate the predator-prey balance from Alaska's national preserves. Each time, the board has refused. So again and again, the National

Park Service is forced to overrule them." Even then the winter-kill of wolves goes on. For those of us who have watched Alaska in dismay these past decades, it seems an endless siege, manipulating all wildlife to inflate game herds for hunters. Public protests and threatened tourism boycotts go unheeded. A National Academy of Sciences review of Alaska predator control in 1997 once predicted that wolf control battles were "likely to continue indefinitely." That prediction still seems apt today.

"Alaska needs a conservation ethic," Alaskan federal wildlife official Vic Ballenberghe has argued. "As the stewards of America's largest wild wolf population, Alaskans simply must find ways to manage and conserve their wolves, in a manner that is in step with the rest of the world, where presently the dominant theme is to conserve wolves where they occur and restore them in areas where they are gone."

Along with so many of Alaska's wolves, one of the wolves' strongest protectors is also gone. One day in 2009 Gordon Haber's research plane crashed, bursting into flames and killing the scientist who had devoted four decades to protecting Alaskan wolves. Two longtime Alaska residents heard Haber's plane circling, then eerie silence. Wolves began to howl and howl. They howled, the people said, longer than they had ever before been heard howling. What might Haber think if he were still alive to hear the news that the East Fork pack of Denali National Park may now all be dead? A spring 2016 report noted that the last radio-collared male wolf was shot when he ventured near a hunting camp. His mate and their two pups have vanished, their den abandoned, "empty and overgrown."

This East Fork pack was one of the largest of the nine monitored wolf families in the Denali. "The pack's decline was fast and drastic," notes the *Washington Post*. "About 75 percent of deaths in the East Fork pack in the past year were caused by human trapping and hunting," explained park biologist Bridget Borg. This loss is so significant because its seventy years of continuous study of large mammal families, beginning in 1939, rivals Jane Goodall's long-term study of chimpanzees in Gombe.

The National Park Service has proposed a ban in Alaska on killing wolves with pups. It is also asking for a rule that preemptively forbids managing wolves "with the intent or potential to alter or manipulate natural predator-prey dynamics." In other words, stop managing wildlife only for game hunters. And the USFW in 2016 banned the hunting of top predators in Alaska's sixteen wildlife refuges unless needed "in response to a conservation concern." USFW director Dan Ashe said the new restrictions were a response to the Alaska Board and Game's continued "intensive predator management." Ashe explained that Alaska BOG intense predator management was not based on sound science of predator-prey relations. "Over the past several years," Ashe wrote in an op-ed for *The Huffington Post*, "the Alaska Board of Game has unleashed a withering attack on bears and wolves that is wholly at odds with America's long tradition of ethical, sportsmanlike, fair-chase hunting." He concluded, "There comes a time when the U.S. Fish & Wildlife Service must stand up for the authorities and principles that underpin our work and say 'no.'"

A new governor, independent Bill Walker, is somewhat more ecologically sensitive; he has actually gone on record as opposing open-pit copper mining. He promises that the state will finally face climate change realistically. What will he do with wildlife management in this new century? In a 2015 ceremony the Tlingit and Haida Indian tribes of Alaska adopted Walker into their Kaagwaantaan Clan, which means "Wolf Clan." It's a rare honor for Alaskan officials. His honorary clan name is Gooch Waak, which translates as "Wolf Eyes."

Will Governor Walker, like the former Democratic governor Tony Knowles, curtail lethal control? Will he ever work more collaboratively with the National Park Service to protect Denali wolves again? More and more Alaskan people are demanding a new way of sharing wilderness with wildlife. When wildlife enthusiasts balance hunting interests, then perhaps wildlife policy in Alaska will finally reflect all of our voices, including those who speak for wolves. Until then Alaska's Last Frontier is still a taxidermist's dream. And a nightmare for wolves.

SEVERAL YEARS AGO I was invited to speak at a conference sponsored by the Center of the American West. On a panel to discuss new ways of looking at wildlife, our moderator was historian Patricia Nelson Limerick, author of *The Legacy of Conquest: The Unbroken Past of the American West*. She asked all panelists this question:

"If somehow we could go back in history and interview our ancestors in the West from one hundred years ago, we might ask them, 'What is the most astonishing thing that has happened since your time?' What might they say?"

Limerick, a MacArthur Fellow, concluded our panel by answering her own question. "The most radical change is not the inventions such as automobiles or planes nor the amazing technology we take for granted nowadays," she said. "The most astonishing fact to one of those early settlers or frontiersmen or farm/ranchers would be this: that animals now have lawyers representing their rights. This advocacy would most amaze those of the Old West."

At that Alaska Wolf Summit, now almost quarter century ago, we were just on the cusp of wild wolves being reintroduced to the lower forty-eight in Yellowstone, a return of a top predator that a majority of Americans fervently supported then—and now. This rewilding of wolves in America would amaze us all.

part three

# RECOVERY AND BACKLASH

# 5. YELLOWSTONE: "A WOLF'S PARADISE"

**H**ow many people in the whole world ever get to see a wolf in the wild?" a burly man whispered and offered me my turn at the telescope.

Eagerly reaching for the scope on its tripod, I struggled to keep my balance on the seven-thousand-foot hillside above Yellowstone's vast Lamar Valley. My ice boots slid on the slick slope. Dawn light was rising, a golden gleam wavering over winter mountains. It was April of 1995, and we were witness to the very first wolves returning to Yellowstone in seventy years. Fourteen wolves from Alberta, Canada, had been captured, radio collared, and moved to acclimation pens in Yellowstone in January. These so-called founder wolves, a mix of adults and pups, began what would come to be recognized as the greatest conservation success story in America.

Below us six wolves were trotting together across a snow-draped meadow. Most of the wolves were shades of charcoal, but one of the largest was streaked with gray. Single-file, the wolves splashed and swam across the icy Lamar River. On the riverbank four yearlings leapt and chased each other. Tails raised, they wrestled in a rough-and-tumble tussle.

"It's the whole darn pack!" exclaimed a woman who had been there every day that winter watching wolves. "They're playing."

Someone gently hushed her. Even though we were a mile away from the wolves, our park ranger, Rick McIntyre, biological technician for the Yellowstone Wolf Project and veteran "wolf interpreter," had warned us that the wolves could smell, hear, and see us.

"It's their decision to allow us to see them," McIntyre explained, his voice low. "I'm really surprised we get to see all six of the Crystal Creek pack. It's our great good luck!"

"I've been studying wolves for ten years, and I've never seen anything like this," whispered Suzanne Laverty of the Wolf Education and Research Center in Ketchum, Idaho. She stood next to me watching through another telescope. "They're letting us see their real, everyday family lives."

"Right," McIntyre echoed with a wide smile, his mane of red hair tinged with frost. "That's something most wildlife biologists don't even get to see in decades of study."

This was no zoo, where wolves were limited to adaptive and captive behaviors. This was the wild, which wolves had once claimed as their territory, to which they now rightfully returned.

"You see the large light gray wolf in the center of them all?" McIntyre asked, adjusting my scope. Unlike the yearlings, the tall female was intent, her snout raised high to catch the wind. "This Crystal Creek pack is lucky to be led by a dominant female. We call her F5—that's her scientific stud name. She and her male mate are older and experienced. That will really help the four younger pups survive here."

McIntyre smiled when he told us that F5 had leapt and raced straight out of her shipping kennel when she first arrived at Yellowstone. After nine weeks in their acclimation pens other Crystal Creek wolves—sometimes called the Crystal Bench pack—had been hesitant, even somewhat shy to explore this new wilderness. At the vernal equinox, after their pen was opened and an elk carcass offered for incentive, the Crystal Creek family took ten days to finally leave their pen. They slipped out at night to hunt and then returned to safety. I remembered reading a *New York Times* article, "Wolves Leave Pens at Yellowstone and Appear to Celebrate," in which National Park Service senior biologist Douglas Smith described witnessing this Crystal Creek family at last outside their pens. Standing on a hillside, they surveyed their new territory. "They were cavorting, playing, and checking things out," Smith noted, and their frolicking "suggests recent liberation."

"Will these wolves really stay here in Yellowstone?" someone asked McIntyre.

There was always the fear that these Canadian wolves would leave the park, tracking their way back home. Biologists had fitted them all with radio collars. The hope was that these transplanted Canadian wolves would find mates and produce new generations, returning Yellowstone to its birthright of wild wolves.

McIntyre smiled, "F5 is a real explorer."

Even now in the Lamar Valley she loped a little ahead of the family, focused on finding something our human senses couldn't identify. But obviously F5 could. She raised her magnificent head, sniffed, and then all but galloped around excitedly.

"She's scouting around for a coyote den," McIntyre whispered. "The female leader makes the big choices for the whole family—when to travel and rest, where to hunt."

Two telescopes veered to focus on the beautiful alpha female Number 5. Suddenly she leapt up, then pounced on a small, raised hummock of earth. She dug and clawed furiously until at last she crawled on her belly deep into the den. With tail raised high, back haunches pulling, she backed out slowly with a squiggling furry ball in her teeth. A small coyote.

"Oh, I can't watch this!" someone said.

"We're not in Disneyland," another murmured. "It's like us going to McDonald's."

I ignored the comments, focusing instead on the vivid drama below us. The wolf sank her teeth into the little coyote, whose legs pumped helplessly, still trying to flee. I watched as she dragged out several more coyotes, killed them with an efficient shaking and clamp of her jaw. The four yearling wolf pups watched every move of their alpha female, learning the generational wisdom of the hunt.

Wolves and coyotes compete in a healthy ecosystem. Usually wolves simply run coyotes off their territory, but sometimes they will kill and eat these smaller canines. For these first wolves to return to Yellowstone, the coyotes were easy prey. They were abundant from decades of living without wolves. In fact, in Yellowstone there was an unusual wealth of prey animals for wolves to choose to hunt—all hoofed animals from elk to deer as well as beaver, hares, and even bison. "The Yellowstone landscape those first animals stumbled into back in 1995 was surely the wolf version of paradise," notes biologist and author Douglas Smith, who has studied Yellowstone's wolves since their arrival.

The presence of these wild wolves now at work and play within our sights also made Yellowstone a paradise for people. "We've had more than two thousand people lucky enough to spot wolves so far this first year," McIntyre told us proudly. "We're watching history here."

For the next two decades of wolf reintroduction in Yellowstone this devoted wolf researcher would rarely miss a single day of wolf watching in the park. With his radio antennae held up to track the wolves' movement and his 3:45 A.M. wake-up calls to wolf watchers, McIntyre was as steady and dependable as Old Faithful itself. McIntyre would document and help thousands of visitors witness wolves every year in Yellowstone National Park. He would become as well known as the wolves themselves. *Outside* magazine would call him "Pack Man," and in his best-selling book *Beyond Words*, Carl Safina profiled Rick McIntyre as the man who "has had his eyes on wild wolves for more hours than any human ever has, quite possibly more than any living creature that isn't a wolf."

That winter in 1995, when the very first wolves were reintroduced to Yellowstone, McIntyre was already building upon decades of wolf research as well as his own family history. Lean and loquacious, McIntyre's Scottish heritage showed in his friendly, freckled face and his storytelling skills. McIntyre comes by his wolf bond from generations of Highland ancestors. McIntyre's Glen Noe ancestors lived in their Highland valley for eight centuries, but when the British threw tenant farmers off their land, they were forced to work as predator-control agents and wolf killers for the conquering upper class. In his preface, "Witness to Ecological Murder," to his classic book, *War Against the Wolf*, McIntyre wrote, "The last Highland wolf reportedly was destroyed in 1743. . . . The thanks my ancestors received for their diligent wolf control work was the loss of their land to sheep."

I'd first interviewed McIntyre in 1993 for a *Seattle Times* article after the Alaska Wolf Summit. McIntyre gave me a story that surprised many readers then but has proven now to be well-documented science.

"The Portland Zoo had hired a thirteen-year-old girl to observe captive wolves," McIntyre said. "But her reports enraged the zoo biologist because she noted that the alpha female wolf was actually the leader of the family pack. The biologist was just about to fire the girl. But then he decided to go back into the field and observe with her. Sure enough, the alpha female was leading her pack."

At the time there was much less research about how an alpha female leads her family. Most wolf biologists were men like David Mech, Vic Ballenberghe, Rolf Peterson, or Mike Phillips. Diane Boyd, a woman scientist who had studied wolves in the field for two decades in Montana's Glacier National Park, was a notable exception. "I have struggled with the perceived conflict of objective science vs. advocacy for twenty years," she admitted. "I have concluded that it is OK to have feelings about the animals you study, without risking damage to your scientific credibility. . . . Objectivity and passion about study animals are not mutually exclusive; I wouldn't have devoted my life to studying wolves if I didn't love them."

On that first winter of the wolves reclaiming Yellowstone McIntyre's stories captivated us so deeply that we forgot about the early-morning chill. Even though our thermos coffee was tepid, our feet numb, our ears crackling with the cold, we wouldn't budge from the telescopes or our hillside viewpoint. The sunlight now glistened on the snow, glancing off the rapid Lamar River. On the muddy bank the Crystal Creek wolf family lazed together, their hunger sated. Two of the yearling males jaw wrestled, yipping and nipping. The male and female leaders leaned together nearby, watching over their family with the fond indulgence of any parents.

Before I surrendered my scope to another wolf watcher on the hill I was surprised to see a few huge bison asleep just hundreds of feet from the busy wolf family. The bison snoozed, their shaggy sides heaving blissfully.

"Why are they so easy with wolves around?" I asked McIntyre.

Rick grinned, "Unlike us, wolves know when they've eaten their fill." He tapped my shoulder to signal me to glance up from the scope. "Over there by the woods," he pointed.

I glued my eye back to the chilly telescope and just caught one of the yearling wolves wagging his tail as an elk chased him up a snow bank. Surely a predator-prey role reversal—and one that both elk and yearling wolf seemed to enjoy.

"Elk, deer, and pronghorn sheep can all outrun a wolf," McIntyre explained. "Bison can outfight wolves. Sheep can outclimb them. Wolves have to work really hard for their supper. So often they go hungry."

The Yellowstone wolves would prove to ace their version of *The Hunger Games* in this national park. And as they thinned the overpopulated elk and deer, their family numbers would increase, then stabilize, and then level off to a yearly average of 10 percent growth. By May 2016 the wolf population remained stable, with ninety-nine wolves in ten packs. Because usually only the breeding male and female give birth to offspring in any family, wolves are self-regulating. In their own reproductive self-control as well as their hunger, wolves know when and what is enough. They avoid having so many pups that they eat themselves out of den and home. Their long-term survival depends upon this physical prescience. In lean years, when there is little prey, the wolves often can die of hunger; they simply decide not to breed. In Yellowstone wolves mostly prey upon elk, but as bison numbers have increased, the wolves are also scavenging on bison dead from winter-kill and accidents.

"My turn," someone tapped me lightly on the shoulder, and I surrendered the telescope to Suzanne Laverty.

Suzanne adjusted the scope for her eyes and focused on the alpha female. That charcoal, massive wolf now raised her head. Intently, she scented the air, keenly focused in our direction.

"She's assessing our danger to her pack," McIntyre whispered.

Suzanne let out a long, soft whistle. "Wolves look right through you, don't they?" she whispered as the female's mate jumped up to join her in studying our hillside.

None of us moved a muscle. We did not want to startle the wolves and lose them to the forest. I no longer had the technological intimacy of the telescope, and without the artificial eyes, I could feel more directly their fixed gaze—as if a laser beam of heat and light shot into my body. Wolves are also watching us, I realized. The female and male pair sniffed, analyzing our human scents, our distance, our intent. We were all locked in the unsettling intimacy of equal predators.

AS WE KEPT OUR SCOPES FIXED on the Crystal Creek pack's après-picnic nap, McIntyre told us about the other original packs here in Yellowstone—the Soda Butte and the Rose Creek packs. The Soda Buttes were four adults and a pup; the Rose Creeks were two adults and one pup. These fourteen Alberta wolves would be the first wolves to reclaim territory and to give birth in Yellowstone in almost a century.

"The Rose Creeks are up north of the Crystal Creek pack," McIntyre explained. "The alpha male, Number 10, was really special. In the acclimation pen he immediately bonded with an unfamiliar adult female, Number 9, and her yearling daughter. When the biologists opened that pen to set the wolves free, Number 10 quickly left. But the two females were afraid to venture out. Number 10 was so calm and committed to his mate that he patiently waited several days for her." McIntyre grinned. "Finally she followed him out of the pen. Together they explored their new home. A month later, just as his mate was about to give birth, Number 10 went out hunting for her" McIntyre said.

Number 10 was the largest and most confident of all the reintroduced Yellowstone wolves. Biologists respected and admired him because he showed no fear when they ventured near his acclimation pen. Douglas Smith noted that the large dark-gray wolf possessed a "startling, muscular show of authority . . . Number 10 wasn't just free. He was back in charge." Once established as the alpha male in the three-member Rose Creek family, Number 10 was loyal, nurturing, and self-assured. He was often seen silhouetted in full view of people along a mountain ridge, howling for his family.

That's how a Red Lodge, Montana, bear hunter, Chad Kirch McKittrick, first spotted Number 10. McKittrick and a buddy, Dusty

Steinmasel, were having a morning beer and trying to extract McKittrick's pickup from where it had gotten stuck in the mud. Thomas McNamee recounts what happened in an *Outside* magazine article.

> "That's a wolf, Dusty," he says. "I'm going to shoot it."
> "Are you sure?" Steinmasel says. "It might be a dog."
> "No," McKittrick says, "it's a wolf."
> "Chad, no," Steinmasel pleads. "What if it's somebody's dog?"
> "Yeah, right," McKittrick says. He takes aim . . .
> Dusty Steinmasel sees the wolf spin around, bite at the wound high on his back, fall, kick his legs twice, and then lie still.
> "Why?" he cries out.

The men face a decision. The wolf's radio collar is still transmitting, and the federal authorities are always monitoring. After stringing the wolf up to skin him, they strip Number 10 of his radio collar. McKittrick decides he wants to keep the wolf skull, so he stows the head and hides it in a garbage bag bound for home. Steinmasel is still arguing that they report the wolf kill to the authorities, but McKittrick decides to go bear hunting. Feeling guilty and ambivalent, Steinmasel throws the radio collar in a creek. He wonders whether it is still transmitting. "He wants Chad McKittrick to be caught," writes McNamee. "He wants to be caught himself."

Steinmasel and McKittrick do not know that Number 10's radio collar is now transmitting in mortality mode and the Fish and Wildlife Service (USFW) is already trying to find it. Meanwhile Number 10's mate, Number 9, who was also radio collared, has gone into her den to prepare to give birth to the first native-born Yellowstone wolves in six decades. She doesn't know her mate will never return to her to help raise their pups. Without Number 10 the family will be in jeopardy. With no father to hunt and regurgitate the meat for his mate, would she have enough strength and nourishment to nurse her pups? Wolf biologist and Montana project leader for USFW Joe Fontaine begins to bring roadkill to Number 9's den in the hope she will not be frightened and abandon her pups.

The USFW, Defenders of Wildlife, and National Audubon Society offer rewards for information on the wolf killer. Meanwhile Fontaine keeps radio track of Number 9's movements. One early May day he discovers a small snow-bed dug out under a spruce. Inside is a whimpering litter of eight newborn wolf pups. Nearby someone finds and reports a huge, headless wolf carcass skinned and tangled in bailing twine—Number 9 has dug her den next to the dead body of her mate. Later the biologists determine that the same day Number 10 was killed his mate gave birth to his pups. If there is any hope that Number 9 and her eight pups will survive, the Yellowstone biologists decide, she and her pups must be captured and restored to their acclimation pens for later release.

McKittrick and Steinmasel are also captured and confess to the killing, though McKittrick claims he thought he was shooting a feral dog. Locally McKittrick has many admirers who consider his wolf killing a heroic act and buy him beers, asking for autographs. Some even urge him to run for governor. But McKittrick is deteriorating into drunken and bizarre binges. Although a judge has admonished McKittrick to forego firearms and to stay close to home, "he is seen shooting into the air, often wearing a black cowboy hat and no shirt." A Montana jury of his peers finds McKittrick guilty of killing Number 10. He will serve three months in a detention center, six months in prison, and a year of supervised release. When he again has an income, McKittrick will be fined $10,000 to cover the costs of capturing, monitoring, and releasing Number 10.

Wolf biologist Douglas Smith eulogized Number 10 in his remarkable book *Decade of the Wolf:*

> He remains in many ways an ideal icon of this reintroduction: both a symbol of the extraordinary strength of wolves—their ability to thrive if given half a chance—and at the same time, a reminder of how frail such vitality can be in the face of humans who would wipe them from the earth.

Number 9 and 10's first litter of pups thrived in the acclimation pen. And another male wolf, Number 8, a yearling from the Crystal

Creek pack, often came to visit outside the pen, befriending the pups and their mother. By the time Number 9 and her eight pups were ready for release, they had a young but devoted Number 8 waiting to claim them as his new family.

Rick McIntyre sent me a photo that shows not only a legacy of Number 10's power but also the way these wolves are changing the world—and us. Standing against the backdrop of a snow-encircled mountain, biologist Joe Fontaine proudly holds up a three-week-old, five-pound wolf pup from the first litter born in Yellowstone—the offspring of Number 9 and Number 10. Golden fur, intense but tiny black eyes looking straight out at the camera, the pup's little paws clutching Fontaine's fingers. Joe Fontaine is well known for his expertise in the maternal call of wolf parent to pups. The newborns recognized him and often responded to his calls. The proud expression of this young and bearded biologist could be that of any Montana trapper or hunter showing off his trophy of the wild. But there is no carcass draped over this man's shoulders, no rifle or metal trap to advertise his hunting prowess. Instead, Fontaine is faintly smiling as he protectively lifts up the pup for all the world to see. Like a proud father.

Fontaine wrote that when he discovered Number 9's den, "I wanted to yell to the whole world that Number 9 had produced the first litter of wolf pups in the Yellowstone ecosystem in sixty years, but there was only me, the pups, and the silence of the forest." Giving credit to all those who had helped return wolves to this national park, Fontaine concluded, "I felt humble and proud to be a part of that team, a team that has just won a championship game in wildlife management."

 ON THAT HILLSIDE IN 1995 we did not yet know the fate of Number 9 and 10's pups, but we hoped they would thrive and survive to parent more generations.

"Oh, man, this is just awesome!" the burly man next to me whispered. "Check out the mom and her pups."

We all swung our telescopes toward F5 and two pups who were now jumping on her. She simply rolled over, exposing her belly not to nurse but just to allow them to play at being alpha. We couldn't know that one of these yearling males would soon step up to be the young father to Number 9 and 10's pups. There was a murmur among our small group of wolf watchers as F5 finally leapt up and, with one giant but gentle paw, subdued her usurper pups. Then the whole family bounded off again across the river, their splashes rising like little geysers in the chill air.

Several of these people on the Yellowstone hillside with me had come from far away to see their first wild wolves. Others were, like McIntyre, regulars who watched wolves daily, memorizing their stories and following certain wolves like rock stars. Because so many millions of people would witness wolves in the wild over the next twenty years—4.1 million in 2015 alone—certain wolves emerged as major characters in long-running narratives. Their intense family bonds and power struggles echo our human societies. *New York Times* science writer William K. Stevens noted that wolves "are as various in their personalities as dogs, their lineal descendants—and as humans. Their social life within the pack is a mixture of dominance and what people would call affection."

McIntyre echoed this when he told us, "There are no two species so similar in behavior as wolves and human beings." He would later tell a reporter, "Certain wolves I've known—they were better at being a wolf than I've been at being a person."

These first fourteen wolves introduced to Yellowstone from Canada would go on to endlessly enthrall watchers and storytellers. Longtime and respected wolf advocates such as Laurie Lyman have kept daily wolf journals and blogs, like her *Yellowstone Reports*, which are read by many devoted readers. What are we following so obsessively when we watch wolves? We watch the wolf families' territorial struggles, their passions, and tragic losses. Most wolves in the wild die violently, rarely of old age. Anyone who has ardently tuned in to *Game of Thrones* has only to watch these Yellowstone wolves to see mirrored our same human struggle for power, dominance, and alliance acted out every day in the wild. In fact, the author of the wildly popular *Game of Thrones* series, George R. R. Martin, is a loyal wolf advocate. In 2015 Martin sponsored a contest to benefit a New Mexico wolf sanctuary, "offering two donors the chance to be written into (and then killed off!) in the *Winds of Winter*, marks his forthcoming book.

One of the most riveting characters among the Yellowstone wolf families was the lean and charcoal-colored Number 42, also called the Yellowstone Cinderella. Hers is a saga of jealousy, competition, and a violent sibling rivalry that mirrors our most enduring stories. Among wolves, as with humans, competition between siblings for parental attention, food, and rank begins at birth. In Yellowstone the Druids, another group of the original Canadian wolves, were perhaps the most closely watched wolf family in the world. In 1996 the Druids' matriarch, Number 40, was so fierce and dominant that she even deposed her own mother, Number 39—who was then forced to flee her family. Wandering alone outside the park boundaries, Number 39 was mistaken for a coyote and shot. Between 1997 and 2000 Number 40 then reigned over her subordinate sister, Number 42, with an "iron-pawed leadership." More tyrant than sibling, Number 40 took every opportunity to thrash, harass, and humiliate her sister. Dubbed "Cinderella" for her forbearance of such mistreatment, Number 42 never fought back—not even when her temperamental alpha sister repeatedly trounced her. But she, a fan favorite of wolf watchers, sensibly created benign alliances with other female wolves in the family, including two older sisters, Numbers 103 and 105.

When Cinderella tried to make her own nearby den, Number 40 tracked her down and viciously attacked her. Again, Cinderella did not defend herself; instead, she simply submitted to the brutal dominance display, passively lying down for the beating. She abandoned her den. Biologists wondered whether the tyrannical Number 40 had actually killed Cinderella's new litter or if Cinderella's denning was a "pseudo-pregnancy." If Cinderella did, indeed, have pups, none of them survived. Douglas Smith, in his "Portrait of Wolf Number 42," notes that the "foul-tempered" Number 40 ruled her siblings with absolute authority. But when Number 40 gave birth to her own pups, the wolf received no help from her siblings; instead, the oppressive matriarch had to depend upon her mate, "the fine, alpha male, a wolf long on patience, Number 21."

As in human families, eventually there is often a come-uppance for sibling cruelty. It's what we wait for in our stories—that moment when a righteous justice prevails and the tyrant is deposed. We long for the underdog to rise up and defeat the bully. We cheer when a dictator's massive statues are toppled by a people's revolt. We find hope when an autocrat is finally imprisoned in the same way he or she has condemned so many others.

When Cinderella finally did give birth to her own pups, she was attended by her many allies, including the loyal sisters Numbers 103 and 105. They brought Cinderella much-needed food to sustain her in nursing the newborns. The matriarch, Number 40, also had another litter of pups nearby. After about five weeks a mother wolf will wean her pups, but until then she is often confined to the den. One day, when her pups were about six weeks old, Cinderella, with her clan of female allies, ventured out for her first foray after motherhood. Unfortunately Cinderella and Number 105 were discovered by Number 40, the cruel matriarch, and tromped upon, as usual. Then Number 40 headed straight for Cinderella's den and her vulnerable pups. As night fell, the Yellowstone biologists dreaded that the Druid matriarch would, true to her almost mythical jealousy, kill all of Cinderella's newborns.

It was an anxious night. But the chill morning brought an unexpected discovery. The long-ruling Number 40 was found bloody and barely able to stand, her jugular vein ruptured, the bite wounds on the back of her neck so deep that biologist Douglas Smith said he "could bury my index finger all the way to the knuckle." At first the biologists believed Number 40 had been horribly wounded by a car. Because it was assumed to be a human-caused injury, an "unnatural event," biologists decided to intervene and tend to her wound. But as Number 40, the once-mighty and malicious matriarch, was lifted into the back of a pickup truck, she drew her last breath.

Biologists then pieced together what must have happened that night when Number 40 raced to Cinderella's den, perhaps intent on murder and infanticide. Cinderella's long and faithful alliance with the two supportive sisters, Numbers 103 and 105, proved to be a despot's undoing. "For Number 40, allies were in short supply,"

Doug Smith commented. "It was payback time." This revolt against an authoritarian Number 40 was "the first time in the scientific record that an alpha wolf has been killed by her own subordinates." *Ding dong, the witch is dead.* The endlessly dominated but enduring Cinderella, Number 42, rose to alpha female in the Druid family. A time of benevolence and peace within the family assured that by 2001 there were three more litters born, and the Druids became the largest Yellowstone wolf pack ever documented.

 TO BALANCE THE MURDEROUS TALES of sibling rivalry we hear stories of wolf family loyalty, sibling cooperation, and survival.

The same alpha male, wolf Number 21, who brought food for his cruel matriarch, Number 40, upon her death took his place as the mate and coleader with Cinderella of the Druid pack. Together Cinderella and Number 21 raised Number 40's motherless pups as their own. Rick McIntyre lauded Number 21 as a true peer with Cinderella in generously leading their thriving family. It's not about dominance, McIntyre pointed out. The true alpha male demonstrates a "quiet confidence and self-assurance. . . . You know what's best for your pack. You lead by example. . . . You have a calming effect."

McIntyre pointed out in a *New York Times* interview that he has rarely seen an alpha male "act aggressively toward the pack's other members, including mate, offspring, or siblings." Number 21's strength was equaled by his kindness, especially toward newborn pups. Number 21 and Number 42 were benevolent toward and fierce in defense of their Druid family. Under their leadership of the Druid dynasty there was almost half a decade of peace and prosperity.

But in 2004 the Druids would face off with another original pack, the Crystal Creeks—the very same pack we watched in 1995 from the Lamar Valley hillside. The Crystal Creek family would become the Mollies. Though smaller, this family would take on the Druid family in a boundary dispute. And prevail. Cinderella would die—not as she had lived, in relative peace and nonviolence, but in a battle with a rival family for territory. When biologist Douglas Smith told regular wolf watchers that Cinderella—their beloved and gentle matriarch—had died, many wept. With her passing, none of the original founder wolves restored to Yellowstone were left. But their descendants lived on to delight and mesmerize many millions of Park visitors.

In 1995, as we perched on that cold hillside, focusing our telescopes on the Crystal Creek family, I realized even then that it was an honor and an initiation to be witness to these founder wolves in Yellowstone. One day that I'll always remember is watching the Crystal Creek pack raise their heads in harmony and begin to sing together—eerie and intricate harmonies that echoed between mountains, a ricochet of high-pitched howls that rose and then fell into a throaty elegy. Wolves can hear each other's howls from as far away as nine miles in the open spaces and over six miles in dense forests. From our Lamar Valley hillside, a mile away, we could easily hear the wolf chorus. The howls faded, only to begin again with one yip or long withheld treble notes. At the last, the wolf music was joined and anchored by a long moan.

It was the first time I'd ever heard real wolves in the wild, having listened for their voices all my life. Hearing wolves in Yellowstone, I remembered the Celtic melody "Winter Wolf," with its rich, woven harmonies:

High above the timberline
Call and echo
Watching, waiting

"For nearly sixty years there has been an unnatural silence in Yellowstone, the absence of this sound that would have been heard here every day for thousands of years," McIntyre said softly. "This year that silence is broken."

At last the Crystal Creek pack loped off into the forest, pups prancing with their tails held high. What adventure awaited them? A hunt? A nap? More play? As we gathered our gear to descend back to the warmth and predictability of our lodges, McIntyre reminded us that wolves devote much of their daily lives to play. Then he took me aside and asked me to follow him back to his parked truck. From under a well-worn tarp he pulled out a full wolf skin and handed it to me carefully.

"I carry this with me for show-and-tell when I give educational talks to schoolkids," he said with a smile. "Children always want to touch the wolf skin and feel this rich, winter fur. It's like something of the wolf is still here."

I held the surprisingly heavy wolf skin, running my fingers through the silver-gray fur of the thick tail.

"Here," McIntyre said quietly, "this is how it should be worn." He draped the massive wolf's head over mine, stretched the long skin down my back like a cape, and then tucked the forelegs around me.

The thick pelt embraced me with its warmth, its responsibility. McIntyre laid a hand lightly on the wolf skin over my shoulder.

"The wolf needs storytellers," he said.

# 6. TROPHIC CASCADES: A NOT-SO-SIMPLE STORY

S cience is not only built upon always evolving research; it is also based upon theories that are continually updated and increasingly complex. The trophic cascades theory is one such continuing story. In the years before wolves were reintroduced to Yellowstone and during the two decades of their gradual return, different scenarios kept playing out in ecosystems.

**Scenario One: Wilderness Areas Without Wolves**
On the eroded riverbank a large gathering of elk rarely glances around in fear. Nonchalantly they nibble new-grown willow and cottonwood right down to the roots. The sparse trees get little chance to grow tall, so beaver can't find enough wood for their river dams. Silted and awash in loose soil, rivers flow slower, offering habitat for fewer native fish, frogs, and amphibians. Deer stroll unchecked through valleys, grazing so greedily because they are starving as their populations are exploding past sustainability. In rain forests fern prairies smother the earthen floor, strangling the healthy underbrush and nurse logs.

In my home state of Washington the ancient Hoh Forest still seems magnificent, but the old-growth trees, rivers, and animals have suffered much since the last wolf was killed in 1920. "We think this ecosystem is unraveling in the absence of wolves," Oregon State University ecologist William Ripple warned in 2009. The Mount Olympus National Monument was created in 1909 by President Theodore Roosevelt to conserve an elk population of about three to five thousand animals. But without wolves to control elk populations, the Hoh Rain Forest within Mount Olympus is now "totally out of whack." Another OSU researcher, Robert Beschta, points out that after wolves were eliminated from the forest, few seedlings made it "past the knee-high stage," and in one area "not a single new cottonwood survived the ravenous elk in the last half-century." He warned that "the degradation we're seeing in the park is profound. It's catastrophic." Where once flowed mighty rivers dense with trees for shade, fertile with underbrush and logs to spawn the Northwest's iconic salmon, there are now sadly diminished waterways with slip-sliding-away banks.

### Scenario Two: Wilderness Reclaimed by Wolves

Exposed again to a top predator, elk and deer retreat from river banks and meadows. These prey animals are wary of the wolf eyes that track them from hillsides or hide behind now-thriving underbrush. Without the rapacious bite and strip of elk, new cottonwood saplings, willows, hemlock, and maples sprout up. The green, vegetable world again flourishes to renew forests and securely root river banks. Beavers, those essential "ecosystem engineers," find wood to build their nourishing dams; these watery woodpiles create cool eddies and pools for ducks, fish, and reptiles. Weasels and foxes feast on what was left of the prey the wolves left behind. Butterflies skitter and sway across nourishing meadows now bright with wildflowers and pollen. Bears discover more delicious berries in the surging bushes. Songbirds alight and sing in thriving trees where they can again make their nests. Because wolves keep the coyotes from overbreeding, there are multitudes more mice and rabbits. Mile-high in the sky, soaring hawks and eagles no longer glide past the degraded forest; instead, they spy the squiggling ground prey and decide to build their nests here in stalwart trees. Ravens flock back. Rivers return to life.

Since the reintroduction of wild wolves to Yellowstone and beyond, this new story of how wolves enhance and help nourish a whole ecosystem has been told again and again. As it turns out, wolves are perhaps the best wildlife and habitat managers of all. After twenty years of wolf recovery in Yellowstone and elsewhere, the wild lands where wolves returned have changed dramatically. "The whole ecosystem re-sorted itself after those wolf populations got large enough," said David Graber, the regional chief scientist for the National Park Service.

Scientists call the benefit of restoring top predators the trophic cascade effect. University of Washington ecologist Robert T. Paine was the first to coin the terms "trophic cascades" and "keystone species." When wolves limit their prey's grazing and behavior, this opens their shared habitat to more richness and diversity. Conservation biologist Cristina Eisenberg of Oregon State University describes a trophic cascade as a dynamic waterfall that flows through the entire food web once keystone species such as wolves are restored. "Trophic cascades are an ecosystem writ large upon aquatic and terrestrial landscapes," she writes in *The Wolf's Tooth: Keystone Predators, Trophic Cascades, and Biodiversity*. Wolves and other top predators can help restore our wild lands into "landscapes of hope."

This trophic cascade concept has deep roots in the green world hypothesis first proposed in 1960—that top predators help keep the world verdant and healthy. It also draws from cutting-edge research on how keystone species such as wolves help bring stability to degraded ecosystems by regenerating healthy soil, vegetation, and even cleaner water. "Wolves nurture the entire ecosystem," Eisenberg explains. "If we eradicate wolves or lower their numbers, the whole system will grow impoverished and collapse."

Eisenberg is part of the vanguard of researchers documenting why wolves matter so much to healthy ecosystems. Eisenberg's research and writing have revolutionized the way we see wolves. I first met her in 2008 when we taught together at Iowa State's symposium "Wildness, Wilderness, and the Creative Imagination." Flying into Iowa in February, I barely beat a blizzard and spent a lot of time freezing. But the heavy snow meant that Cristina and I, along with the other writers—including the late Irish author Patricia Monaghan, cofounder of Black Earth Institute with Michael McDermott, and Iowa poet laureate/memoirist, Mary Swander— enjoyed a lot of time stranded inside cozy cabins. We gathered close around Amish rock-hewn fireplaces coaxed to burn high with perfectly dried and seasoned wood. Surrounded by such inspiring writers, we told stories—mostly about wild animals—during the snowbound night.

Slender with thick, dark hair down to her shoulders and an engaging, open face, Cristina's Mexican heritage also shows in her gracious and welcoming manner. Cristina told me about her grandfather, who both won and later lost his vast ranch in remote Chihuahua near the Sierra Madre Occidental. This was near the same Sonoran border wilderness where Aldo Leopold studied wolves in the 1930s. Cristina's father spent his summers working the ranch with the cattle and hunting wild game to feed the cowboys. In his saddlebag he carried his favorite wild animal stories by Ernest Thompson Seton. Although he was ordered to kill any wolves he spotted, Cristina's father noted that the wolves didn't bother the cattle and were never aggressive toward him.

In *The Wolf's Tooth* Cristina would later write about her father and how he never could bring himself to shoot a wolf because they "always seemed to be moving through the herd on their way to someplace else. . . . And there was something about them, their eyes, in the way they carried themselves, that compelled him to let them go peacefully." Her father "realized that his direct experiences with wolves did not resemble my grandfather's nor the ranch hand's, so he kept them to himself."

Cristina's story made me wonder how many other ranchers observe wolves simply moving benignly through cattle territory on their way to kill their preferred prey of elk and deer. Wolves are actually responsible for very little livestock predation—many more livestock are killed by disease, coyotes, dogs, bears, and mountain lions than wolves. And in the case of wolf predation, livestock producers can receive compensation for their losses. If these statistics were more commonly known and if more ranchers like Cristina's father told their stories about wolves, more accurate information might replace the stereotype of the vicious wolf devastating cattle.

As Cristina and I spoke by the fire I asked her how she first chose to study wolves or whether they had simply called her to this work. I've noticed that many wolf researchers have a first-contact story about wolves, an encounter that initiates them into their lifelong studies of what many cultures consider the most spiritual animal. Cristina had such a story and also said that her science is a form of service.

As we talked I often felt that I was in the hands of not only an expert scientist but also a fine storyteller. "My husband and daughters and I moved to Montana in the early 1990s, when wolves had reintroduced themselves naturally, migrating down from Canada," Cristina began. "Our Montana cabin was remote, really wild country. The land bordered the Bob Marshall and Great Bear Wildernesses. It was like having millions of acres of wilderness for a backyard. One night I heard a sound that was both primal and totally familiar. Wolves howling. I ran to the window to listen . . . and those wild voices were comforting, like 'Welcome home.'"

Local rangers and researchers had assured Cristina that there were no wolves left anywhere around. But if there were wolves, there were very few and just now returning. Her family hadn't moved to Montana to study wolves. "They were just another animal to me," she explained. "But then everything changed."

One summer morning Cristina and her daughters were weeding their garden. It abutted three acres of lush mountain meadow. Often they'd watch elk standing around for hours, nibbling the nutrient-rich grasses and trees. "We didn't realize that there was something really wrong with that picture of elk fearlessly grazing, standing around like lawn ornaments," she laughed. "I wasn't an ecologist then. The land taught me about ecology."

Suddenly the nearby forest exploded with sound—a lean deer lunging and racing, her legs stretched out like a terrified thoroughbred horse. On her flying hooves were two wolves, one big black wolf and one smaller gray wolf. "The deer ran right toward us, as if for protection," Cristina said. "Came within twenty feet of our garden and then veered off to the other side of the meadow. Disappeared into the forest. We were in total shock. Never seen anything like that. We just stood there in the garden until one of my kids said, 'Let's go track them!'"

Cristina had taught her children how to recognize the tracks of grizzly bears and cougars to protect themselves when hiking and playing around their remote wilderness cabin. These skills meant they never felt threatened by predators. "So we tracked the wolf chasing that deer," Cristina continued, her voice quickening. "We could smell the wolves—a beautiful, earthy scent. And we noticed the grass was springing up already after the imprint of hooves and paws. We even tracked exactly when the gray wolf turned back to look at us following her. That slight shift in her shoulder changed her gait, and we saw the change in her tracks. I had to wonder: How many times had this wolf hunt gone on around our cabin and we'd just never even noticed?"

"So what happened next?" I asked.

"The wolves had left shreds of fur in the bushes as they loped past. I took the fur in a little plastic baggie to the Forest Service guy. He said, 'Oh, lady, that's fur from big dogs.'"

Although the Forest Service ranger dismissed her field sample, Tom Meier with the Wolf Project was very curious to see her evidence. Had wolves really recolonized themselves to their former Montana territory? "Tom looked at the fur for a really long time. Then he turned to me and smiled. 'Want to track them for me?' he asked."

That was the beginning of Cristina Eisenberg's research, work that led her to become one of the top wolf specialists in the world. "After our first sighting of wolves that summer," Cristina concludes, "we noticed that our meadow completely changed. Within three years the meadow was deeply filled in with shrubs and trees. We'd always counted birds for Cornell University. Now all these new warblers showed up, the kind who only live in the thick understory of young, thriving forests. That's how I got into studying trophic cascades."

As for the black and the gray wolves she first saw, Cristina says, "They turned out to be the breeding male and female. Two or three years later they came by with their pups. It was as if they were introducing their family to our family," Cristina said.

Cristina would also study "the ecology of fear" in the relationship between apex predators, like wolves and grizzlies, and their prey. When predators are missing from an ecosystem, their prey can overpopulate, like the elk and deer in Yellowstone. According to Cristina, "fear is an essential and very healthy force in nature.

We—including humans—coevolved as species that lived in a land-scape of fear. This kept us in check and enabled a form of equilib-rium in the natural world. Take that fear away, and we are remov-ing wildness, part of what makes us humans and an important part of what makes the world function . . . like those elk in our meadow, complacently mowing down the shrubs and saplings."

 OVER THE YEARS I kept up a lively correspondence with Cristina about wolf issues. It was to her I turned in the win-ter of 2016 to help me understand when some new research on trophic cascades surfaced that needed her clear thinking.

With any widespread theory like trophic cascades, there will be debate. Science is always revising and adding nuances to its the-ories. A few researchers recently argued that wolves are not the only factor reducing elk and deer populations and restoring Yel-lowstone's degraded ecosystem. Field biologist Arthur Middleton claims that "wolves have made less of a difference than previously expected." Willow and aspen haven't recovered as much as some claimed, he says. "A few patches of Yellowstone's trees do appear to have benefited from elk declines," he admits. "But wolves are not the only cause of those declines. Human hunting, growing bear numbers and severe drought have also reduced elk populations." Rather than being the single cause of elk populations dropping in Yellowstone, they are one among several important influences, Middleton concludes. He urges scientists and conservationists to focus on "pragmatic efforts that help people learn how to live with large carnivores. In the long run, we will conserve ecosystems not only with simple fixes, like reintroducing species, but by seeking ways to mitigate the conflicts that originally caused their loss."

Another article in *Nature* also questions any overly simplistic interpretation of how wolves and trophic cascades affect com-plex ecosystems. It finds that "the more-complicated story of how beavers and changes in hydrology" might be even more im-portant than wolves to help willows recover: "Restoring an eco-logically complete ecosystem in Yellowstone requires the return of willows—and with them beaver. There's a clear threshold for ecosystem recovery. Willow stands must be more than 6 feet tall, the scientists found. That height is important. . . . Then willows are beyond the reach of browsing elk, and can serve as seed sources for new young willows."

A 2010 study of Yellowstone aspen by the Wyoming Cooperative Fish and Wildlife Research Unit concluded that "the major influence on the trees is the size of the elk population, rather than elk behavior in response to wolves. And though wolves influence elk numbers, many other factors play a part"—like grizzly bears, drought, and elk migrating out of the park in winter.

Cristina echoes this *Nature* article, adding, "We've been trained as a culture for generations that there is a simple solution to everything. When we introduced wolves to Yellowstone there were noticeable impacts ecologically within three to four years. Elk suddenly had to be wary instead of standing around overgrazing. Conservation organizations, myself included, thought, 'What a great story. Makes perfect sense.'"

But more research led to more complexity in understanding not only how wolves change their habitat and the behavior of other animals but also how factors like climate change and, especially, drought affect the ecosystem. "Climate change reduced frost-free days by 33 percent in the park," Cristina explains. "This increased the growth of willows, which then created dryer stress for aspen in Yellowstone's Lamar Valley. Added to that, the aspen hadn't burned since the park's 1988 fires. So fire was another big factor in understanding Yellowstone. It's really an ecological mosaic."

Researchers noted that in some areas of Yellowstone, like river banks, aspen flourished, growing in healthy thickets. Meanwhile on the Lamar Valley floor, aspen trees were struggling. Further studies of elk populations revealed even more complexity: climate change affected the elk's food source. "Heat in the spring determines how elk survive the winter," Cristina says. "In May and early June the grasses sprout up and are at the peak of their nutrient-rich protein. That's right before the elk give birth, so this protein-rich grass is essential in healthy birth rates. If the grass is not at its nutritional peak because of climate change, elk births and survival rates go down."

In the 1990s Yellowstone elk populations were at a high of twenty thousand. By 2015 those numbers had dropped to four to five thousand. Some scientists think that this lower number of elk is the true carrying capacity for the park. Meanwhile, the bison population has quadrupled in the last twenty years, so much so that the Yellowstone biologists are conducting controversial culls of bison herds. "Wolf numbers are also changing," Cristina notes. Wolf birth rates in Yellowstone fluctuated because of resumed hunting in 2012 after the federal government returned wolf management to states, with some often hostile to wolves. "Wolves have learned what they need to do to stay alive," Cristina remarks. "The first year of the wolf hunts, wolves were naïve, and there were losses."

In 2003 wolf populations peaked and then crashed. Pups went from a high of around 160 down to only 3. One year only one wolf pup survived. That had to do with a wave of parvo, or distemper, which is very dangerous for all canines. Cristina explains that scientists call these big population changes the stochastic effect, meaning unexpected, uncontrollable events that you can't predict or control. Storms, drought, disease—all of these contribute to what Darwin described as nature's very complex "tangled bank."

Cristina elaborates. "Our stories and science about nature must be as complex and sophisticated as the natural world itself. Science works incrementally, taking us ever deeper into nature's tangled bank as we investigate ecological questions. Each study answers some questions and begets new ones."

In her own continuing research into keystone species and trophic cascades, Cristina is now including new studies of how fire dramatically changes an ecosystem. In her Alberta, Canada, fieldwork, Cristina documents the after-effects of setting fires in a system that has a high density of elk and two wolf packs. When you combine wolves and fire, she explains, you get really powerful trophic cascades.

Fire, climate change, drought, hunting, elk and willow growth, wolves, bison, beaver—all of these elements work together to shape story-as-ecology. And science needs time to understand and tell these not-so-simple stories. The Yellowstone wolf recovery is still in its infancy, even after twenty years. Several years into wolf recovery, when Yellowstone's ecosystem was changing, it was very tempting to tell a simplistic story of wolves single-handedly saving Yellowstone, for elk numbers dropping and, thus, more vegetation, thriving trees, more songbirds, beaver, and even changing riverbanks. The trophic cascades theory, with its apex predators as top-down determinants of ecosystems, replaced the bottom-up, plant-based previous theories.

As the scientists debate whether trophic cascades are most influenced by predator/top-down or plant/bottom-up processes, as they try to determine whether it is wolves or beaver or climate change that most shapes and changes an ecosystem like Yellowstone, they all agree on one thing: the "great complexity of ecosystems and the likelihood that the truth lies somewhere in the middle." The scientists agree that wolves do matter—but they are "not alone on the ecological dance floor." Wolves are not enough to restore a degraded ecosystem like Yellowstone.

Cristina Eisenberg reminds us that "science's job is to come close to the truth." If a simplistic trophic cascades theory that wolves alone save ecosystems is shown to be false, it gives ammunition to those who don't want wolves. Unlike many scientists who thrive on conflict and competition, Cristina often talks about finding "the middle path" between diverse scientific factions. It's also her style when working with Congress, ranchers, and conservationists. Certainly her successful and well-funded research grants—including her latest 2015–2016 grants from the Kainai Nation, Earthwatch Institute, several foundations, and Parks Canada to study wolves and how they interact with forces of nature such as fire—reveal that scientists, like wild animals and humans, can coexist with each other. Since 2008 Cristina has been experimenting with large, landscape-scale fires in Waterton Lakes National Park in a place that has a thriving wolf population and one of the highest elk densities ever recorded in North America.

Interestingly, even with that many elk, the wolves keep them on the move and, along with fire, keep both aspen and grasslands in superb health. Now she is working with First Nations to look at a third force of nature: bison. Because bison were historically present—along with wolves and fire—before European settlement of this area, the animals probably combined work with these other forces to maintain this landscape in a balanced condition. In this work Cristina is using cutting-edge science to demonstrate how traditional ecological knowledge practiced by indigenous people in managing this landscape still applies today. And the wolf is integral to all of it.

Coexistence is a huge factor in any story about wolf recovery and habitat restoration. We need to talk about returning wolves not only to national parks but also to their former territories, which covered two-thirds of North America. "National Parks and preserves are not the answer," Cristina says, "because even places like Yellowstone amount to being little more than a postage stamp of protected land in the scheme of things."

A recent example is the long-suffering red wolf in North Carolina. After federal protection for red wolves languished and there were only fifty wild red wolves remaining in the world, local support for red wolf recovery surprised many trying to abandon red wolf recovery. In early 2016 a group of private landowners signed a petition asking the USFW to support keeping endangered red wolves on their land. It's this kind of cooperation from those who are the most affected by wolf recovery that offers hope for wolves returning to their native territories in this country.

As science continues to discover new wrinkles in the trophic cascade and wolf recovery story, climate change overshadows this more sophisticated story. Many scientists believe that we are now in the sixth extinction, which is driven by climate change. If you have a system that is as resilient as possible, with top predators like wolves allowed to function ecologically by evolution, that in turn boosts biodiversity.

Cristina explains that rich and vibrant biodiversity is our insurance policy when dealing with climate change. "So it makes perfect sense to preserve these apex predators if we want to have a resilient world for future generations." She gives this example: What if you have ten species of sparrows, and by 2100 you lose 25 percent of them—that ecosystem is still going to function. But if you only have two species of sparrows and climate change hits, you're out of luck.

In an increasingly changing world, why not take out every ecological insurance policy possible for our own health and the health
of our planet? Wolves, as keystone species, are a vital part of that
insurance. "Bringing keystones back, because of their far-reaching
effects, is one of the simplest ways to improve ecosystem function
and increase biodiversity," says Cristina. "They are major players
in any thriving natural world."

Cristina reminds us, "We need to tell a more sophisticated story
in which wolves are part of the picture but also work together with
other animals and elements in the ecosystem."

**Scenario Three: A Possible Future of Wolves and Trophic Cascades**
Wolves chase an elk herd back into the forest and away from the
riverbank willows. Elk graze now in the higher meadows, bright
with mountain wildflowers—purple iris and forget-me-nots, pink
shooting stars, and rosy paintbrush—but where aspen still struggle
to survive. Cool streams and creeks move more slowly now, dense
and bogged with willows where returning beaver busily build their
homes. These industrious beaver ponds, with their intricate lattice-
work of willow and other woods, sift down more sediment that
roots even more healthy willows. In the nearby valley a fire is set
to temper and encourage the forest to open up to more space and
sunshine. Huckleberries, which bears feast on, grow more heartily
after the burn; the ash fertilizes the soil to root and nourish even
more vegetation and healthier trees.

In winter the elk and even antelope thrive on these thick grasses
and shrubs. After the fire even more wildflowers astonish and attract bees, birds, songbirds. The controlled fire also cleanses the
forest floor where decomposing logs were once too slow to rot, so
they had been fuel for future wildfires. With increased drought
and climate change, these forests, without the natural benefits of
flames, might otherwise burn uncontrollably. After burns, new
and fresh grasses, herbs, shrubs, and trees nourish new generations of wildlife. Cougars, grizzlies, coyotes, foxes, and wolves survive together, no more species missing, both top predators and rich
habitat beginning the restoration.

Conservationists working on the recovery of wolves hope to see them recolonize their original territory. Many imagine North America's wild lands once again balanced and restored with the help of this fellow predator. Many hope their grandchildren will hear the howling, the call to community of the wild wolves. Even now scientists are drawing maps of North America with projected future wild wolf ranges widely expanded throughout much of the West, the Rockies, the Great Lakes, and the Northeast. To return wolves to their native lands will take not just time but also a change in cultural values—an evolution in the American character.

# 7. 06: THE WORLD'S MOST FAMOUS WOLF

Some wolves, like humans, are legends—larger than life and yet strangely vulnerable. This was true for one Yellowstone wolf, 832F, also named 06 for the year she was born. She was strong and self-sufficient, especially for a female. With buff, gray-black, and agouti-colored fur, in summer she bore a silver-tinged saddle over her impressive shoulders. Her long-legged lope was a blur of copper and white underbelly, with a dark, distinguishing black marking on her thick tail—the sign of the wolf. Most striking were her deep brown eyes, fierce yet expressive, always watching. Nothing was lost on her. It was easy to see early on that she would be resilient and remarkable, the alpha of Yellowstone's Lamar Canyon family, that she would enthrall not one but two chosen mates, that she would successfully hunt for and defend her own pups—even when all around other wolf families came close to starving. This mother wolf, this charismatic clan leader would never be captured for longer than it took to radio collar her. Instead, she captured us.

Scientists don't name their study animals, much preferring scientific stud names like "832F." Once we name animals, we give them an identity and character, a recognition of their individual lives. It's our human nature to call by name those we love—and so 832F came to be known by her nickname, "06." She was born to the stately Agate pack. Because the Yellowstone wolves have been so intensely studied for twenty years, their genealogies are well documented. Tracking a Yellowstone wolf's heritage is like reading a lineage of royal bloodlines. Each pack, their ancestors, age, and social position can be traced to the very first families—the founder wolves—reintroduced in 1995.

06 was the granddaughter of the alpha male of the famous Druid pack, 21M and 42F, the female wolf nicknamed Cinderella who rose up against her tyrannical sister (see Chapter 5). Wolf watchers in the park noticed something different about this young female, heir to a lineage of strong females. Even as a pup 06 was powerful and inquisitive. There was an electricity about her that translated into a local buzz among the scientists and watchers and then a growing reputation.

Laurie Lyman, a retired teacher who has been documenting Yellowstone wolves for years, first photographed 06 with her mother and sister when 06 was two years old. "She attracted males from everywhere," Lyman said. "At that time we should have known that she was going to be exceptional. . . . The action was nonstop."

Although 06's Agate family was one of the most dominant in Yellowstone, it was not immune to tragedy. When she was two years old her father, the alpha male, died. The loss threw his family into chaos. His alpha female mate and her young pups faced a winter of dwindling prey because elk numbers were down. The family fell apart as some of the wolves dispersed and others died of starvation. Of the original seventeen wolves in 06's Agate family, very few survived. 06 barely endured. But with such a sadly diminished family, it was also time for her to leave in search of a mate.

Wolves have a strong instinct against interbreeding and often must leave their families in search of an unrelated mate. If a solitary female finds a willing male, she must win him by dominating his current female in a battle for his affection. Usually a female finds a willing mate within months. Not so with 06. Was it because she was so singular in her own clout and curiosity? She was destined for more than a subordinate status with an alpha male. Without a family to hunt alongside her, 06 had to content herself with rodents like prairie dogs. Those who watched saw her ribs sharply etched with hunger, her flanks scarred from mange, her characteristic lope and trot hobbled by fatigue. Many lesser wolves would have simply given up and died alone, bereft of family and food. For over a year 06 braved a dangerous and solitary life in Yellowstone.

Observers watching 06 struggle feared she would be missing come spring. But somehow 06 was skilled enough to survive blizzards, rival packs, and disappearing prey. By spring she was seen galloping around meadows aglow with wildflowers, still looking for a mate, still very selective about her suitors. "One particular mating season, she had five different suitors—as far as I know, that's a world record for a wild wolf," Rick McIntyre noted, "and she dumped every one of them."

One bright spring day in 2010 06 was spotted in the company of two yearling brothers who followed her like the rock star she was becoming—self-possessed, discerning, gorgeous, the "Angelina Jolie of wolves," as Rick McIntyre called her. Through word of mouth, social media, and YouTube, people around the world were watching 06, later calling her "The Legend of Lamar Valley."

When it did come time for 06 at last to accept one of her many suitors, she bewildered researchers by finally accepting a pair of immature brothers, 754M and 755M, shaggy but strong charcoal wolves with silver snouts and sturdy, streamlined legs. These two brothers forsook seven sisters in a pack they'd been courting to follow 06. It takes only two wolves to form a family, so the trio of 06, a massive gray female wolf, attended by two young brothers was a sight many wolf watchers most longed to see. When 06 chose to mate with 755M, the pups were also eagerly anticipated by wolf watchers. Although the alpha female, 06, and her alpha mate, 755M, became the main breeding pair, 754M was an accommodating and amiable uncle—and sometimes a mate.

But soon researchers noted that the young brothers were rather clueless about fathering, more involved in jaw wrestling and playing with one another than providing for any of their pups. Because 06 denned so closely to the road, wolf watchers could follow her valiant struggles to raise her black and gray pups, many hoping that the two bad-boy mates would finally figure out their responsibilities.

In one scene in the documentary about 06, *She-Wolf*, she struggles to steal a shank of elk carcass from a bear's kill. Her body is still heavy from birthing, her teats swollen and worn from feeding greedy newborns, her gait a little uneven from exhaustion. Nearby the brothers don't know or don't care enough to guard the carcass for future feedings; instead, they romp around together. So 06 wearily picks her way over rocky ground. Her jaws clench the red meat she will eat, regurgitate, and feed her pups. But while she is in a slow midstride, a huge eagle zooms down, grabs the meat right out of 06's mouth, and flies off with her supper. Stunned, there is nothing for 06 to do but return to the carcass. Now a bear is guarding the precious food and, with a ferocious growl, chases her off. The matriarch and her pups will go hungry a little longer.

The brothers were so immature that they also rarely helped 06 in the hunt. Wolves usually hunt in groups. It often takes four 120-pound wolves to bring down a two-thousand-pound bull bison, with the largest leading the chase from behind their prey. 06 had to develop her own solitary style, what McIntyre called "face-to-face, direct combat-to-the-death." This is the most dangerous hunting strategy. A seven-hundred-pound bull elk can stomp a wolf, toss her helplessly into the air, and then gore her once she hits the ground. But 06 was quick and efficient and soon learned to avoid any counterattack. Instead, she leapt high into the air, spun sideways, and sank her sharp teeth into an elk's throat—a quick kill. Once McIntyre witnessed 06, weakened after giving birth, take down two elk in ten minutes. Sightings of 06 in her independent wanderings through the lush Lamar Valley were enough to keep any other wolves away from her territory.

Watching 06's family, one wonders about her strategy to choose two companion males. The brothers could learn to play double male roles, father and devoted uncle. If one of the brothers were killed, there would still be another mate. As the brothers settled down and matured, 06 taught them and their pups how to hunt as a family. Three litters of pups—thirteen newborns—grew their family. Of the offspring in 06's very first litter, three were surprisingly gray, considering their father was so dark. Not unexpectedly, the four pups were self-reliant and robust, especially the daughters. One of the female pups was called Middle Gray to differentiate her from her siblings by color. There was also Light Gray and Dark

Gray. Many of 06's sons dispersed from the family to find their own mates. After some years the Lamar Canyon family was vibrant, endlessly playful, and thriving.

But that didn't mean their struggle was over. Nearby lived their rivals, the Mollies—formerly the original Crystal Creek family whose ancestors I'd first witnessed in 1995. The Mollies were deadly enemies of 06's family, each patrolling and possessively guarding their close territories. McIntyre tells the story of their fateful encounter in 2012. In her den 06 was nursing her newborns, still weak from having given birth. As if sensing her vulnerability, the Mollies sniffed out her den, sixteen adult wolves circling, ready to attack. Suddenly observers saw a large wolf desperately racing out of the forest, trailed by the rival Mollies. It was 06 running for her life toward a cliff. She would either have to leap to her death or turn around and face off sixteen furious wolves.

Even a formidable fighter like 06 could not survive so many attackers. Through his telescope McIntyre watched the battle unfolding below with resignation. McIntyre believed 06 was doomed, that he was "going to see her torn apart." Then 06 sprinted down a narrow gulley, invisible to the Mollies. They couldn't follow 06, but they could follow 06's scent back to her den and simply destroy all of her newborn pups.

What happened next, McIntyre said, shows that "all those years of training that she put into her family finally paid off." One of 06's well-trained older daughters suddenly stepped out of the forest to reveal herself to the Mollies. A decoy. Distraction. Also, a possible self-sacrifice. Like her mother, 06's daughter was extremely fleet footed. But would she be fast enough to escape sixteen wolves biting at her heels? The Mollies veered away from 06's defenseless den and sped after 06's daughter. They all raced east, yipping and growling. But 06's daughter "just left them in the dust," said McIntyre. "The Mollies' wolves gave up in frustration. Went home. And they never bothered 06's family again."

That might have been the happy ending for 06, her motley mates, and her strong offspring. But 06 had more to contend with than just rival wolves. She had us humans. Her fame had spread worldwide, thanks to stories retold by wolf watchers and social media. Before reintroduction biologists believed wolves would be mostly hidden from view. But wolf families often chose dens near the roads, near throngs of people with telescopes. Wolves carried on their mesmerizing daily lives for thousands to witness. It was better than any miniseries or movie, these complex episodes of territorial wars, death-defying hunts, and always the timeless and familiar struggle of caretaking their young. Soon 06 was beloved not only in Yellowstone but also all over America, Europe, and Asia. She was a legend. And some legends don't outlive their stories.

 DID HER FAME make 06 more vulnerable? Was it our rapt attention that so singled her out that made her life much riskier—like any public figure or rock star whose popularity also exposes them to danger? Douglas Smith, a Yellowstone biologist who, like McIntyre, has studied these wolves since reintroduction, told NPR about the moral dilemma he faced when trying to attach a radio collar to 06 and so make her even more visible. For three years Smith had tried to chase down 06 from a helicopter, dart her with a tranquilizer, and fit her with a radio collar for science. The goal is not only to protect but also to study wild wolves to better understand their behavior, biology, and natures. But 06 managed to outwit Smith every time he tried to spot her. She'd disappear suddenly into a forest or leap into underbrush.

"She would look at me with disdain," Smith said. "Most other wolves just ran. But she would look at me and our eyes would connect. And the look she would give would be, 'I don't like you at all, and I'm going to outsmart you.'"

Just as 06 had outsmarted the Mollies, she also outwitted the radio collaring. Until one day she didn't. Ironically, by that time Smith had quit wanting to capture 06, even for the minutes it took to strap a radio collar around her neck. "When you get to know another species like we all did her, you just begin to kind of respect that individual," he said.

But at last 06 made a mistake and let herself be caught. At first Smith didn't realize it was 06 he'd darted with the tranquilizer gun. He thought he'd caught up with 06's swift daughter. But once she was lying on the ground Smith realized *this* was the iconic Lamar Canyon breeding female. "I didn't want to collar her. I dreaded it," he explained. "But there was just so much at stake because from the perspective of science . . . of learning about these animals that we so much want to help, this is the number one wolf you want to get."

Even with the ungainly radio collar, 06 was still a beauty. Her middle-aged teeth were still "clean, sharp, and fully intact." She was so healthy and strong that it was easy to see how 06 had passed for one of her daughters. Several days after 06 was mistakenly radio collared, the alpha female led her family to face off again with the Mollies. The long-standing battle for territory between 06's Lamar Canyon family and the Mollies erupted in a full-scale battle. One of the wolf watchers, Dr. Nathan Varley, witnessed the life-and-death struggle. Like two small armies, the Mollies and the Lamars galloped straight toward each other, clashing headlong in a furry blur of bared teeth, pummeling paws, and massive shoulders. From a nearby viewpoint wolf watchers were mesmerized by the violence and skill of these rival families as they fought for their lives and territory.

Finally 06's family was "crushed, driven before a superior force that scattered its opponents in chaos." One of 06's pups was overwhelmed by the Mollies, and onlookers feared they were witnessing a death in the Lamar Canyon family. After seventeen years of wolves in Yellowstone, elk populations were not as high as those first years when Yellowstone was "a wolf's paradise." Wolf predation on other wolves is another way population growth is regulated in any territory. But the wounded wolf pup in 06's group did somehow survive the Mollies' attack and fled away with his family. Varley concludes his report, "With the fury with which these two big wolf packs clashed, I felt like there would be few survivors. Yet, they are as always, resilient animals."

Veteran wolf observer Rick Lamplugh, author of *In the Temple of the Wolves*, has written about Yellowstone's fascinating families. He describes how they leave scent marks to ward off rival wolves, setting a firm boundary for these animals whose sense of smell is one hundred times that of humans. He chronicled another epic battle between 06's Lamar Canyon family and a solitary wolf who either missed their scent marks or was attempting to join their pack. It is always risky for a lone wolf to disperse from his or her own family and go in search of a mate, especially if that mate is already part of a tight-knit group. The biological drive in wolves, as in humans, is to find a mate, territory, and family. Like us, wolves are hard-wired for community. Yet they also are wary of outsiders.

06's companion males, the brothers 754M and 755M, immediately spot the lone wolf approaching their hillside. The now-mature males protectively plunge down through the snow banks, their charcoal mantles rising and falling as they run toward the solitary stranger. Backing them up are the Lamar Canyon pups, two males and two females. At the rear, keeping her eye out for any other wolves, is 06. The lone wolf waits, standing his ground, and the Lamar Canyon brothers suddenly stop, tentative. In the snow one wolf faces seven Lamars in a tense silence. Will there be an attack or an acceptance of this new wolf? Onlookers hold their breaths collectively in the chill air.

"Suddenly," Lamplugh writes, "the brothers attack the lone wolf with no mercy. The pups join in, with the males more active than the females. 06 joins the fray and all seven wolves ravage the loner, now on his back in the snow, his body covered by a writhing mass of biting wolves."

The lone wolf somehow manages to grip one of 06's pups with his fierce, razor-like teeth—and suddenly the melee is over. The pups back off from the battle, leaving only the two brothers to finish the fight. 06 was not very active in the struggle, as she'd been continually scanning for any other rival wolves. The solitary wolf stands in the snow, shakes himself off, and simply walks away from the Lamar Canyon family. Very little blood, but later researchers will discover he hemorrhaged from puncture wounds from canine teeth. Still, he is lucky to survive at all.

Wolf-on-wolf aggression in Yellowstone has been documented by researchers like Kira Cassidy of the Yellowstone Wolf Project, who videotaped this whole encounter between the lone wolf and 06's family. Cassidy's research between 1995 and 2011 documented 292 "aggressive chases" between wolves, 72 of which "escalated to physical attack." But in only 13 of these attacks was a wolf actually killed. In the case of the lone wolf vs. the Lamar Canyon family, this particular wolf did indeed survive his wounds and was later seen wandering around Yellowstone. His search for a mate and family continued.

The Lamar Canyon family also continued to grow until, at the age of six, 06 was a formidable matriarch. Usually wild wolves live about eight to ten years. The matriarch's successful mothering of so many pups made her the wolf to witness in Yellowstone. Of the thousands of park visitors, many came in the hope of catching just a glimpse of 06 and her flourishing family. Some visitors made yearly visits to Yellowstone, and the wolves' lives became intertwined with their own. Anne and Douglas Griggs first visited Yellowstone in the early 1990s and returned annually, but after the reintroduction of wolves to the park in 1995 the Griggs began visiting Yellowstone twice a year. "Our visits were always at the end of May," Anne told me. Not only were the wolves a touchstone for this couple, they also made many friends among the wolf enthusiasts, nature photographers, and naturalists from all over the world. These friendships spanned countries and languages.

Two of Anne's favorite wolves were 06 and 42F, the Cinderella female wolf of the ancestral Druid pack and grandmother to 06 and her Agate family. "One of my favorite memories," Anne recalled, "was seeing almost all of the Druids in their rendezvous site, the puppies in a great pile." This memorable sighting was just before Anne's husband, Douglas, a cardiologist, learned he had liver cancer. In the spring of 2008 Anne and her sons and sister climbed that very hill in the Lamar Valley to scatter Douglas's ashes. She wrote me about their ceremony: "Clouds lowered and snow threatened. All was quiet, except for the call of ravens and the sounds of the Lamar River. At the crest of the hill there was a single wolf paw print. Returning to the Lamar Valley has become a pilgrimage for me."

In letters, blogs, website posts, Facebook pages, and tweets too numerous to name, lives of the Yellowstone wolves have become intimately interwoven with human stories. This intimacy with a wild animal is what makes the seemingly endless struggle for wolf recovery take on such a personal nature. Well-known and loved wolves become extended family.

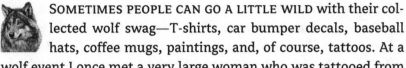 SOMETIMES PEOPLE CAN GO A LITTLE WILD with their collected wolf swag—T-shirts, car bumper decals, baseball hats, coffee mugs, paintings, and, of course, tattoos. At a wolf event I once met a very large woman who was tattooed from neck to toe in elaborate wolf images. Her skin was like a living mural featuring on her back a blue planet held aloft by a howling wolf, on her arm a huge wolf paw, and finally, over her chest, a black wolf portrait that pulsed with her every heartbeat. I was a little taken aback when she invited me into the restroom to view other wolf tattoos hidden under her skimpy, sleeveless scarlet dress.

What happens when affection and sometimes-intense identification with wild animals clashes with the fear that makes others see the return of a wolf as a threat to their own lives? This territorial battle is taking place not only in the human heart and imagination but also in public wild lands.

In the spring of 2011 a political rider to delist wolves from the Endangered Species List in Eastern Washington, Eastern Oregon, Idaho, Montana, and Northern Utah was attached to a piece of unrelated congressional legislation. It passed, setting a disturbing precedent. This was the first time since the passage of the Endangered Species Act that politics, not science, succeeded in determining the fate of wild wolves on public lands. Denying wolves previous federal protection meant that the states bordering Yellowstone took over wolf recovery. Usually with any ESA delisting there is a sixty-day period for public comment and litigation. But within days of the wolf delisting, Idaho's governor, Butch Otter, signed a bill declaring populations of gray wolves a "disaster emergency," giving him more authority over his own state if wolves were ever relisted as endangered. Other states, like Montana, followed suit and sanctioned legal wolf hunts. These hunts were very popular with those who had always resisted returning wolves, and it was dreaded by those who cherished wild wolves returning to their native territories.

At first none of these political wars made a difference for Yellowstone wolves. They recognized no boundaries except those they marked as their own. 06 and her Lamar Canyon family rarely ventured out of the park. But during the late fall of 2012, when the elk populations were again dwindling, 06 led her family out of the protected land to hunt. It must have seemed to wolves like stumbling onto another planet—asphalt roads, ranch houses, the choke of automobile exhaust, and, most of all, the scent of humans. The Lamar Canyon wolves had scented humans from the road, from the helicopters, from the valleys all their lives. Until this moment they had no reason to fear us. Humans had always existed near wolves in Yellowstone.

So 06, always walking point ahead of her pack, ventured into this alien wilderness outside Yellowstone. Suddenly the forest throbbed with a crackling explosion. Had 06 ever heard a gunshot? Her sharp ears could pick up sound from six miles away. But as Rick McIntyre poignantly noted, Yellowstone wolves "didn't know the difference between the click of a camera and the click of a gun."

If she didn't understand human hunting now, 06 instantly recognized a fellow predator as 754M fell down, wounded. No rival pack, no fierce fangs or hot fur or the thud and growl of bodies hurled against each other. The charcoal wolf simply dropped to the ground as if struck by lightning or some other invisible force. This doting uncle, 754M, who had played with and protected so many of 06's many pups, was dead. Quickly 06's family fled back into Yellowstone.

Douglas Smith and other biologists hoped that 06 and her Lamar Canyon family had "learned their lesson." Smith explained, "I thought she was immune. But it's naïve to think that we have a wolf running around in Yellowstone that's untouched by humans."

One December day in 2012 hunger again drove 06 to lead her mate, 755M, and family seventeen miles outside the park. There she too met a bullet. In an instant this majestic matriarch, who had inspired such devotion, was gone. Legally shot down by a hunter. He refused to be identified to the public or to claim his wolf trophy because he had killed the world's most famous and beloved wolf. As some of the protests said, "One hunter now has a trophy, while 100,000 wolf watchers and visitors mourn her death."

Reaction was instantaneous and mostly negative. The *New York Times* eulogized 06 as "beloved by many tourists and valued by scientists." She was the eighth radio-collared wolf killed by state-sanctioned hunts. Many people questioned whether the $4,000 radio collar she wore made 06 a susceptible and valuable target for antiwolf factions. Of the total ten Yellowstone wolves killed that year outside the park, five wore expensive research collars.

Editorials and social media weighed in with the suspicion that wolf hunters had unfairly targeted wolves with radio collars. Yellowstone Wolf Project volunteer Laurie Lyman told reporters, "I've been standing on the side of the road watching wolves and had people pull up and say to me, 'Lady, you better take a picture of those wolves because they're the last you're ever going to see.'"

Many veteran wolf watchers believe the hunters targeted 06 because she was so famous. Scoring a kill on such a well-known wolf was a kind of coup for antiwolf protesters. For evidence of this unethical tracking via radio collars by nonscientists, *Outside* magazine reprinted a 2010 post (now withdrawn) from the website www.huntwolves.com.

The post advised wolf hunters to hunt late into the night and scan for collars at a specific frequency. Although biologists made those wolf frequencies classified, it was not difficult to illegally hack into the radio-collar research and exactly locate a wolf. The post also explained how to turn off a radio collar by using a strong magnet. Destroying the radio collars of dead wolves meant that scientists also lost vital research.

The revival of legal wolf hunts and the loss of 06 sparked international outcry. There was such universal dismay about 06's death that Montana's wildlife agency briefly suspended hunting and the imminent trapping season. Many wolf advocates wanted to expand the park's boundaries to give wolves more protection. But others resisted giving wolves any more room to roam. Legal wolf hunting now continues in states bordering Yellowstone, with official kill quotas set for each Wolf Management Unit. In 2012, the year 06 was shot, the quota for wolf kills was thirty, about one-third of the eighty wolves who still survived in Yellowstone. That same year the Montana State House of Representatives voted one hundred-to-zero against creating buffer zones around the park to protect wolves from traps and guns. So the wolf hunts go on. In

2016 the Montana Fish and Wildlife Commission considered a request to increase wolf killing quotas from two wolves to six in one of the Yellowstone management units that borders Yellowstone, an area that has seen many wolves killed or poached.

 FOR THE BIOLOGISTS who have studied Yellowstone wolves for two decades, the loss of even a single wolf, especially one as much cherished and documented as 06, is profound. We are just beginning to understand wolf biology. Douglas Smith, the director of the Yellowstone Wolf Project, notes that studies of the social life of wolves are vital and still in the early stages. "Social means you have leaders and subordinates," he explains. "We're now looking at what the impacts are of a lead wolf dying vs. a subordinate wolf. Because wolves are social, one wolf is more important than another. . . . What happens to the pack after that leader is lost?"

After 06 was shot, her mate, 755M, left his family. He'd not spent a single day without his brother, whom he'd lost only weeks before. Animals mourn. We know that now from much-documented research about animal emotions and behavior. Elephants will stand over a slain matriarch, touching her body with their sensitive trunks in what appears to be funeral rites; dolphin mothers will carry a stillborn, nudging and balancing the tiny offspring, until the baby disintegrates; gorillas, like the famous KoKo, now have the sign language to express delight over a pet kitten and then sorrow over her loss. Wolves, one of the most social animals of all, grieve over the death of a family member by howling alone. According to evolutionary biologist Marc Bekoff, wolves mourning a death often lose their spirit of playfulness, lowering their tails and heads when they near a place where one of their own was killed. Like our domesticated dogs, wolves' expressions clearly show their emotions—from grief to pleasure.

Wolves also have an innate moral compass, says Bekoff. This is revealed in their strong social ties, complex communication, empathy, sense of fairness, and cooperation. Bekoff cites research from veteran wolf researcher David Mech that "pack size in wolves is regulated by social and not food-related factors." Family size in wolves depends on how many individual wolves can "closely bond." The recognition of ethics and emotions in other animals is revising the way we see our fellow creatures. This new research holds us to a higher ethical standard in our own treatment of other species.

"We had her in our sights," Laurie Lyman said, eulogizing 06. "We knew her and were so able to see how everything fell apart after her death. . . . Her death was sad, but the breakup of her pack—nothing good comes of it."

Without their leaders, the Lamar Canyon family fragmented, many of her daughters dispersing. Lyman tells the story of one of 06's daughters, 820, who was killed outside the park while preying on a chicken. Like 06, she was alone, trying to feed two pups. If she'd been with her family, she'd have recognized by now that leaving the park was too dangerous and that chickens were not as good a prey as elk or deer. But 06's young daughter had "no leadership or supervision." Her family was now like a "classroom without a teacher."

Because 755M couldn't mate with his daughters, he was forced to go in search of another mate. His quest was dangerous. Rick McIntyre notes that he and his colleagues had watched two other of "those big, tough males die in the attempt to start over."

But a year and a half after he lost 06, her mate finally found a bond with two females from the Mollie family—traditionally the Lamars' deadly rivals. Another trio formed, this time between two sisters and an alpha male. Both sisters were pregnant, but one of them died. The other gave birth to a new family. After years under the wise tutelage of 06, her mate, 755M, was a master hunter and good father. He has helped raise three litters. But when 755M attempted to return to his original Lamar Canyon family with his new mate, he was not welcomed back. 06's daughters now had new mates who threatened 755M and killed his mate. They drove the once-alpha male away from the Lamars. In 2014 he was again a lone wolf.

In the Lamar Canyon pack one of 06's formidable daughters has now risen to leader and continues the strong matriarchy that runs through 06's bloodlines. And so the legacy of 06 lives on—not only in her family line but also in our science and storytelling. They can kill the wolf, but they can't end her story. Any quick Internet search reveals memorials still updated annually on the anniversary of 06's death. Her family has been nicknamed "The Royals" of Yellowstone National Park and are chronicled with the same fascination as with other royalty. Watching the lives and deaths of royal families is in our human DNA and history. What's different now is extending that fascination to the dramatic rise and fall, the lineage and blood-lines, the alliances, mates, and conquests of other animals.

Jane Goodall defied scientific dogma by naming her study animals so that they became characters in their own dramas—Fifi, the nurturing and wise matriarch; Frodo, her strong and confident son; and on through their generations. In her talks before standing ovations Goodall often pant-hoots before she speaks. When she tells stories of the Gombe chimps, audiences lean forward as if she is telling us about our own families, our fears, our fates. In a remote Chinese village Goodall was once approached by a peasant woman who desperately grabbed her arm, demanding, "How is Fifi?"

The bonds that such stories create can be both compelling and threatening. The president of the Montana Shooting Sports Association, Gary Marbut, complains, "One of the ploys of the wolf advocates is to personify wolves . . . by giving them names and making them look like cute and fuzzy creatures. They generate acceptance of wolves by people who don't have to live with wolves. I see that as the chief motive for making them famous."

This fame and this intimate alliance with the other, with the animal, is exactly what those who want to eradicate wolves fear most. For so long the wolf has been declared "public enemy number one" that any other storyline is a big threat. To declare a person or an animal an enemy requires dehumanizing the other. Language plays a vital part in this process, like the propaganda of World War II when Americans reduced all Japanese to "Japs" and Germans to "Krauts." When we wish to exterminate any animal species we call them "pests" or "nuisance animals" or worse. Once other creatures have been demonized, rendered less than us, we are free to destroy them.

The British writer Alexander Pope once said, "All looks jaundiced to the jaundiced eye." If generations have called the wolf nothing but a ruthless killer, then of course that obscures any other view. In the same way, for those raised watching movies like *Never Cry Wolf*, in which the biologist begins to respect and even revere the wild wolf, that is the lens through which wolves are seen. In addition, because wild wolves' lives mirror our own in certain ways, we have difficulty seeing this fellow creature as separate and distinct from our own projections.

The powerful female wolf 06 was a fierce and protective matriarch who killed her prey and her foes with equal expertise. She was neither a ruthless killing machine nor a sentimental icon. She was simply going about the daily business of being a wolf—leading her family, feeding her young, and ferociously guarding her postage-stamp territory. Our dwindling wilderness was too small for such a singular and adventuresome wolf. Just as 06 had pushed the boundaries of her own strengths in her solitary hunts, just as she had chosen not only one but two males to make a family, just as she was immediately recognized as a charismatic leader, it was probably her destiny to be gunned down as soon as she left the protected park to explore and perhaps even claim more territory. 06 was too big for Yellowstone, too much larger than life to fit into our human lens. Main characters like 06 demand our timeless stories. We make myths of those we identify as the best or worst versions of ourselves. Whatever our point of view, the main character in any myth is either villain or hero. It all depends on who is telling the story—and when and where. But that lens is shifting: the more people who witness wolves, who watch their lives, who follow their generations, who understand their ecological role, the more clearly we'll see and act to conserve this fellow creature. The story of the real lives of wolves, as with all good tales, will change the way we see ourselves and our world.

# 8. OLD GROWTH AND YOUNG HOWLS

At midnight on a wild and cold mountain in Blue River, Oregon, in 2011 a small and hopeful human pack cupped our chilly hands around our mouths.

"*Ahhhhhwwwhhooooo*," we howled out into the dense and deep layers of old-growth forest, our voices a soulful blend of throaty baritone and wavering soprano.

We listened to hear if any wolves would answer. Screech owl hoots, a dim airplane roar high above, a startled scattering in the underbrush—but no communal and haunting *Canis lupus* howl came back to us. The same answer heard here for decades—the silence of the wolves.

"But wolves have been slowly coming back here since 2008," whispered a biologist accompanying us from the US Forest Service's enlightened HJ Andrews Experimental Forest. "In Oregon we now have a pretty sane and sensible management program. Yes, the wolves are still hiding out. Of course, they're always very wary of us. Who can blame them?"

Who indeed? Only three weeks earlier, in April 2011, the Republican Congress had passed a "wolf rider" to a budget bill, ending federal protection for wild wolves in Montana, Wisconsin, Idaho, Washington, Utah, and here in Oregon. Wolf management was returned to the states. Already wolf hunts were planned in Idaho, Wyoming, and Montana. The Natural Resources Defense Council was estimating that in Idaho alone, six hundred wolves—or 50 percent of the population—would be destroyed. There were a total of fifteen hundred wolves in all three Rocky Mountain states. In 2010

Idaho ranchers had lost only 148 cattle out of the state's 2.2 million head. The rider set a troubling precedent—politics trumping science in wildlife management. There were many protests: "Howl-ins" and "Phone-ins for Wolves" with people demonstrating from Idaho to Central Park. Friends of Animals president Priscilla Feral declared, "What's about to happen to gray wolves in Idaho, Montana, and Wyoming—who are a vital part of the ecosystem—is vile. Governors of those states are subjecting wolves to pogroms from the Middle Ages."

I had just written a *Seattle Times* article on the federal delisting, "Wolves Endangered by Political Predators." The *Times* headline was my editor's, not mine. Even the former director of the USFW, Jamie Rappaport Clark, was dismayed by the proposed delisting: "The service is saying, 'We're done. Game over. Whatever happens to wolves in the U.S. is a state thing.' They are declaring victory long before science would tell them to do so."

In Montana one outfitter advertised, "maximize your predator experience . . . add a fall black bear to your wolf hunt." It offered a "proven predator calling technique" to lure the wolf, bear, mountain lion, coyote, foxes, "and more" into your crosshairs. Those of us now howling in the forest were well aware of the violent backlash against wolves in other states. We believed that Oregon, still then in the early stages of wolf recovery, would handle wolf management in a more enlightened and far-sighted way.

"*Ahhhhhwwwhhooooo*," again, our plaintive and hopeful howls echoed through the valley. Below us the McKenzie River flowed fast and steep.

No wolves.

I wondered whether the wolves slowly returning on their own to this western Cascade Range might actually be nearby, scenting and waiting to figure out whether we were the dangerous kind of humans: guns instead of cameras, shooting instead of singing. Some scientists believe that wolves not only can smell danger, but they also can scent our moods, like our long-socialized and companionable dogs. I'd just read new research that wolves were able to follow a human's gaze—a surprising sign of social partnership. This skill at following a human's gaze is a difficult test for most animals and something that only apes, rooks, ravens, and wolves achieved in research tests. We already knew that wolves could easily follow our voices and could choose to respond to our human howling. So we sang on, a chorus engaging in an interspecies call and response as ancient and enduring as these trees.

"Listen!" someone whispered as a far-off howl ricocheted through the woods. Without our flashlights, it was astonishingly dark. An immense blackness, lit only by very distant stars. We closed our eyes tightly to open our ears.

"Oh," we sigh in disappointment, recognizing the hoarse whine and howl. "It's just a dog way down in the valley."

"At least we got some kind of canine callback," a man said, and we could hear him grinning.

Some of my companions were robust and knowledgeable Forest Service folks gathered for a weekend workshop in the HJ Andrews Forest. I was here as the spring's 2011 writer-in-residence. Wisely set aside in 1948, this forest, with its moss-draped canopies of Douglas fir, cedar, and hemlock, is a complex mix of old-growth and mature trees, from one hundred to five hundred years old. Much spotted owl research was conducted in these remarkable woods, an example of what happens when a forest is set aside not just for "multiple use" but also for long-term study.

It was so restorative to return to this Pacific Northwest forest only three hundred miles north of my High Sierra birthplace. Every day we trooped off into the old growth to study nurse logs and forest decay. In the evenings we gathered to talk about forests and wildlife. One of the participants read us a tenth-century Chinese dynasty poem called "Little Pines."

A thousand years from now
Who will stroll among these trees
Fashioning poems on their ancient dragon shapes?

Living among these old trees was indeed like being surrounded by giant, green dragons. It reminded me of my first forest and my father calling these massive red cedars "The Standing People."

Suddenly on our hike we heard a voice. "Don't be afraid. You can do it!" A boy in red overalls and blue down jacket was standing at the foot of a 250-foot Douglas fir and shouting up into the thick forest canopy.

I followed his gaze and saw seven ten-year-olds in full climbing gear—white helmets and black-strapped harnesses—all hanging from various heights along the huge tree. Cinching their metal clamps with their feet, they were inching up skillfully like little monkeys. Every now and then they dangled and swayed far out on their long red ropes to rest and chatter. Several adults hung between the climbers, expertly safeguarding the kids.

"If I die, you can have my cell phone!" one kid yelled down at another trying to catch up with him.

All the climbers burst out laughing. Squirrels chittered, and several ravens swept out of the canopy with complaining caws. Wings whooshed above.

Several of the kids were so high in the stalwart Douglas fir that I could see only their tennis shoes pushing off playfully against the moss-draped trunk. But one rather round and terrified boy was paralyzed, stuck only about fifteen feet up the tree. His eyes were riveted on the forest floor as if willing himself back on the soft ground.

"Lift up with your knees," quietly instructed the guide, who was hanging right above the frightened boy. "Then push up one step at a time on the rope." He rappelled down a few feet and reached out a hand to steady the boy's nervous sway. Again he showed the boy how to squat down as if in a fetal position and then step into the metal hardware attached to his rope to ascend one more body length up this rope's lifeline.

Very slowly the boy lifted his heavy body up one step at a time, cheered on by the other climbers above and below him. After a few successful lifts the boy's expression was pure delight as he finally got the hang of the rope and harness. In a surprising burst of speed, he climbed straight up with the grace of our primate ancestors. Everyone cheered and hollered and hooted their welcome.

"Now, it's your turn," the guide turned to me with a grin and offered me all the gear.

I hesitated. It had been decades since I'd scampered up a tree—and never one this enormous.

Almost all of the kids were climbing up to the very top of the tree, where lichen-rich boughs were streaked with sunlight, while I was still down here in the shade.

"Don't you want to get up there in the canopy where so few people ever get to be?"

Yes, of course I longed to be way up there with all the other kids, seeing this wondrous green world from the highest treetop like a raven or a red vole. I knew all about forest canopy research from reading Jerry Franklin's work; Franklin is a forestry professor at the University of Washington who first pioneered studying these old-growth forests from the top down instead of looking at trees from the bottom up. Franklin called his research "a clarification of the architecture of the forest," and it was a revelation for foresters.

I reached for the helmet, and the guide expertly tightened the harness around my hips, tugging it to make sure it was secure. I was surprised that my legs seemed to remember the firm push-down and powerful lift-up of a climbing rope as I slowly ascended the huge fir. It was hard and very physical work, and soon my muscles were warm, aching a little.

"Hey, kids," the guide called out to us all. "Let's take a rest and just be totally quiet for two minutes. Can you do it? Listen to what the trees and the animals hear this high up.

Not a giggle or a grunt. The kids fell into the same soaring stillness of the ancient trees that held them midair. In that spacious silence was a sense of timelessness. I remembered the Andrews forest biologist telling us, "Every tree has a resonance. When wind blows at that exact vibration, then the tree and the wind are in resonance. It's like music."

The wind makes a different song moving through each tree. This Douglas fir tree's song was sonorous, with a reassuring bass tone from standing tall for five hundred years. It had ventured up from the forest floor as a sapling, long before the European settlers came to these shores. In my lifetime 80 percent of these old-growth trees have fallen down in Pacific Northwest forests, and like the wild wolves who once roamed here, forests survive on only a fraction of their former territory. But this fir was still a mighty presence. And the wolves—at least here in Oregon—were still protected. I dearly hoped this Douglas fir would stand until these kids swaying far above me so silently were themselves great-great-grandparents.

Dangling there below all the children I realized that these little ones would live longer than I did. They see much farther than I do, I thought. They are already far in the future. What would their green world be like? Would these ancient trees survive them? Would wild animals like wolves still be a vital part of their lives and lands?

At last we all rappelled down, one by one, with an exhilarating zip-zip-zip of our ropes. There was a time to talk under the trees. I asked several of the kids about how it felt to climb so high into the mysterious forest canopy.

"We're on top of the world!" said one beaming girl, her pigtails matted with lichen and twigs.

"Awesome!" a boy echoed. He didn't want to give back his very cool helmet with the tree design on it.

"What are you doing here?" one asked me.

I told them I'd been listening for and writing about wolves. Before I could say another word the entire pack of children simultaneously startled howling. It was a higher-pitched but more melodious chorus than our howl in the forest the night before. I realized then that although the wolves may have gone almost extinct in our Pacific Northwest forests, the wolf in these children's imaginations had never been lost.

"What do you think about the wolves returning here?" I asked when they'd finished their long, group howl.

"It's cool!" they again all cried out together, still in tune from their howling.

"Yeah, I saw wolves in Yellowstone," one of the kids spoke up, happy to have bragging rights. "They were hunting!"

Not to be outdone, a girl searching in her backpack for her big glasses enthused, "Our whole class just adopted a wolf from the Wolf Education Center!" There was pride in her tone and immediate interest from the other kids when she talked about the wolf sisters, Motoki and Ayet. "Motoki is really shy and gets dominated a lot by her sister." The girl told the story of the two surviving wolves as if they were her own family members.

She explained that in her science class they had studied wolves and watched the documentary *Living with Wolves* about the Sawtooth wolf pack, the world's most famous captive wolves. Filmmakers and wolf researchers Jim and Jamie Dutcher spent six years living alongside the wolf family in a tent camp high up in this wild and remote wilderness. Their work offers a rare and intimate glimpse into wolf biology and behavior. Idaho's Sawtooth Mountains were five hundred miles west of our Oregon experimental forest. But those tree-climbing kids had already made plans to go visit Motoki and sister Ayet in their retirement at the Nez Perce tribe's Wolf Education and Conservation Center in Winchester, Idaho.

Many of the kids climbing the trees already knew about the wolf rider and the hunts scheduled to begin that winter in Rocky Mountain states.

"We're gonna stop these wolf hunts if they ever try it here in Oregon," the girl seemed to speak for all the kids. "We can do it!"

Standing there in the benevolent shadow of the majestic old trees, I truly believed they could.

THIS REUNION WITH the old trees and the determined children was a memory I held onto all during the next disturbing years as wolf hunts again became part of my daily news. Wolf hunting in the Rocky Mountain states began again in the winter of 2011–2012, and they were eagerly sanctioned by many state wildlife officials.

Ed Bangs, a retired coordinator for the USFW Wolf Recovery Program, commented that killing wolves was not sound and "isn't wildlife management—it's farming. You are farming for elk hunters." He added that the return to wolf hunts to "placate hunters" was telling: "A little blood satisfies a lot of anger," he said.

Bloodlust and backlash against wolves again had its day. In Montana there were 166 wolves killed out of a quota of 220. Most of the wolves weighed less than 100 pounds. Even after the official season in Montana was over in 2012, their Department of Fish, Wildlife, and Parks extended the hunt past the December 31 deadline because "not enough wolves were shot during the season. Just 105 wolves have been taken so far . . . and officials wanted hunters to harvest 220." Wyoming hunters used snares and leg traps that inhumanely and very slowly strangle the wolf who tries to escape. Idaho, the self-described "ground zero" for wolves, gunned down radio-collared wolves from helicopters—a strategy that Governor Butch Otter still champions and Wildlife Services tragically employs today.

Even in my home state of Washington, where wolves are still federally protected, at least in the western region, antiwolf factions again targeted the wolf. Ranchers suggested that wolves would attack livestock, pets, and people. They urged wolf recovery only in the urban, western part of the state, where liberal cities like Seattle passionately support it. To put this in historical perspective, in the past hundred years in North America only two people have allegedly been killed by wild wolves. Yet since 2002 bears have killed thirty-five people, and cougars have killed eleven people since 1990. In the United States domestic dogs kill twenty to thirty people every year. And human hunters kill nearly one hundred people in the United States and Canada every year and injure around one thousand. Even domestic cows kill more people than wolves do.

As the wolf wars raged on under states' control between 2011 and 2016, I caught up with wolf researchers Jim and Jamie Dutcher at their "Hidden Lives of Wolves" National Geographic presentation. In the standing-room-only Seattle concert hall, twelve thousand people listened to the Dutchers tell stories and show video about their field research on the Sawtooth wolves. Half of the audience was children—five thousand of them. Kids and adults were both spellbound as the Dutchers introduced us to wolves they'd come to know so well that they could recognize each one by their howls and could read their expressions, from fear to delight to wariness.

"We've really learned a lot from the return of wolves," Jamie explained. With her jet-black hair and small, wiry frame, she paced the stage. Jim was content to perch on a stool at the lectern. His silver hair reflected the subdued light of the grand hall. "In fact, it was the wolves who allowed us to become civilized. Over time, when we domesticated dogs—who descended from an extinct but common wolf ancestor—they helped us domesticate cattle and sheep. So we became a stable, agricultural society."

Jim Dutcher added, "Many people don't yet know that wolves mate for life."

In their Living with Wolves website and many books the Dutchers tell the story of our long history of prejudice. "We completely misunderstand and reserve a spectral hatred for wolves that we show no other animal," Jamie noted.

When she told the kids about the rampant wolf hunting then underway in the Rocky Mountain states, they all screamed out in one strong voice: "Noooooooooo!"

The fatal statistics for just that year of 2014 for all predator deaths were harrowing: Wildlife Services killed 322 wolves, 61,702 coyotes, 580 black bears, 305 mountain lions, 796 bobcats, 454 river otters, 2,930 foxes, 1,330 hawks, and 22,496 beavers. And the tab that taxpayers paid for Wildlife Services to destroy all of these wild animals was $1 billion. Jamie announced that at this date—the spring of 2014—over 2,262 wolves had already been killed since the 2011 federal delisting. She explained that Idaho governor Butch Otter proposed to reduce the wolf population to an unsustainable 100 animals. (This proposal would soon pass the Idaho State Senate.)

For years the Dutchers' research has been helpful in countering the regressive default to wolf hunting on the part of wildlife managers. "It's a policy that shows no science or real understanding of the species' survival," Jim Dutcher told me in a follow-up interview. "We can't treat wolves like rabbits or deer or like something that simply grows back. Just imagine if you killed off most of the members of your family—and expected the animals to go on as if nothing devastating had happened?"

It was an analogy that brought home just how complex and integrated wolf families are. Like us. His experience replicates what new research is proving—that wolf culling may actually end up hurting ranchers.

"When you decimate a pack—especially the experienced alphas—you end up with a younger, dysfunctional, and smaller family," Jim concluded. "The young wolves really don't know how to take care of themselves or hunt down larger prey. So they go after slower, easier animals—like the rancher's livestock."

"Wolves are such highly intelligent and social animals," Jamie echoed. "But we don't want to acknowledge that . . . because it makes it so much easier to hate them."

Then she explained that when a wolf pack loses one of the family members, their howls actually change. "When the Sawtooth lost their omega wolf to a cougar attack, the whole pack mourned his loss. They moped around, tails tucked, ears back. For six weeks they even stopped playing. Their howls took on a searching and mournful quality."

The Dutchers' work has revealed new insights into the close-knit family bonds among wolves. "We once found a wolf skull with signs of a broken jaw," Jamie explained. "But the jawbones had mended, and the wolf continued to live for several years after the injury. The only way that wolf could have survived is if the other family members fed him, regurgitating for him and refusing to leave him behind."

It was not so dissimilar, Jim said, as when a human dies and their dog grows depressed and howls. Jim told the story of when a wolf was shot down, "the whole family howled for days and days. The wolves then traveled in figure-eight patterns as if searching for that lost wolf."

We talked about the future for wolves in America. "Remember that half your Seattle audience was children," Jamie reminded me. "Do you know about Kids4Wolves and their social media campaigns to help wolves?"

I was reminded of the tree-climbing kids in the Oregon forest and their keen interest in wolf recovery. I had never heard of Kids 4Wolves or its hugely popular Instagram, Twitter, and Facebook sites that went live in 2013 and now have twenty-one thousand followers.

"I really think we might have to wait another generation," Jamie concluded. "The hope is in the children."

THAT NEXT GENERATION of wolf educators and advocates is here and already at work saving wild wolves. Washington State high schooler Story Warren, who was awarded a 2016 President's Environmental Youth Award, is the founder of Kids4Wolves. I finally caught up with this busy young woman in the early summer of 2016 right before she was journeying to the nation's capital to accept the PEYA at the White House. At my waterfront studio one of the first things she did was borrow my binoculars to watch an osprey diving and clutching a wriggling fish in its beak.

Story understands predator-prey relationships as a natural cycle of life. She has a biologist's perspective that comes from long hours studying wolves in the wild. "The first time I saw a wild wolf in Yellowstone I was six years old," she recalls, her voice clear, her dark blue eyes still riveted on the waves—and perhaps spotting another osprey fishing the Salish Sea. "The wolf was just a black dot in the telescope, but I kept following that dot in the snow."

That first glimpse of a wolf leaping in the snow captured Story's attention. She has been observing and following wild wolves ever since. Her family returned to Yellowstone every few years after that. "But pretty soon," Story smiles, "we started visiting the Yellowstone wolves three times a year . . . whenever I had more than a week off from school."

Story launches into a detailed and very impressive record of Yellowstone wolf genealogies, complete with what she calls "all the crazy plot twists" of family dynamics. Listening to Story expound on her research, it's impossible to tell her apart from any wolf biologist I've known. There is the same passion and practicality. Story can easily rattle off statistics—wolf depredation by territory or pack, wolves poached from each family, legislation that threatens the wolf recovery in each region, from red wolves in North Carolina to the recent killing of an Oregon alpha male, OR-4. Someone taking on the responsibility of educating her twenty-one thousand followers on Instagram needs this comprehensive knowledge.

"Why did you start Kids4Wolves?" I ask her.

Story's face darkens. "After they shot the female matriarch, 06, and 754M, her mate's brother, outside the Yellowstone Park boundaries," she says, "I was so upset that I went to my parents and said, 'I'm sick of you adults not getting anything done. Can I open an Instagram page for kids and wolves?'"

That was in December 2012, and now Story spends more than an hour a day handling her Kids4Wolves online grassroots organization. That's in addition to her homework. For this young science student wildlife is not just a study; it is already a calling, an avocation. On weekends she lugs a heavy backpack through knee-deep snow to track and document a wild wolf pack now claiming territory in Washington's mountains. Story started looking for the wolves in 2013 and didn't find any until the summer of 2014.

"The wolf pack has gone through a lot," Story explains, her voice shifting into a rather somber tone. "At least one member was poached, and there were no puppies last year."

"How is it different tracking wolves in Washington instead of just observing them someplace like Yellowstone?" I ask her.

"It's really different," Story says. "Remember, Yellowstone Park has no cattle. But when you're tracking wolves on the ground here, where there's a lot of cattle grazing on public land, you see how often wolves and cattle are actually in contact. The wolves are raising their pups among cattle. For the most part, wolves don't see the cattle as prey, and sometimes the living situation can continue for years."

The wolf family that Story has been diligently tracking has successfully shared the land with cattle for the past five to six years without a single known depredation until last year. Story has noticed that the cattle have adapted to the wolves recently by becoming much more alert. "Cows act more like elk. Now, with wolves around, cows will huddle together facing outward," Story explains. "And I've heard of situations where mother cows will actually chase off wolves to protect their calves—just like elk do. . . . Wolves don't chase cows who meet their advance. Cows will often hightail it after the wolves!"

Like any good wildlife biologist in the field, Story is keeping data on her wolf tracking. "Every single day wolves and cattle are together during the summer grazing season," Story reminds me, speaking quickly and earnestly. "We see cows right where we see wolf tracks. No way for wolves to live there without being among cattle all the time . . . sharing territory."

Story credits the Washington State ranchers for their use of proactive, nonlethal techniques to ward off wolves from their free-ranging cattle grazing on public land. "Many ranchers are using range riders to patrol their cattle and only ask for a wolf to be killed as a last resort."

Story would like to train as a range rider herself and in the future work with ranchers to facilitate wolf recovery. She already engages with ranch kids who respond to her blogs or Facebook posts.

"When I first hear from a young rancher or hunter," Story says wryly, "it usually starts with something hateful or violent . . . and I always try to begin a civil conversation. If I ask them questions about why they dislike wolves, then I can also learn a lot." She pauses thoughtfully. "Sometimes when I talk to these other kids and show them actual data . . . like how many cattle wolves actually kill or examples of ranchers successfully using nonlethal tools . . . there is a chance for an open exchange. Kids know what their parents tell them, and often there's no other point of view in their communities. So I just listen and keep asking them what their experience with wolves is. Then I tell them mine. If they prove me wrong, well, then I've learned something." Story, however, doesn't mince words when it comes to speaking out strongly about something she finds disturbing—like the Wildlife Services' use of "Judas wolves" in their culling strategies.

"Most of the time I can see why wildlife managers do what they do, and sometimes it's hard to know what is the right course of action in a wildlife situation," says Story. "But when it comes to a species as social and intelligent as wolves, I believe science as well as ethics should be a major consideration. There are some situations where I'm just not seeing that." In her Kids4Wolves blog Story wrote:

Sometimes these wolves were collared for research, but sometimes they are collared specifically so they can later lead the helicopters to their packs. After the sharpshooters have killed as many members of that wolf's family as they can, they leave the collared wolf alive. The hope is that this collared wolf will later join up with other wolves or form its own pack, and the helicopters can come back the next year, using the collared wolf to track down and kill its family yet again. Conceivably this collared wolf could go year after year watching its pack die, oblivious that it is the one leading the helicopters straight to them. These wolves are sometimes called Judas wolves.

This Judas wolf strategy is officially called "collaring for later control" by the Idaho wildlife managers. Imagine losing all of your family—over and over again. The lone wolf repeatedly loses his family for the four-year life of the radio-collar batteries. It's one of the most inhumane wolf-control practices, harking back to the Old-West days when cowboys on horseback would each lasso a trapped wolf and then ride off in four different directions, literally tearing the wolf limb from limb.

One of the most poignant and remarkable of Story's Kids4Wolves/YouTube channel posts is, "Kids to Secretary Jewell: Follow the Science." These brief but powerful video comments feature kids, from ages seven to eighteen, all across the country opposing Secretary of the Interior Sally Jewell's 2014 proposal to delist the gray wolf from the Endangered Species List. In their videos the kids point out that Jewell has promised to abide by "the best available science" on wolf recovery. Yet the scientists have rejected this delisting proposal, and the kids demand, "Who will inherit the benefits or consequences of your decision?"

Watching these kids ask of us a future that includes wild wolves, I'm reminded of the venerable author Ursula LeGuin at a recent Seattle reading. When a teen stood up to ask LeGuin, "What is the most important thing your generation can give ours?" LeGuin answered without hesitation, "Hope."

Does Story feel hopeful about the future of wildlife—especially wolves—in America?

The young woman surprises me with her direct and honest answer. "I'm a pretty cynical person," she says. "I doubt I'll ever accomplish anything concrete with Kids4Wolves." Story pauses and then continues, "There is still so much hatred in rural cultures, and it seems to be passed down through the generations." She adds with more energy, "But there is progress, especially here in Washington. I see the most hope here with all the stakeholders talking to each other, like with the Wolf Advisory Group." A recent Kids 4Wolves website post notes that Idaho ranks forty-ninth on school spending in the United States and forty-sixth in overall education. "Makes you wonder," it asks, "if that $400,000 per year from the legislature to be spent exclusively for killing wolves could be better spent on educating Idaho's kids."

It's a good question. What if these state monies spent on lethal control of wolves were redirected to educating the next generation? Or given to ranchers to fund nonlethal wolf deterrence? The federal delisting of wolves in Idaho and other states through a congressional budget rider set a dangerous precedent for the future of wild animals and for our own children's' heritage, and it foreshadowed the now-repeated attempts to gut the popular Endangered Species Act by a Congress overrun by the Tea Party's trigger-itch for budget cuts.

There is change and some signs of hope in America's ever-shifting attitudes toward wolves. "Hey, there, Little Red Riding Hood," a car commercial opens with the throaty pop song as a sleek red car zooms along a darkly wooded highway. Suddenly the driver stops. In the road stands a wild wolf. This is no deer caught in the headlights. True to centuries of our demonization, the wolf is growling, sharp teeth bared as if for attack.

If this scene were happening in the Wyoming or Idaho woods or any of the states determined to again sanction lethal wolf control, the man could simply get out of his car and shoot the wolf on sight—because state law has declared open season on wolves. But the ad takes a surprising turn: the driver simply veers around the wolf and zooms away. Then the driver turns to the backseat, where we see his little daughter, clad in a red-hooded jacket.

"What does the wolf say?" he asks her.

"Ahhwhooooooooo!" his little girl howls back, speaking the universal language of wolf.

part four

# WOLF NATION

# 9. WOLVES AND THE NATIONAL COMMONS

On my family's first cross-continent drive from California to Boston we children restlessly endured Kansas. In the most maddeningly monotonous state of all, sibilant green and yellow corn rows and cud-chewing cows lasted *forever*. Every now and then, when a scarecrow flapped in his red plaid shirt, strewing straw from his crazy arms, we woke from our hallucinatory flatlands daze. There were no trees for our Forest Service facts-on-file father to make us name and memorize, no dazzling mountain lakes, no grizzlies or mountain lions, and, of course, no wolves. Only humans and boring farm animals.

Our whining about the dull farmland allowed my father one of his famous lectures about how public lands—like national parks or forests—must be set aside for the future. There were hardly any wilderness areas in the Midwest, he explained. It had all been settled. Civilized.

My father had no bias against farmers, having come from a farming family in the Ozarks. But his years in the US Forest Service had inspired in him a lifelong passion and protection for federally managed wilderness. In fact, in a few years he would be part of passing the landmark 1964 Wilderness Act—legislation that protected large areas, especially in the West. This landmark legislation, the first in the world, would be the model for many other countries, inspiring them to declare and set aside wild lands for future generations.

On that cross-country drive my father continued his soliloquy to a captive audience of his children agitated by sugar and small bladders. But for once I was really tuning in. My father informed us that in the whole world, 99 percent of the people lived on just 1 percent of the land.

It was easy to believe this shocking statistic while driving empty Kansas highways. But it also looked to me like 100 percent of Kansas was farmed. Every inch of the Midwest was a patchwork of cookie-cutter crops, irrigation ditches, battered barns, and occasional trim, almost always white farmhouses. For a forest-born child reared in the mysterious shadow of Mt. Shasta, the sameness of Kansas seemed the very visual definition of the verb *domesticate*. I was in third grade and had just learned this word. For my recent school essay decrying the cruel treatment of horses, I had looked in the dictionary and discovered that a synonym for *domesticated* was *tamed* or *broken*. That's what this Kansas country looked like to me—broken into big squares, scarred through with dirt roads, and relentlessly tamed. Horses were broken, cows were, well, *cowed*. It was a farmer's paradise, a rancher's realm. Although there were endless horizons, there was no room for wilderness. No space for any animal who did not serve us.

As an adult traveling through Europe I would again be dismayed at how developed and domesticated land in Italy or Germany was, except for their unbroken mountains. How *spoken for* and neatly disciplined the public lands were, arranged into gardens, parks, tidy forests. Europe was beautiful and green—but completely subdued. Managed. By the time European settlers sailed to the New World of North America, all of their old-growth forests had been cut down. I longed to return to America with what was left of our old-growth forests and wild animals. Though there are some very modest attempts to reintroduce wolves to Europe, especially in Spain, Italy, and Romania, they have lost most of what was once wild.

Americans are now hotly debating whether we will go the domesticated way of Europe or preserve some wildness in our public lands, our characters, our souls. The Northeast and the South's public lands are older, with fewer top predators, but the battle for wildness and predator recovery is being played out in the Northern Rockies and the West. The pro- and antiwolf struggle is a particularly American passion play and identity crisis.

Are Americans lone cowboys out on the range with just sheep and cattle for company? Or are we urbanites who, having lost so much of what's wild, call passionately for rewilding? Are we rugged rural individuals who prize our gun rights more than our own safety? Or are we part of a larger community that negotiates cultural change and can tolerate outsiders and even other top predators? The fault lines are clearly and often tensely drawn. Will wolf reintroduction survive the inevitable backlash, the aftershocks of change?

Time and again the national polls tell us that a large majority of Americans want wolf recovery, especially on public lands—which belong to all of us, not just ranchers or farmers. In 2013, when the Obama administration proposed permanently stripping wolves of federal protection across most of the United States (except for the highly endangered Mexican gray wolf in Arizona and New Mexico), only one in three voters supported this delisting proposal. Many wildlife scientists vehemently decried the delisting plan. In a letter to Secretary of the Interior Sally Jewell scientists argued that wolves "have only just begun to recover in some regions and not at all in others," so federal protection must continue for the health of natural ecosystems. A *New York Times* op-ed by Jim and Jamie Dutcher, "Don't Forsake the Gray Wolf," noted that wolf management "continues to be hijacked by hunting and livestock interests" and concluded with the poignant question: "Have we brought wolves back for the sole purpose of hunting them down?"

A story from the Alaska Wolf Summit still haunts me and typifies a fading Last Frontier mentality. One of the wildlife managers at that backroom bar meeting mused, "My granddaddy was an old-time trapper up north. Once he discovered this big wolf with a paw clamped shut in the metal teeth of his trap. 'The wolf just stood there looking at me,' Granddaddy said. 'He just kept staring at me and wagging his doggone tail like that—until I finally shot him.'"

I never got a chance to ask the wildlife manager, "Would you too have shot that trapped wolf?" I could intuit by his expression—at once proud and yet troubled—that he might have at least considered making a different choice. He was more than a little haunted by his grandfather's story.

AFTER 2012 wolf management was returned to the state
wildlife commissions in Michigan, Minnesota, Wisconsin,
Idaho, Wyoming, and Montana—where 97 percent of gray
wolves in the lower forty-eight live—wolf trapping and hunting
was again quickly declared legal. All manner of bounties, hunts,
and trapping was allowed, and by 2014 fifteen hundred wolves
were killed in the Great Lakes region. In Idaho, during the winter of
2016, a virulently antiwolf Governor Butch Otter and the state's
Department of Fish and Game gunned down twenty radio-collared
wolves in a hunt that was kept secret from the public until it was
over. This hunt was intended to boost the state's elk population.

By the end of 2015 a federal judge, Beryl Howell, reversed the
feds' earlier decision to remove the gray wolf population from the
Endangered Species List. This was the fourth time a judge had over-
turned attempts to delist the gray wolf. Judge Howell noted that a
court "must lean forward from the bench to let an agency know, in
no uncertain terms, that enough is enough." Judge Howell ordered
wolves in Michigan, Minnesota, and Wisconsin restored to the Endangered Species List.

Although scientists and conservationists welcomed this decision,
a hostile Republican Congress immediately introduced legislation
in the form of yet another political rider attached to the budget bill.
This rider, like the successful one in 2012, would have again stripped
wolves of Endangered status and reversed Judge Howell's order.
There was another caveat to this 2015 rider: if passed, the legislation
would prevent any more judicial protection of wolves in the Great
Lakes states. At the last minute in early 2016 the rider was dropped
and the budget bill passed with wolves still under federal protection.

In 2016 the federal delisting proposal for all wolves in the United
States was still pending, and the seemingly endless backlash
against wolves went on. Oklahoma Republican senator Jim Inhofe,
who has also long claimed that climate change is a "hoax," chaired
the US Fish and Wildlife Service committees before the 2016 presidential election. He and other congressional Republicans were
"plotting separate courses for how to dial back the Endangered
Species Act," which included removing protections for many
endangered species. The GOP's 2016 presidential convention's

platform targeted the gray wolf as one of three species to delist. "The main objection to species conservation," noted *National Geographic*'s "Why These Rare Species Are Targeted by GOP," was that wolf conservation limits jobs and property rights. "But much of the public is uncomfortable with the idea of killing iconic species just as soon as they make a recovery," the article concludes. "Perhaps the GOP's mention of these species in their platform has more to do with wider cultural wars than wildlife science."

Democrats, such as California's Barbara Boxer, pledged to stop any weakening of the Endangered Species Act. "We will have hand-to-hand combat on the floor if these bills get that far," she vowed. Between the federal delisting in 2012 and 2016 over four thousand wolves were killed in the United States, according to the Center for Biological Diversity. And even though in 2016 only five to six thousand wolves now occupy less than 10 percent of their original range in the lower forty-eight states, there was again legislation—ironically called "Bipartisan Sportsmen's Act"—to "permanently end Endangered Species Act protections for gray wolves in Wyoming and the western Great Lake states."

Who is really fighting in this war? For over two decades I've listened to these voices and been on the front lines of what some are calling "the forever war." Because of a childhood raised not among wolves but among hunters and wildlife managers, I am very familiar with those who believe wolves must be lethally controlled. Because I've been covering wolves for so long, I receive many letters. People don't hesitate to tell me their opinions. To give voice to these people, I've chosen several to profile here. These individuals stand out either because of their representative or their unique points of view. Each of them offers more perspective than a simple pro- or antiwolf position. Think of them as the gray areas in the gray wolf controversy.

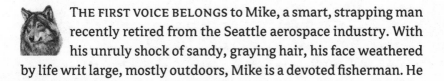 THE FIRST VOICE BELONGS to Mike, a smart, strapping man recently retired from the Seattle aerospace industry. With his unruly shock of sandy, graying hair, his face weathered by life writ large, mostly outdoors, Mike is a devoted fisherman. He

and his brother have enjoyed many elk- or deer-hunting treks. A rugged and outspoken researcher, he respects science, even while pointing out that it is changeable and endlessly revised. Mike is deaf but can easily read lips and speaks out articulately about his very strong opinions. His baritone voice carries even in a crowd. A stickler for facts and not one to tolerate fools, Mike often drily notes that public opinion is rarely based on reality. I've often met with Mike and his wife, Mary, who expertly translates for him in sign language if that is needed to clarify our dialogues. Mike resists political labels and prides himself on voting for the person, not the party. Mike has much to say about wolves returning to our lands.

We met for lunch at his home where his big motorboat, his pride and project, almost eclipsed the driveway. As a conversation appetizer Mike offered one of his favorite hunting stories.

"I was hunting up in Alaska with my good buddies but somehow ended up alone on the ridge with a grizzly nearby and a pack of wolves just below me." Mike paused to register my keen interest and then commented drolly, "Not the best position with night and bitter cold coming on. I tell you, I was afraid of those wolves, and one of them was acting kinda crazy, spinning around and howling. Maybe he was playing."

Mike had to risk hiking down to camp. Most of the pack moved behind him. "But I had to scoot right past that lone wolf"—he pauses with a smile and the punch line—"and when I got back to camp it was my buddies who were the real threat. They duct taped me in my sleeping bag—and then they threw me in the river."

Mike so reminded me of my father and his Forest Service friends with their hunting memories, told around a campfire or supper table. To a child these vivid and sometimes wry man-against-nature or wild animals stories were much better than fairy tales because they happened to be true. I enjoyed listening to Mike in the same way I was riveted to those stalwart hunters in my childhood.

"There's no real tradition in American history for wolf reintroduction," Mike's gruff voice took on a more serious tone as we met on his veranda that spring day. He adjusted his large glasses and fixed me with an intensity that perhaps came from often being misunderstood or dismissed because of his deafness. "Wolf recovery is all brand-spanking new to us! And before you judge hunters for re-sisting wolf recovery, I want to remind you that the press shouldn't always lump hunters and ranchers together. Don't you know that most hunting groups actually don't like ranchers?"

"Why not?" I asked.

"Ranchers don't like people shooting around their cows and sheep. That's why." Mike eyed me like a critical science teacher. "A huge amount of public land that is great for hunters and also hab-itat for bears and wolves is leased out for grazing to ranchers." He sat back and winked. "Of course, shooting cows is frowned upon!"

Mike told the story of a grizzly recovery project years ago. "A rancher was complaining to me about how he had to put up with bears threatening his herd on *his* land," Mike gave a short, dismis-sive snort. "I pointed out that I agreed with him—he should move all his cows off the public land and forfeit his lease in favor of the bears." Mike grinned and continued, "His comeback was to ask me, 'What's most important to you? The people making a living or the bears?'" Mike paused for greatest effect. "So what do you think I answered?"

"Dunno. Tell me."

"Well, I told him, 'The *people* are most important. Since the peo-ple own the land, it shouldn't be used to profit just one rancher!'" Mike sat back on his lawn chair and surveyed his impeccably sculpted backyard, complete with garden, cupola, and even a foun-tain—all made with his own hands. He concluded with a satisfied nod, "Later that night the rancher threatened to beat me up. He said he'd shoot me if he ever caught me near *his* land."

When I asked Mike what his bottom-line opinion of wolf re-covery was, he unhesitatingly informed me, "A lot of us hunters love wolves and want to see them restored where they belong. But we also believe wolves should always be controlled. And we don't buy all that bullshit about wolves having rights. Like land or trees, wolves are property of the state."

We paused to enjoy a little lunch together and throw bits of food to Mike's exceptionally well-trained black Labrador retriever. "You know, recently there was a coyote living in one of the gullies right near *your* apartment, wasn't there?"

I remembered the story of a female coyote in an old-growth Seattle park near where I live, blamed for killing several pet cats and getting into garbage cans. She was, indeed, killed by Animal Control.

Mike pounced on the predator comparison with glee, "Your Seattle neighborhood won't even tolerate a coyote in your backyards—so how do you think ranchers feel when wolves go after their sheep or cows? I also don't want any wolves wandering around in my neighborhood and would shoot any wolf, dog, or person who harmed my own dog here." He laid a protective large hand on his Labrador's head. "The thing is, you have to understand these ranchers, what they're afraid of losing. They're not the enemy. Just good, decent, and hard-working people trying to get along and make a living. And there really is no war against the wolf," he fervently claimed. "Just regular people trying to figure out how to survive with wolves right in their own backyards."

I pointed out that most of the rancher's livestock was already destined to be slaughtered. And that there were governmental and conservation groups like Defenders of Wildlife who had already paid out thousands of dollars to compensate ranchers for their losses to fairly minimal wolf predation over the last twenty years.

Mike waved my arguments aside and insisted, "But that's often a real hassle for ranchers to prove that it was actually a wolf that killed their cows. And ranchers are the ones who have wolves now as neighbors. They have to live with them.

"Conservationists must win their support, or the recovery efforts is either doomed or will be so restricted as to be pointless," he told me.

"But how to do that?"

"Keep talking," Mike advised. "You might be surprised at how many ranchers are really tolerant of wolf recovery but just afraid to speak out publicly because of peer pressure."

 I TOOK MIKE'S ADVICE that I talk with ranchers and farmers coexisting with predators when I met Elizabeth. She was visiting Seattle for a few months with her husband for his tech job. The couple and their three sons work a modest cattle farm in Virginia, where her grandmother's family has farmed since the 1600s. A lean and wiry woman with an energetic smile and a grounded intelligence, Elizabeth is in her midforties. She's passionate and well versed about sustainable farming.

"To me, sustainable farming is all about working with nature, not against it," Elizabeth told me, her expression intent. This is a farmer who is up many nights birthing calves. She's had to educate herself in veterinary skills because the closest vet is an hour's drive away. She's also a mom who tries to teach her sons about farming.

"When we're out building fences or moving cows and we'll hear a coyote howl or see raccoon tracks in the mud, I always tell my boys that producing food doesn't mean you have to eradicate all the wildlife around you. Instead, we welcome wildlife here. Coyotes keep rodent, rabbit, and groundhog populations down, which also benefits our farm."

"So coyotes are the main predators in Virginia?" I asked.

Elizabeth nodded, "There is really nothing more upsetting to a rancher than having our livestock killed by predators, so I understand wanting to kill off wolves. As a cattle farmer myself, I also imagine it's hard for ranchers to hear people who don't make their living off the land calling for a return of the wolves to the wild."

Elizabeth paused thoughtfully. "But in the East, where my family raises cattle, we simply have to take a different approach from the mass slaughter of wildlife." She leaned forward, her dark eyes reflecting a characteristic enthusiasm. "Instead, our strategy is to protect our livestock from predation. We don't leave our cows way out in the woods or out in the furthest pasture during calving season. We bring our cows closer to home to protect them."

"But what happens if you lose a cow to a coyote?"

Elizabeth sat back and considers this for a while. Her tanned face fell into an attentive stillness. "Well, if a wild animal makes a kill, then we know we've been slack and have to reevaluate our management strategy. In the last fifteen years we've never killed a single wild animal."

"That's really impressive. What do you think about the wolf-recovery issues here in the West?"

Elizabeth frowned and shook her head ruefully. "Western ranchers who graze on public land—something we don't have the luxury to do in the East—have come to have an entitlement attitude, giving all farmers a bad name."

"How so?"

"Well, if we have to work hard to protect our livestock while western ranchers use land subsidized by taxpayers and then demand that public agencies use public money to kill off wolves rather than tightening up their own management strategies—then clearly they've moved from being so-called cowboys to standing in the welfare lines."

"Strong words from a fellow farmer."

"Yes," she nodded. "Strong words because farmers are straight-talking people. We tell it like it is. The bottom line is that western ranchers can also learn to take more responsibility for protecting their own sheep or cattle. It's just part of the job."

More and more ranchers and farmers are understanding and implementing what Elizabeth's farm models—active protection of their livestock from predators. In my home state of Washington wolves are still on the Endangered Species List, and there is the hope that in the far West we will, as Elizabeth said, do it differently, more sustainably, and less acrimoniously from the endless wolf wars of the Rockies.

 IN 2015 the Pacific Wolf Coalition reported that one hundred thousand West Coast residents joined 1 million citizens from across the country to urge the federal government to maintain federal protection for gray wolves.

"Washington has the best wolf management plan in the West," notes Conservation Northwest's Mitchell Friedman. "We don't want wolves to be just another divisive urban-rural, green-brown issue," he added. Friedman wants to use dialogue between ranchers and wolf advocates to build "a sense of community around doing the right thing so we can have recovered wolf populations and healthy wild ecosystems right along with successful ranches and agricultural production."

Friedman takes part in the collaborative work of the Wolf Advisory Group, which includes sportsmen, ranchers, and wolf advocates. In Washington, Oregon, and California, ranchers are learning nonlethal ways to protect their livestock. They hire range riders and don't graze their sheep near known wolf ranges. Ranchers can sign an agreement with Washington wildlife officials to practice "conflict avoidance." This collaboration offers participating ranchers daily radio-collar alerts to signal when wolves are near grazing livestock.

Washington rancher Sam Kayser, who pastures his cows on public land, explains that he's working with the state to adapt to wolves. His ranch is one hundred miles east of Seattle. When wolves killed one of his cows in the summer of 2015 Kayser told the *Capital Press*, the West's ag website, that "he still believes his cattle can coexist with the returning predators." Kayser is not a wildlife advocate; he's a realist. "I'm not excited about it," he says of wolf recovery, "but it doesn't matter whether I'm excited. We're stuck with them. I want to think there's room for all of us out there."

Kayser's cattle ranch is in Central Washington near wolves known as the Teanaway pack. Of the six wolves in this family, three were fitted with radio collars. Three times a day these collars transmit the wolves' location to Kayser's veteran range rider, Bill Johnson. The Teanaway pack is still protected by the federal Endangered Species Act because it ranges in Western Washington. Shooting these wolves, even if they prey on livestock, is not allowed. So the ranchers have to learn nonlethal alternatives. Necessity does become the mother of invention—and if not acceptance, tolerance. Range rider Johnson has been protecting Kayser's five hundred head of cattle since 2011. On one of his patrols he stopped to check out scat and noted that the wolves had dined on elk, rodents, and robin's eggs. Not livestock. Johnson's work is partially supported by Conservation Northwest. As a professional range rider, Johnson now considers himself prowolf.

Jay Kehne of Conservation Northwest explains, "Wolves bring up so many emotions on all sides. We wanted to find that middle ground and work with ranchers to give them the best possible tools for nonlethal deterrence." Some of those deterrents include bright flashing lights, sirens, stun pistols, barking guard dogs, and red, flapping strips of cloth called "fladry," which seem to frighten off wolves. One of the most effective ways to ward off wolves is simple: remove carcasses so as not to attract any predators. In Washington a new facility is being built where ranchers can drop off dead livestock for composting.

Range rider Johnson credits the wolves for their keen intelligence. "It doesn't matter where we run the cattle—the wolves have a way of knowing." They don't appear to be afraid of him on his horse as he keeps vigil over the herds. Johnson's and others' range-riding work uses the timeless tactics of any cowboy or shepherd—human protection. Move cattle for grazing and to avoid possible wolf presence. Every morning Johnson checks the computer for radio-collar signals from the wolves. Working with his well-trained border collie, Nip, Johnson protects the cattle from probing wolf packs.

Washington State fully compensated Kayser for his loss of this one cow. "I appreciate that, and that's the way it should be," he says. "I shouldn't have to carry the financial burden for the public getting to have wolves." More wolf depredation may occur, but "we'll cross that bridge when we come to it." Kayser concludes, "So far we've been successful. But we have enough habitat for the wolves we have."

In the summer of 2016 Washington hosted nineteen wolf families, which included ninety wolves with eight breeding pairs. Conservation Northwest has contracted to hire five more range riders throughout the state, but although they can protect livestock from wolves, they can't protect wolves from illegal hunting. Sadly, within a year after wolves killed Kayser's calf, a poacher killed the alpha female of the Teanaway pack.

Fellow ranchers have accused both Kayser and Johnson of selling out because Kayser has signed the agreement with the state to work together to adapt to wolf recovery. Kayser protests this accusation. "I call B.S. on that. To me the goal is coexistence."

 ALTHOUGH A VERY VOCAL and historically dominant minority of antiwolf ranchers, who have thus far determined wildlife policies, still have much influence, new demographics challenges their power.

Our changing American identity will profoundly affect how we see other top predators. By the year 2020 "more than half of the nation's children are expected to be part of a minority race or ethnic group," says the Census Bureau. Whereas 72 percent of Baby Boomers are white, Americans born after 2000 are only 50 percent white. Hispanic populations will triple by 2050, and Asian and African American numbers are also growing. As the United States grows more diverse and urban, our politics and policies concerning public lands and wildlife will change.

In another shift, there are now as many Millennials (those born between 1982 and 2004) of voting age as Baby Boomers, and they are only 56 percent white. Millennials are "the most educated, the most diverse, and one of the most liberal generations ever." This demographic is also "the largest generation in American history." This is the generation of Occupy Wall Street and Black Lives Matter, people who value authenticity and integrity in candidates for political office, a collective voice well schooled in social media.

An interesting note is that while few Millennials label themselves as "environmentalists," they are, in their politics and preferences, the most environmental generation ever. They support sustainable companies, and solar and wind energy, and approve of stronger governmental regulation. In fact, Millennials are open to more and bigger government involvement in everything from food labeling to humanely raised meat and dairy to conservation. Millennials eat less meat than previous generations and are more active in local, grassroots green organizations. Two-thirds of Millennials believe that human-caused global warming is real and that climate change needs to be addressed; only 25 percent believe that the United States should expand oil, coal, and natural gas production. This so-called Green generation bodes a different future for both conservation and animal welfare. As one Millennial writer noted, "Environmentalism and modern, urban lifestyles are not mutually exclusive. . . . I'd argue that Millennials have begun to shed the mindset that having concern for the future of our planet and species is specific to environmentalists alone."

A Millennial I interviewed in North Carolina on wildlife issues exemplifies this new generation's broader reach. Courtney is in her late twenties, slender and amiable but with a welcome dark sense of humor. She has written essays published in *The Huffington Post* on everything from pets to chronic anxiety. She met her husband, Isaac, while both were interning at a dolphin-research facility in the Florida Keys. As a child Courtney wanted to be a dolphin trainer, so spending her summer days with dolphins was a dream come true. Like many of her Y Generation, Courtney suffers from asthma and intense food allergies; she's had to study food labels and is hyperaware of both air pollution and dangerous additives in foods. After graduating college with a degree in psychology, Courtney was the director of Student Services at a medical arts college in Winston-Salem, North Carolina, and she now works at a local nonprofit teaching life skills to socially challenged kids, like those with autism or developmental disorders.

"I struggled with social skills as a child," Courtney told me, "but thankfully my parents recognized this and placed me in a program where I could learn them."

With her vivid bright blue eyes and easy laughter, it's hard to imagine that Courtney ever had any difficulty with "social skills." But there is an edginess to her admittedly droll and ironic take on life. She is a chronic sleepwalker and has a recurring nightmare that she is "sleeping on a pile of puppies who need rescuing."

Like Courtney, giving back and community are two of the major themes of many of these globally minded and hyperconnected Millennials. Check out any Instagram, Facebook, or Tumblr page, and you'll find calls for everything from pet adoption to river restoration to protecting endangered species. Courtney loves all animals but is allergic to most dogs. Her husband presented her one day with a nonallergenic labradoodle puppy named Henri. Chocolate colored with curly hair, Henri is one of the most personable canines I've ever met, her black eyes eerily human. Courtney and Isaac used their dolphin-training skills to raise Henri to be so socially gifted that she is now an official therapy dog. Courtney brings Henri to elementary schools to help kids learn how to read, and Henri is equally embraced by enthusiastic and grateful elders at a local senior center.

When I interviewed Courtney, her labradoodle was leaning against my knee, gazing up at me with an almost unsettling attention. Although Henri is certainly domesticated, she has the alertness and intensity of her *Canis lupus* distant cousins.

When I asked Courtney what she thought about wolves being restored to their former ranges in America, she replied, "I really support wolves being returned to their homes and former territories. We've taken so much out of the wild—why not try to restore wolves and other animals to where they belong?"

I asked Courtney what she thought about the controversial efforts to restore the red wolf, the most highly endangered wolf of all, to North Carolina—the only place in the world where red wolves are not extinct. North Carolina once had an engaged wolf recovery program, but the federal agencies charged with their reintroduction have recently abandoned efforts to release captive-born red wolves into the wild. Conservation groups are filing an emergency petition and suing the USFWS to save a red wolf population that is going extinct on their watch.

As we talked about this sad decline in red wolves in her state, Courtney said, "I only hope we can give them the space and respect they deserve. I live in a city, but it's good to know that wild animals are still surviving in my homeland. Maybe my children will one day hear or even see a red wolf in the wild."

WE MAY NOW BE WITNESSING the last days of ranchers, hunters, and farmers dominating public lands and wildlife management. In fact, livestock grazing on federal lands has decreased over the last half century—from 18 million foraging acres in 1953 to only 8 million in 2014. Ranchers' influence in politics is also shrinking. This doesn't, however, mean the transition and evolution of our American lands and identity won't be turbulent and troubling. Or violent.

One of the new battlefields emerging is between the states and the federal government over control of public lands. State campaigns to "take back" public lands and resistance to federal wolf recovery programs are inexorably linked. That struggle is embodied in the occupation of the Malheur National Wildlife Refuge in Oregon's high desert in January of 2016 by militants crusading against federal "ownership" of those remote 187,757-acre public lands. The militants were an offshoot of an earlier protest by Nevada rancher Cliven Bundy because the feds had removed his cattle from public lands after Bundy refused to pay long-overdue grazing fees. Bundy's sons staged the Malheur wildlife refuge occupation.

In that bleak, midwinter wilderness militant protesters cut down trail signs with a chain saw and burned them. They confiscated a USFW vehicle and threatened violence. Patrolling the remote visitor center, heavily armed men in cowboy hats guarded the wildlife refuge on horseback waving an American flag, while others held up signs reading, "Take Back Oregon" and "BLM—Another Intrusive, Tyrannical Government Entity Doing What They Do Best ABUSING POWER & Oppressing the Backbone of America." (BLM is the Bureau of Land Management.) Are these angry protesters really the "backbone of America"? Does their cause reflect our true American character, or are the protesters a fringe group, a throwback to the past? Whatever the answer, they certainly represent the confrontations ahead over public lands and wildlife management, especially in the West.

The wildlife refuge takeover revealed several old and new twists in a states vs. feds battle. An irony that the occupiers seemed to miss when they proclaimed that Malheur was "taken illegally by the federal government" from the "more than 100 ranchers and farmers [who] used to work this land" is that the refuge stands on ancestral land still sacred to the Paiute tribe. Their ancestors lived on this land nine thousand years ago, but the federal government forced them off their land after signing the treaty of 1879.

In knee-deep snow the tribe was loaded into wagons, and "they literally walked our people, children, and women off our lands," said Paiute tribal council member Jarvis Kennedy. The two-hundred-member tribe still struggles to get by in this isolated Oregon landscape that is especially desolate in winter. In Kennedy's view, if his tribe were trying to take over the wildlife refuge, "We'd be already shot up, blown up, or in jail. They are white men. That is the difference."

One of the most vivid reactions to the Malheur antigovernment occupiers came not from tribes or politicians but from wildlife advocates—especially birders. Conservationists have long cherished Malheur as a mecca for its multitudinous bird life—from great horned and barred owls to elegant ibis, from western snowy plover to white heron. The Malheur Wildlife Refuge is "home to 320 species of birds and 58 mammal species" and a birders' delight, according to veteran birder Noah Strycker, who spotted 50 species of birds at the refuge in one day.

An outraged letter from a longtime birder, "Warning from the Birding Community to the Terrorists in Oregon: We're Watching You," went viral and spawned a #takebackmalheur campaign. The letter called out the Malheur occupiers and claimed "your decades of constant poaching of protected wildlife around Malheur and other wildlife refuges, national parks, national forests and BLM lands has been well-documented." The letter also pointed out that "Wildlife photographers and wildlife/bird watchers now number some 40 million people in the USA and feed many rural western economies with our tourism dollars" and promised that "we are watching you and our years of birding photography have made us endlessly patient and determined."

It wasn't just angry birders who condemned the Malheur occupation. CNN security analyst Juliette Kayyem, a Harvard professor and former assistant secretary in the Department of Homeland Security, called the Oregon antigovernment occupiers "domestic terrorists." Kayyem wrote, "They are dangerous, they are unforgiving, they are flouting federal law . . . they are clearly willing to use violence to get their way." She reminded the occupying militia that "if a federal agent or public safety official is harmed or killed during any siege . . . they all will be accomplices to first-degree murder." She advised the feds to wait out the occupiers who were, after all, in a snowy, remote area and having trouble even getting supplies from sympathizers. "We're not in Iraq," she concluded.

After all the media coverage, there was very little public solidarity for these cowboy militants taking over a wildlife refuge. Oregon locals held town halls demanding that the antigovernment pro-testers at the wildlife refuge "Go home!" The majority consensus on the occupation was echoed in a *Christian Science Monitor* article on the Malheur occupation as "political theater that paints their fellow Westerners in a poor light and disregards—and even under-mines—the approach favored by many who seek to reshape the West's future without a revolution." The article was sympathetic to small-town ranchers and farmers who are struggling, losing farms, and having trouble adapting to new economic trends.

In fact, *High Country News* points out that since frontier days the American West has the highest suicide rates in the country among white males aged forty-five to sixty-four; most shoot themselves. That was the same age and ethnicity of the Malheur occupiers, many who fully expected they might die violently at the hand of the feds. These men feel disenfranchised by swift cultural and eco-nomic changes that leave them marginalized and powerless. Their armed takeover of a wildlife refuge and threatened violence was a kind of last stand for a way of life that is fading. Their outrage, enti-tlement, and violence reveal a kind of adaptive disorder, an inabil-ity to change. Many of the Malheur occupiers mistakenly believed that grazing on public lands was a right guaranteed in the Consti-tution, not a contract that required payment.

When interviewed, the occupiers had neither a sense of this land's history nor what might become of it and its wildlife if fed-eral lands were divested to state and private owners. If that hap-pens, the likely result would be a rapacious land rush and real take-over that would ruthlessly eliminate small farms, ranchers—and wildlife. After such a private and corporate land rush the federal government might be remembered as benign by comparison.

Many white settlers were originally called to the West when the federal government granted free land for homesteading. "The fate of the West has, almost from the very beginning of the country, been tied to Washington." So the irony that those who were once given free land by the feds and for over a century have been using our public lands for grazing are now raising a rebellion against the government is not lost on many westerners. An editorial, "Cow-boy Nihilism," in the *Seattle Weekly* reminded readers that it was

Republican president Theodore Roosevelt who first created the Malheur reserve in 1908 to protect native bird populations devastated by plume hunters for feathers used in women's hats. Roosevelt wrote that whenever he heard the phrase "destruction of species," he "felt just as if all of the works of some great writer had perished."

The fact that wildlife conservationists played a big part in opposing the Malheur occupation is a vital sign of how important wildlife has become to the American public and our evolving identity. It wasn't just environmentalists who decried the Malheur wildlife refuge takeover; many hunters and anglers "worry that their elk-hunting grounds and trout streams would be sold to private hands and developed," notes the *New York Times*. "Unlike the federal government, many states require that their land be used as profitably as possible." The Malheur occupation, in the tradition of the Sagebrush Insurgency before it, is significant because it is a highly visible drama that symbolizes the smoldering state vs. federal government tensions flaring up in the West like the record-setting summer wildfires.

After about six weeks the Malheur occupiers were jailed with one death—a protester who resisted arrest at a stop sign. When the Malheur armed takeover was winding down in February 2016, troubling news broke of the "dark money" funneled by the American billionaire Koch brothers into other public-land-seizure efforts by some state politicians to wrest away control of national forests, monuments, and public lands and transfer them to states. This "land grab" movement, often called "Free the Lands," is well funded by the Koch Brothers and "has forged an alliance with groups and individuals who have militia ties and share extreme antigovernment ideologies." Unlike the small band of militants who took over the Malheur Wildlife Refuge, this showdown is a national and very robustly financed campaign to transfer public lands back to increasingly belligerent state officials who oppose federal protection of lands and wildlife, calling conservationists "pro-animal extremists." In the federal trial, all of the Malheur Wildlife Refuge occupiers were acquitted—a verdict that shocked many conservationists. David Yarnold, president of the National Audubon Society, commented, "Wild lands belong to all of us, not the people who hold them at gunpoint."

Tracing the roots and often shadowy players in this state rebellion against federal protection of public lands and wildlife is important because it is the states that are now mainly calling the shots on wildlife in the United States. And in the West some of those states—especially the ones that are increasingly resistant to wolf recovery—are being run by legislators sympathetic to paramilitary uprisings against federal management of public lands. During the Malheur occupation several Republican House representatives from Utah and Oregon, active in a group calling themselves COWS (Coalition of Western States), visited the Malheur occupiers against the express request from the FBI and a local judge to keep away from the refuge stand-off. NPR covered the story and noted that the COWS visit "was the last step in an ongoing and organized campaign by these lawmakers, essentially the political arm of the militant movement, to make a once-radical political cause part of the mainstream."

That cause, proclaimed on the COWS website, is to "restore management of public lands to the States where it constitutionally belongs." With press releases that declare "This is a war on rural America," COWS found sympathy in a Republican-controlled Congress where several Utah representatives demanded that the Bureau of Land Management (BLM) and the US Forest Service be stripped of their law enforcement authorities. In 2014 Texas senator Ted Cruz proposed "preventing the federal government from owning more than half of any state's land." Much of the West is under federal management. Population stats echo what my father once told us: "5 percent of westerners live, nearly alone, on half the West's land."

After the Malheur occupation there were news reports that the ultra-right-wing Koch brothers—who inherited their fortunes from industries in chemicals, jet fuel, fertilizer, and electronics—had actually funded the Bundy land seizure movement through various lobbying groups. "Is this why efforts are continually blocked when trying to stop the brutal slaughter of our wolves, bison, wild horses and other imperiled species and places?" asked Examiner

.com. "Could they also be covertly blocking endangered species designations or enforcement? Could they, in fact, be instrumental in facilitating the removal of America's native wildlife from public lands, in favor of mining, drilling, logging, hunting and ranching interests?"

*High Country News*, which covers the entire West, notes in a cover story, "Inside the Sagebrush Insurgency," that both the Malheur occupiers and the Sagebrush Rebels who've been fighting the feds since the 1970s aren't really that representative of ranchers and farmers. There were very few ranchers among the occupiers, and the Bundy family actually owns a truck-fleet business. Bundy told reporters that he was not only speaking out for "the ranchers, the loggers, and the farmers" but also "the auto industry, the health-care industry, and financial advisors." That's quite a large and more urban swath of Americana that has little to do with public lands or wildlife. The *High Country News* report points out that the states vs. feds struggle over public lands is "a nationwide confluence of right-wing and libertarian extremists. Many of them have little interest in grazing allotments, mining laws, or the Wilderness Act. It's what these things symbolize that matters: A tyrannical federal government [that] activists can denounce, defy, and perhaps even engage in battle with."

The election of Donald J. Trump in 2016 dealt a serious blow to American wildlife, especially wolf recovery. This was an election characterized by an entire Republican party whose leading candidates denied climate change and consistently voted against ecosystem and wildlife protections. President Trump vows to cut funding for the EPA and has shown no sympathy for America's wild lands or wildlife. Under his pro-business, anti-environment administration, the Endangered Species Act may finally be gutted by a Republican congress. And that would be bad news for wolves and all endangered species.

 AMERICA'S 640 MILLION ACRES of public lands are treasures and "our national commons," writes author William DeBuys. These vast and diverse wild lands "spread unbroken over great enough distances to offer the connectedness that any plants and animals will require to adapt, to the extent possible, with a warming climate." They offer, as Gretel Erlich reminds us, "the solace of open spaces."

In our evolving American politics and history of land disputes, symbols or symbolic acts have deep roots. For better or worse, the wild wolf has become a vivid symbol of our shifting and often contradictory American identity. What is the American character? Given enough land, we are strong willed and successful settlers of territory; we struggle all our lives for hierarchy and dominance. We are close-knit and loyal to our families; we are sometimes welcoming but more often exclusive and wary of outsiders. We are violent and playful and as yet untamed—like the wild wolf.

There are as many facets to the American character as there are states. Whether it's Mike, the sixty-something fisherman who accepts wolves but not too near his suburban Washington neighborhood; the Virginia cattle farmer, Elizabeth, who prides herself on her nonlethal alternatives to predator control; the Eastern Washington rancher Sam Kayser, who tolerates wolves on his ranch and aims for coexistence; the Millennial urban-dwelling social activist and wolf advocate Courtney who hopes her North Carolina red wolves will survive; or the antiwildlife and states' rights militants who demand that the vast western public lands be managed first and foremost for big business like mining and fracking—these characters will define our national identity, but not without struggle. In a new century the Old West must change its identity to reflect New West realities and values—unless we want to see our wilderness auctioned off into nothing but farm and ranch land. An endless Kansas.

# 10. WOLVES AT PLAY

F or those of us who work with wildlife conservation, there is often a kind of compassion fatigue that settles in amidst the seemingly endless political and legal battles to help save endangered species. One antidote to this malaise is the abiding friendships, the high-spirited play, and even the humor that animal people share. In their company I often find myself howling with laughter, uplifted by their camaraderie, their cooperation with other wolf-recovery organizations, and their generosity. I'm especially in awe of the conservation lawyers who every day fight valiantly for other species. With the relentless congressional efforts to gut the Endangered Species Act and renewed, intense wolf hunting, these lawyers would have the most reason of us all to succumb to despair. Yet they are some of the most buoyant and heroic of all animal people. One of these conservation warriors is Amaroq Weiss, who is based in the San Francisco Bay Area and is the West Coast wolf organizer for the international Center for Biological Diversity. In fact, her name, Amaroq, is Inuktitut for "wolf."

"My client is the wild wolf," Amaroq says with a wide smile. With piercing eyes and jet-black hair woven with silvery strands, Amaroq, like many animal people or pet owners, resembles the animal to whom she has devoted her life, blending her background as a former attorney and biologist.

This is the first time I've met Amaroq in person, although I've often corresponded with her about wolf issues. It's a balmy, sunlit day, and we're meeting at my waterfront studio. Behind us the tide is so high that its waves accompany our dialogue. At my kitchen table over tea she leans forward, literally rolling up her sleeves. "We are winning for the wolf. It just doesn't look like it at times. When I was a defense attorney victories were few and far between. But victories for the wild wolf—when they happen—are really big." She nods with pleasure and well-earned pride.

Amaroq is here in Washington to attend the spring 2016 Wolf Advisory Group (WAG) meeting in Ellensburg. Created by the Washington Department of Fish and Wildlife (WDFW), WAG consists of representatives from the livestock industry, sports-hunting groups, and conservation groups and was convened by WDFW to help it implement the state wolf-conservation and management plan. Part of the state Wolf Plan's objectives is to "minimize conflicts that may occur, recognizing that public acceptance is essential for wolf recovery to succeed." Some of the key strategies and issues in the Wolf Plan that the WAG discusses and fleshes out include compensation for livestock lost to wolf predation and how to encourage livestock producers to "take proactive, preventative measures to decrease the risk of loss." These WAG meetings are open to the public so that anyone who wants to understand how WDFW develops its wolf-management policies and practices can listen in and learn about what different stakeholders are advising in order to best live with wild wolves.

The nonprofit Center for Biological Diversity is a leader in international conservation. It seeks legal protections for endangered animals, including Florida panthers, owls, jaguars, and black bears; fights against rampant fracking on public lands; and uses science, law, and creative media to engage people in saving biodiversity. Its mission statement says, "We want those who come after us to inherit a world where the wild is still alive."

Along with their many successful lawsuits on behalf of imperiled wildlife, the Center for Biological Diversity has come up with some persuasive innovations, such as cell phone ringtones of Mexican wolves, Puerto Rican frogs, Hawaiian monk seals, Texas toads, or humpback whale lullabies, as well as condoms that link overpopulation with wildlife extinction. Each condom features a different animal with slogans like: "Fumbling in the dark? Think of the monarch" or "Before it gets any hotter, remember the sea otter" or my favorite, "When you're feeling tender, think of the hellbender," which features a drawing of a bright orange and slithering aquatic salamander.

When I ask Amaroq about these delightful ways to involve people in conservation, she replies with a grin. "You know wolves find every opportunity to engage in play, yes?"

"Yes, I've read that wolves initiate play about every thirty minutes," I say, delighted we've landed on one of my favorite subjects. My decades with wild dolphins and whales have taught me that play is a powerful antidote to trauma in both humans and animals. Bonding and playing with animals often restores us body and soul. At the Lockwood Animal Rescue Center (LARC) in the Los Padres National Forest near Los Angeles there is a vibrant human-animal healing project. Veterans with PTSD struggling to reunite with their families and adapt to civilian life forge strong bonds with wolves rescued from abusive situations.

"Combat veterans have been paid to be predators, much like wolves," explains the LARC cofounder and ex-Navy man Matthew Simmons. "Many come home with this inner war inside them. They don't know if they're an infantryman or a husband." The wolves, many of them wolf hybrids, are in turmoil because they are torn between their wolf and dog genetics. Partnering these soldiers with wolves at the center brings solace to both traumatized humans and animals.

Together with his own partner, clinical psychologist Dr. Lorin Lindner, Simmons has designed an "eco-therapy program" to help keep both human and wolf "safe, sane, and sober." Many of the veterans are profoundly depressed, addicted, even suicidal after the trauma they've endured and witnessed in war. Like wolves, veterans often are misunderstood and exist at the fringes of our communities. "Some sort of cross-species communication goes on between them," says Simmons, when a soldier and a wolf—often with similar physical and severe trauma troubles—bond together. "Our program heals veterans. The wolves get to live out their lives and maybe share it in a special way with another sentient being who's also suffered. It's magical and special."

A poignant fact for both humans and animals who have been severally traumatized is that they may never play again. For animals play is a survival skill, but it is also so much more. Among gorillas in the Congo researchers discovered that poachers had so emotionally damaged orphaned baby gorillas that they had to be taught how to play. When the orphaned gorillas ventured into play behavior at last, it was a major milestone in their recovery. Rehabilitated gorilla babies would play up to seven hours a day. Every day the Internet is awash with viral videos of wild animals—painting elephants, snow-awed playful pandas, gorillas talking in sign language, captive beluga whales blowing bubbles to amuse themselves and escape boredom. Domestic animals also play in viral videos on the Internet—cats trying to make friends with annoyed dogs, terriers playing pinball machines.

Play is essential to evolution and change. If it were not, why would natural selection have preserved such unabashed, risky behavior? New research in *Science Daily*, "Gambling Wolves Take More Risks than Dogs," notes that dogs, like humans, have an evolutionary preference for "playing it safe" and are "risk-aversive." The study conducted at the Wolf Science Center in Ernsbrunn, Austria, raised dogs and wolves in natural settings. When offered two upside-down bowls, one hiding a predictable but stable "insipid food pellet" and the other offering sometimes just a stone and other times a tasty bite of meat, sausage, or chicken—59 percent of dogs most often chose the less risky food pellet bowl. But wolves chose the risky option of real food 89 percent of the time. The wolves' risk-prone but more fulfilling choice is behavior that "seems to be innate," said Sarah Marshall-Pescini, the study's first author. Risk taking among wild wolves "is consistent with the hypothesis that risk preference evolves as a function of ecology."

The risk-adverse preferences of domestication—whether it's in more cautious dogs or in humans—can have an evolutionary and ecological cost: less exploration, fewer new if radical or brave ideas, and, of course, often much less exciting rewards.

"Wolf pups play not only as preparation for future activities, such as stalking, hunting, and social hierarchy," Amaroq continues. "They play for fun—*every* chance they get." She talks about the

Legend of Lamar website with their many videos of Yellowstone wolves at play. "What appeals most of all to people is wolves—just playing."

She reminds me of video footage taken by wildlife videographer Bob Landis and narrated by Yellowstone biologist Douglas Smith of a young wolf trying to hunt an elk. Amaroq often shows this footage to her audiences to counter all the stereotypes of wolves as efficient killing machines. "It's hilarious because the wolf is only seven or eight months old and goes after the elk," Amaroq explains. "The elk just struts and chases the juvenile away. Then the wolf play-bows to the elk . . . and this 'practice session' of how to hunt continues, with this same sequence repeated multiple times. The elk handily survives, and the young wolf has learned that taking down an elk is no task for ingénues!"

Amaroq and I riff on wolf play and why it engages us so enthusiastically. We touch on the lifework of Dr. Stuart L. Brown, a psychiatrist and clinical researcher who founded the National Institute for Play. Brown has pioneered studies on why play behavior makes our own and other animal species so successful. "Nothing lights up the brain like play," Brown says in his very popular TED talk. His work, especially with animals, has taught him that play is not just about rehearsing for adult skills. "Play has a biological place, just like sleep and dreams do . . . the next step of evolution in mammals and creatures with divinely superfluous neurons will be to play," he predicts.

In his article "Animals at Play," Brown expands on the rewards of play—from play fighting among brown bears to object-play with rocks as toys among New Zealand parrots, social play like somersaults and pirouettes among chimpanzees, playing to learn body language and facial signals among foxes and mountain gorillas, and play as exploring habitat among wolf pups.

James C. Halfpenny's *Yellowstone Wolves in the Wild* runs through the many reasons wolves engage in sophisticated play patterns— racing to build stamina, wrestling to learn how to take down a larger animal, dominance displays, flexibility, creativity, and maintaining social hierarchy. He describes a scene in which fifteen wolves race out of the forest onto a frozen lake. Slipping and skidding across the slick ice, the wolves are like living bumper cars crashing into each other, rolling, and tumbling together in what the biologists could only call gleeful play. Does play always have to have some evolutionary purpose or lesson? As any human will tell you, not at all. Sometimes play is just fun. Sometimes play is just play.

Amaroq surprises me by telling tales of her nearly five years playing competitive women's flat-track roller derby. "It's like a game of chess on wheels," she says. "When the two opposing teams are competing in the rink, it's called a 'pack.' Skaters jam and block and pivot in this really complex, evolving sport." She pauses and laughs, "Roller derby skaters have skate names, and my initial skate name was 'Howl on Wheels.' Now I use that as the team name for me and my huskies when we go urban mushing."

"So is it just animal survival out there on the roller derby skating rink?" I ask.

"It is survival," she says. "But you're not alone. It's teamwork. It's truly like being part of a pack."

Laughter as well as play is hardwired into us. Rats have been re-corded chirping, a primitive form of laughter. Psychologist Robert Provine finds a link between chimpanzee and human laughter. "Laughter is literally the sound of play, with the primal 'pant-pant,'" he says. "The labored breathing of physical play—becoming the human 'ha-ha.'" Laughter is not consciously controlled and therefore rises up from the most ancient and instinctive impulses of our brain. As science continues to search for "the genes that control joy," laughter appears to be a key to understanding—perhaps even treating—human depression.

Laughter is not always the tenor of wolf people, with so many sad statistics and often unbearable tales of generational wolf hatred and increasing wolf hunts. I hadn't expected such a joyful encounter with Amaroq, and I didn't want to remember that the next day she'd sit at the Wolf Advisory Group hearing about what circumstances might justify lethal intervention or "wolf culling." So instead I ask Amaroq about why she thought wolf advocates seem like such a harmonious and noncompetitive group compared to other conservationists I've known. There is a buoyancy and optimism that is inspiring and necessary for those who devote their lives to wolves.

"So many women are involved in wolf advocacy and have been all along," Amaroq says. She explains that women wolf advocates call upon a kind of feminine pragmatism: cooperation, a focus on the long-term health of our shared habitats, and a deep understanding that when it comes to a subject as contentious and controversial as wolf recovery, this is a marathon, not a sprint. Women also truly understand that, for a wolf, it's all about family and pups.

"As a former criminal defense attorney, I know people make decisions based on their emotions," Amaroq emphasizes. "So I think it's more important to talk about how it impoverishes our souls when we kill off so many species. We see more people now open to the idea that animals have intrinsic value all their own."

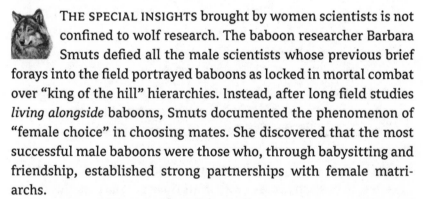 THE SPECIAL INSIGHTS brought by women scientists is not confined to wolf research. The baboon researcher Barbara Smuts defied all the male scientists whose previous brief forays into the field portrayed baboons as locked in mortal combat over "king of the hill" hierarchies. Instead, after long field studies *living alongside* baboons, Smuts documented the phenomenon of "female choice" in choosing mates. She discovered that the most successful male baboons were those who, through babysitting and friendship, established strong partnerships with female matriarchs.

In her essay "What Are Friends For?" Smuts notes that "friendship among animals is not a well-documented phenomenon." She found that "virtually all baboons made friends" and that older males had the most friends. As they groomed each other and shared child-rearing chores, the females and their chosen male friends—not necessarily their mates—forged lifelong friendships. With these male friends, female baboons "exhibited the most reliable sign of true intimacy; she ignored her friend and simply continued whatever she was doing." For a female of any species just to continue what she is doing without having to please, attend to, or serve an alpha male is unusual and liberating.

Wolf families are led by an experienced breeding pair, alpha male and female. Power and responsibility are equally shared. And the relationships among other wolves in the family are not about sex, as only the alpha pair may breed—a form of self-regulating birth control among wolves. So what are those other wolves doing? They are going about their own business—cooperation, babysitting, and ensuring the survival of the family's next generations.

With the return of the wild wolf we're learning more and more about their intimate family lives. Amaroq tells me about USFWS wildlife biologist Cathy Curby, who has been closely observing wolf families in northeast Alaska. In her presentation "A Family of Wolves" Curby notes that she's "spent hundreds of hours watching caribou walk, wild sheep feed, and wolves sleep." One summer Curby camped near a wolf den, using her spotting telescope to observe and record the daily life of a wolf family—eight adults and four pups. All the wolves were tan-brown except the white matriarch, nicknamed "Pearl." The mother wolf was devoted to her four pups but often had to leave them to hunt so she could nurse her hungry young. One balmy day, Pearl didn't return but instead paused to rest a little distance away. A babysitter wolf settled down beside her. Soon the babysitter wolf trotted off to the pups, leaving Pearl a little solitude. Any new mother understands how rare that quiet time is—and Pearl seems to luxuriate, stretching and napping in the sunlit arctic tundra.

For the babysitter wolf there was no such rest. Time after time she tried to coax the pups away from their den, across the sharp, talus rock and scree slopes, back through a quarter mile of willows to their mother. A mother wolf will train her pups to follow her by adjusting her pace: "if she walked away slowly—at the speed short puppy-legs could keep up with—the pups would accompany her; but when she walked away at an adult pace, they learned to stay where they were until her return," notes Curby. But the babysitter wolf hadn't mastered the pace that would convince the puppies to follow her. They have no idea their mother is awaiting them. With each attempt the wolf pups balk at the babysitter wolf's increasingly agitated antics and stubbornly stay close to their den.

For the observing biologist, watching the two hours it took for the babysitter wolf to persuade the four puppies to follow her was like watching a wolf learning lessons in both play and survival. Even after setting all sorts of paces—from awkward and comic slow-motion walks, to pushing the pups from their rear ends, to carrying them by the scruff of their furry necks to try to move them—nothing worked. Finally the babysitter wolf began an energetic, noisy dance of jumping and yipping while moving backward toward the rough rocks. It looks like a "Come and play!" invitation that the puppies at last accepted. All but one of the pups picked their way across the steep rocks, through the thick shrubs to their reward: mother Pearl with her full and milky teats. The pups jumped on her excitedly, now having learned to trust and obey their babysitter—a lesson it takes human children time to learn as well. If in the future the mother were to be killed by hunters, these pups would have to follow another adult to survive.

But one of Pearl's pups was still lingering at the den. Alone. In danger from any predator. Again the babysitter wolf returned and went through her repertoire of enticements for the pup to follow. No movement. In fact, the pup shrank away, lying down as if determined never to budge. Then the babysitter wolf tried something new. Picking up a caribou shank from a recent hunt, the babysitter wolf growled, shaking the bone. Immediately the pup leapt up and engaged in the tug-of-war over the tasty bone. Anyone who has ever played this game with a dog knows how oblivious the pet is to anything but winning this struggle. And that's how the babysitter wolf led the recalcitrant pup, slowly backing up and over the rocks, through the willows, all the while playing a ferocious game of tug-of-war. At last the wolf pup was reunited with Pearl.

"This glimpse into the behavior of a family of wolves taught me a great deal about how wolves interact and solve problems," concludes biologist Curby. "It even taught me many lessons to improve my own mothering and childcare skills."

ANOTHER WOMAN IN WOLF RESEARCH, geneticist Linda Rutledge, at Trent University in Peterborough, Ontario, has tracked changes in wolf populations. In a precedent-setting *New Scientist* article, "Wolf Family Values: Why Wolves Belong Together," Rutledge argues against the wildlife agencies' single-minded focus on wolf populations as the main marker by which they manage and hunt wolves. Just studying the numbers of a wild animal—and then setting wolf-culling goals—is looking at the most superficial and simplistic data. Rutledge insists that wildlife managers "look beyond numbers" and instead make decisions based on "the social dynamics of wild creatures." The more we understand about the social life of wolves and their family values, the better we can live alongside them in the future.

In my studio Amaroq and I have enjoyed our afternoon together. Yet she has several hours to drive across mountain passes to get to the Eastern Washington Wolf Advisory Group meeting. As our time together ends, she says thoughtfully, "What we are doing now is really for future generations—and I do have hope for them and the wolves.

"We really need wildlife commissions with a broader view of wildlife," Amaroq explains. "Not just ranchers, hunters and anglers but those who represent the interests of nonconsumptive users, like tourists, photographers, educators, and conservationists. I even know some hunters who love the idea of wolves not because they want to shoot them but because they want to be out there hunting with the wolves."

Wildlife commissions must represent all of us, says Amaroq, because the lands and animals they control are for all of the public. "The doctrine of the Public Trust has long been applied to waterways and upheld in courts across the country as a right the whole public has—not just the monied few who want to make a buck off of a water project," Amaroq notes. "Wildlife advocates are fighting hard to see this same principle applied by courts in cases pertaining to wildlife," she says firmly. "That is the new reality for wildlife managers and one that conservationists see as making a big difference for the future of wolves on public lands."

Balancing the hopes of "hunters who want to take more wolves and tourists who want to see wolves" is every wildlife commission's job, says a *Bozeman Daily Chronicle* article. Yellowstone has economically benefited from tourism—and many people come just to see wolves. Since the 1995 reintroduction of wild wolves, Idaho, Montana, and Wyoming have received $35 million each year in tourism. In Alaska wildlife viewing brought $2.7 billion in state revenue in 2011.

New reports show that wolf sightings in both Yellowstone and Alaska's Denali National Parks have been cut in half since increased wolf hunts and wolf trapping has been allowed just beyond the protected park borders. Borders are human constructs. Wolves don't know they've crossed out of a protected area into a free-fire zone until it's too late. Visitors were "twice as likely to see a wolf when hunting wasn't permitted adjacent to the parks," the report concludes.

Important new research from scientists such as University of Wisconsin's Dr. Adrian Treves and Ohio State University's Dr. Jeremy Bruskotter reveals that "a great threat to achieving wolf recovery is current lethal management, not intolerance by citizens." Their 2015 open letter to Congress signed by more than seventy other scientists and scholars offers strong evidence that "the vast majority of the U.S. public holds positive attitudes toward wolves and support of the ESA"—79 to 90 percent public support. They point out that public support for wolf recovery has "actually increased substantially over the past three and a half decades." The letter notes that special interest groups that are "vocal, but small in number" have fueled the increasing lethal management of wolves. It concludes by asking that the Great Lakes wolves remain protected under the ESA.

In a spring 2016 follow-up research project Treves and Guillaume Chapron of the Swedish University of Agricultural Sciences studied decreased wolf protection laws in Wisconsin and Michigan between 1995 and 2012—and how that affected wolf populations. One of the rationales for lethal management of wolves, which is often touted by state and federal wildlife agencies, is that it will make local people more tolerant of wildlife living alongside them. This study found that the exact opposite was true: when the wolf population, when culled, declined by one-third, there was actually more poaching. "If poachers see the government killing a protected species," the study found, "they may say to themselves, 'Well, I can do that, too.'" Culling wolves is not the answer, says the study: "You do not reduce looting by allowing shop-lifting, but instead by having zero tolerance."

The authors of this new study expect a backlash from the wildlife manager establishment because it disproves their long-held lethal management practices. But the scientists hold true to their need to serve the public: "The traditions in wildlife management are finally being subjected to scientific scrutiny," they argue, "and we are learning new things that will probably improve co-existence." The study concludes with the truism: "Wolves are quite adaptable to humans. The question is whether humans are adaptable to wolves."

Perhaps it is in the West, the so-called left coast, that we will at last find ourselves more adaptable to wolf recovery than other regions. WAG has hired a veteran conflict mediator, Francine Madden. She prefers the word "conflict transformation." Her subtle but very effective work with WAG is showing signs of success. Madden has helped negotiate a wolf-management agreement between livestock producers and environmentalists that sets new precedents for possible partnerships in the future. Madden told all sides gathered at WAG, "Every one of you is going to have to ask yourselves if you are willing to take a risk to move in a direction of peace rather than staying with what is familiar and really comfortable." She concluded, "There is common ground here. . . . We need to build on that."

 MEANWHILE THE Center for Biological Diversity keeps on with its playful and persuasive antics. Amaroq showed me the YouTube video entitled, "What to Wear at a Wolf Rally," a how-to in which Amaroq, using paper and bold paint, demonstrates how to make your own highly stylized and customized wolf mask.

Amaroq asks, "Have you ever stayed home from a wolf rally because you just didn't have anything to wear?"

"Well, *snap!*" says Amaroq as the video shifts to four wolf people beautifully masquerading with their silver-gray, brown, and bright-red wolf masks, all happily howling.

Amaroq gives step-by-step artistic directions on creating a personal wolf mask, complete with shaggy fur, eyebrows, realistic muzzle, and open eyes. The wolf-making mask video is such a tonic for those of us who have watched way too many films of wolf slaughters or seen one too many downer documentaries that leave us wishing we could leave our own species as easily as we might emigrate to another country. The YouTube video ends with this droll promise: "*Next* time you're going to a wolf rally, my guess is that you'll be the most stylish and sophisticated wolf person at the event."

Amaroq also shared with me a darkly comic video produced by herself and her husband, "One Determined Husky Takes on the Planet's Most Pressing Environmental Problems," in which her Siberian husky, Captain Miranda, play-attacks Republican congressional leaders disguised as endangered species. Posing as a BBC America reporter, Amaroq details the charade. "Some Republicans appear as salamanders," she narrates in her perfectly serious Brit accent. "Others appear as picture-winged flies or rare but dangerous parasites. No one yet knows their motive, but one suspicious-looking wolf approached a reporter and said, 'We're doing just fine, thank you! We don't need further legal protection. No sireee, bob!'"

Enter eco-warrior Captain Miranda. Exclusive video footage shows Miranda pouncing on brightly colored yellow and pink play toys, shaking them into submission, then racing around to destroy more ESA enemies. Growling and howling, Miranda "explains her plan of action" against those who would delist wolves and halt their recovery with punitive legislation. "Inside sources reveal that Captain Miranda flew into action and made quick work of the Republican imposters," Amaroq's faux-BBC reporter explains, "After an exhaustive search, Captain Miranda tracked down Senator James Inhofe, posing as an endangered Southern California mouse."

The dramatic outcome of that encounter shows an image of Minnie Mouse all but buried alive under a fence, her stuffed animal body shredded and torn to pieces, utterly destroyed—just as Senator Inhofe's attacks on endangered species would destroy our country's wildlife. After the 2016 WAG meeting Amaroq would be able to report that the group agreed that in order for WDFW to choose lethal removal, there must be four qualifying wolf depredations in one calendar year or six in two consecutive years. And in order for that depredation by a wolf or wolf pack to count as a strike against it, the rancher must have removed all attractants, such as bone piles or carcasses, and have used at least one method of non-lethal deterrence at the time of the wolf attack.

"These agreements on things that must have been in place *before* lethal removal of wolves can even be considered are essential. Because on-the-ground studies and experience have shown that removing attractants and using deterrent measures—particularly a human presence—are effective means at reducing or altogether preventing livestock conflicts with wolves," says Amaroq. But she is realistic about the work ahead. "The figures agreed to by the WAG on numbers of depredation events and numbers of years are purely social compromises, without taking science into account. People may feel better about each other because they have worked hard to find common ground and come to agreement. And they should feel good about finding common ground—we don't call it the 'Wolf Wars' for nothing. But when science is ignored, wolves frequently lose out. So stakeholder processes can be a double-edged sword, and whether the specific agreements reached in this case will actually aid wolf recovery remains to be seen."

For Amaroq the goal is not just to find a social and political compromise but also to develop protections based on science and the law that will bring lasting benefit to wild wolves.

"What's the most important thing you're doing for wolves, besides these essential lawsuits to stop wolf hunts and your educational programs?" I ask Amaroq.

"When we can bring a lawsuit on behalf of an endangered animal like the wolf, it means they will not be killed for a while longer. And the people living on the land near them will have to use more prevention measures to protect their livestock. It also means that the level of hysteria on each side can calm down while we wait for court decisions."

With her trademark smile and firm nod, Amaroq concludes, "Winning for wolves is really finding ways to give them more time."

# 11. RAISED BY WOLVES

The stories we tell will profoundly shape the fate and future of the wild wolf. There are new stories that are beginning to balance and defy the Big Bad Wolf myths we've recycled for centuries. The "lethal take" graphs of a government's official wolf-culling campaigns or the wolf-trapping trophy tales told around cowboy campfires have been shifting. As wolves begin to repopulate our wild lands, they also roam the most spacious and evolving territory of all: the human imagination.

Authors, artists, and musicians are creating a rich habitat for wolves in their work. It's not just natural history classics like Farley Mowat's *Never Cry Wolf* or Barry Lopez's *Of Wolves and Men* or popular memoirs such as Nick Jans's *A Wolf Called Romeo* that use science to tell a truer and less biased story of wolves. Wolves are also compelling our attention in live-action fictional 3-D films such as China's hugely popular *Wolf Totem*, in the 1972 and 2016 Disney homages to Rudyard Kipling's *The Jungle Book*, in enduring children's classics like *Julie of the Wolves* by Jean Craighead George. Wolves also find their voices echoed in rock music, like guitarist John Sheldon's elegy for Yellowstone's 06 or the haunting Celtic ballad "Winter Wolf." As wolves again take up residence in our wilderness and our storytelling, we return to a more fully imagined kinship with them. One story that returns to captivate each new generation is that of human children raised by wolves. As Shakespeare writes in *The Winter's Tale*:

Come on, poor babe
Some powerful spirit instruct the kites and ravens
To be thy nurses! Wolves and bears, they say,
Casting their savageness aside, have done
Like offices of pity.

The legend of twin brothers Romulus and Remus, who were suckled by a she-wolf and survived to become the founders of Rome, is echoed in fiction such as the 1919 novel *Shasta of the Wolves* about a boy adopted by a wolf pack; the popular *Through the Wolf's Eyes*, Firekeeper series by Jane Lindskold, whose heroine is rescued by wolves and reluctant to return to her own kind; or the 1970s television series *Lucan*, set in Minnesota, in which a boy is raised by wolves and needs ten years to learn to adapt to so-called civilized society.

Perhaps the most famous of all the stories of a child raised by wolves is Rudyard Kipling's "Mowgli's Brothers," collected in *The Jungle Book*. This story of a lost Indian child and his wolf-pack family captured the hearts of generations of adults and children and inspired several films. In her 1988 foreword to Kipling's *The Jungle Book*, children's book author Jane Yolen notes the many stories of feral children—from the eighteenth-century naturalist Linnaeus's scientific definition of a feral man to the Indian news sensation in the 1920s of "a pair of sisters who had supposedly been found by a missionary in a white ant mound along with a she-wolf and her litter of cubs."

Kipling's own father had written stories of Indian children raised by wolves in his 1891 book, *Beast and Man in India*. In many of these accounts the human child, unwanted and abandoned by his parents in the jungle, was nursed by a mother wolf and thrived. But once captured and returned to humankind, the wolf-child was still savage, inconsolable, and unable to adapt. Often, as with the Indian wolf sisters, they died from depression over the loss of their wolf family, even in the care of British missionaries.

Mowgli adapts more successfully, both with his wolf family and after he returns to the human village. As a baby lost in the jungle, Mowgli is accepted into a wolf family by the leaders, Mother Wolf

Raksha and Father Wolf Akela. They are called "The Free People" and teach their man-cub Mowgli the Law of the Jungle, which "never orders anything without a reason." This jungle justice forbids all animals from killing man unless that man is showing his own children how to kill animals. Kipling explains that if the animals kill humans, "everybody in the jungle suffers." Mother Wolf accepts the man-cub because he is never afraid and finds his proper place nursing alongside her other pups. Soon he is swinging through the vines, much like his later imitator Tarzan, and racing through the dense and mysterious jungle with the Seeonee Wolf pack.

Bagheera, the majestic panther in Kipling's story, notices the unique characteristic of this young human: "If he stared hard at any wolf, the wolf would be forced to drop his eyes." The man-cub's direct and unflinching gaze is so powerful, explains the panther, that "Not even I can look thee between the eyes and I was born among men, and I love thee, Little Brother."

The original *Jungle Book* hews close to real wolf biology. As it is with wild wolves, when the leader grows old and too feeble to hunt or command, he can be pushed out or even killed by a younger rival, a fate that soon befalls Kipling's Father Wolf Akela. Once Akela's own pack has voted to kill him, he is allowed to speak on behalf of the adopted boy-cub, Mowgli. He argues, "He has eaten our food. He has slept with us. He has driven game for us. He has broken no word of the Law of the Jungle." Akela honorably offers that if the Wolf Council spares his man-cub, he will not fight off any attack from any next-in-line young wolf.

The pack responds to the doomed leader's cry for mercy for Mowgli, a being who has the fierceness of the wolf and the inventiveness of humankind. Having just witnessed the death of Akela, Mowgli makes a promise to the Wolf Council: "I will be more merciful than ye are. Because I was all but your brother in blood, I promise that when I am a man among men I will not betray ye to men as ye have betrayed me. There shall be no war between any of us in the pack."

Eventually the maturing boy must leave his wolf family for a life with humans. But he first begs a promise from his wolf mother, Raksha: "Ye will not forget me?" Mowgli asks. Raksha promises, "Never while we can follow a trail." She hopes her man-cub will come back soon, "little naked son of mine, for, listen, child of man, I loved thee more than ever I loved my cubs."

The timeless appeal and what the *New York Times* called "immortality" of Kipling's *Jungle Book* in its 2016 cinematic resurrection suggest that multitudes of children—and many adults—have never really left the jungle for the man-village. Many readers easily imagined ourselves part of Mowgli's wolf family—especially those of us raised in rural or wild areas.

Such positive and intimate stories of our historic bond with wolves—both in the territories of our stories and our wild lands—help reverse generations of hatred and negative stereotypes. Of course, the real life of wolves is not like Disney's. But such hugely popular stories offer hope for a new generation's more charitable attitude toward sharing public lands with them.

A more realistic book, informed to some extent by wolf biology, is *Julie of the Wolves*, published in 1972 and still widely read. Julie, a thirteen-year-old Inuit girl, runs away from her boy-husband and her Alaskan village and gets lost on the tundra. She is adopted by a wolf family and learns how to survive and navigate a dangerous wilderness. She builds her own den and begs food scraps from the adults like a wolf pup by licking the face of the alpha wolf, just as our domestic dogs do with us—both a greeting and supplication.

In many subtle ways readers learn wolf biology—the "sweet odor of ambrosia" in a wolf's scent, the leaps and jumps in the complex body language of the "wolf code," and the facial expressions so critical for fitting into wolf family hierarchy. Julie is given the wolf name "Miyax" and allowed to follow the wolf family, led by her wolf father, Amaroq, as they hunt and share the meat. The wolves teach her to howl and sing, to outmaneuver grizzly bears, to find water, and to hide from the human hunters who shadow the tundra in planes. These hunters finally gun down Amaroq and his son, Kapu. There is a bounty on Amaroq's magnificent head, yet when the hunters land their plane, they don't even bother to take their trophy. Kapu is grievously wounded, but the wolf-girl, Miyax, tends him, and he slowly heals to become the new leader. Miyax and Kapu help restore the devastated wolf family after the loss of their leader.

Again, as in all the stories of children raised by wolves, there is grief when Miyax must finally return to her own species. But in *Julie of the Wolves*, unlike *The Jungle Book*, she well and fondly remembers her father, whom she believes is lost at sea, as well as her village. When she hears that her father is still alive, Miyax returns to her village to reunite with him. Yet her father is disturbingly changed. He has taken on the ways of the white man, and he too now hunts wolves from airplanes. This man, Miyax realizes, is "after all, dead to her" like her wolf father, Amaroq. But unlike her human father, Amaroq's wiser spirit still dwells within Miyax and guides her. Again Miyax runs away into the tundra, where she hopes to live with what is left of her wolf family. Miyax sings an elegy for both the soul loss of her father and the real death of the wolf who raised her with much more devotion and constancy:

Amaroq, Amaroq, you are my adopted father.
My feet dance because of you.
My eyes see because of you.
My mind thinks because of you . . .

The theme of humans also befriending and helping wolves survive is the companion story to tales of our children being raised by wolves. It is also the more common tale told throughout the world about wolves. In China *Wolf Totem* is considered *the* best-selling contemporary Chinese novel. The popularity of this autobiographical novel by retired professor Lu Jiamin (pen name Jiang Rong) was unexpected in China, not known for its environmental stewardship or wildlife conservation. Both the book and the movie of *Wolf Totem* were huge successes in the West as well. Their conservation message was very well received by American audiences, who live in a country that leads the world in reintroducing wolves to their native habitat.

*Wolf Totem* is set in the grasslands of Inner Mongolia, where the wolves are thought to be one of the reasons the great Mongol warrior, Genghis Khan, was so successful in his conquests. The Mongols, once a great nation and now a minority, live in China's far north. They believe their original ancestor was abandoned in the wild and raised by a fiercely maternal mother wolf. Because of this wolf-human ancestry, the Mongol herdsmen both revere and struggle with the wolf, called Chono. Sometimes they must also cruelly kill these powerful and otherworldly animals—even the pups in their dens—to protect their livestock. This harsh balance between Mongols and these ancient wolves is threatened when the Chinese Communist government, under Chairman Mao, orders *all* Mongolian wolves exterminated to make space for massive farming projects. The Mongol culture, like their wolves, is endangered. Soon imported Chinese farmers will overwhelm the traditional herdsmen's vast open lands. Into this troubled mix of Chinese encroachment and Mongolian survival enters a young intellectual Han student, Chen Zhen, who has been "sent down" by the 1960s Cultural Revolution to learn herding from the nomadic Mongolians.

Zhen is from Beijing and marvels at the breathtaking beauty of the steppes and wild grasslands of Inner Mongolia. While apprenticing himself to an elder herdsman, Zhen is fascinated by the wolves. He is deeply troubled by his Mongolian mentor's ritual killing of a newborn wolf litter—by piling the puppies in a bag and then hurling them skyward to plunge down to their deaths. Zhen manages to save the last pup. Secretly Zhen hides his cherished wolf pup from the herdsmen and the Communist official in charge of developing the land for farmers. But as the young wolf grows strong under his care, Zhen's treasure is discovered. He, the Mongols, and the wolves suffer from the encroaching Chinese. When the wolves hide their carcasses in deep snow to save for summer, the frozen sheep are dug up and stolen by a greedy Chinese official—setting off the wolf-human conflict.

The Chinese eradication of the wolves destroys the natural predator-prey balance, so the wild sheep overgraze the grasslands to dust, and rats plague the people. Jiang based the book on his own decade in Mongolia when he too was sent down by the Cultural Revolution. In 1989 he participated in the Tiananmen Square protests and was thrown in jail for a time. His novel is controversial because he intended it as a "critique of thousands of years of Chinese culture" when officials expected a public to be "obedient as sheep."

In *Wolf Totem* the wolves are the heroes of another kind of revolution—the Mongolians' fight for sovereignty and cultural survival—and the wolves' own struggle to survive the original invaders, humans. These lean and fleet grassland wolves are the symbol of a whole people and their fierce spirit—in the face of modernization and rapacious development. The book was translated into thirty-nine languages. In China it was so popular that it sailed past the censors. Amy Qin of the *New York Times* wrote, "Political dissenters found anti-Communist messages in the novel . . . while corporations gave it to employees to encourage them to work together like wolves."

In a moving interview Jiang explained the traditional Mongolian ritual of offering bodies at death to feed wolves. "They do this because they believe wolves return to heaven," he said. "So when wolves die, they bring the human souls with them to heaven." The venerable role of the wild animal as psycho-pomp—one who crosses over and helps other souls to cross over—is echoed in other cultures, like the ancient Greek dolphins who carry souls to the next world or in Tibet, where vultures lift the dead souls into the sky.

When I saw the gorgeous 3-D film adapted from *Wolf Totem*, directed by French filmmaker Jean-Jacques Annaud, in a Seattle theater, every seat was filled. Here on the Pacific Rim the audience included many Asian viewers. One of my Chinese American students was amazed and delighted at both the book and the film's strong condemnation of wolf killing.

"China is responsible for buying so much of the illegal traffic in wildlife," she told me. "From paying poachers for endangered rhino horns to elephant tusks to Moon Bear bladders to capturing marine mammals for Chinese aquariums." She really didn't expect such a rapturous and sympathetic portrayal of the Mongolian wolves. Or the powerful ecological message about saving wolves.

The book and the film have very different endings. In the book the young hero kills his cherished wolf pup because he "doesn't want the wolf to become a servant to man," explains the author. Because the wolf pup is ill and the Chinese occupation of his ancient territory threatening, the wolf must "die like a soldier, not die like a dog." Jiang understands why, in the film version, the wolf pup must be set free in a wrenching scene between man and wolf. "Westerners would not be able to bear this," he told the *New York Times*. "So having the main character release the wolf, this provides a little warmth and hope to viewers."

That warmth and hope for the future survival of both the Mongols and their Chono is well drawn throughout both book and film. In the film, director Annaud employs real Mongolian wolves, not animation, to bring their story to vivid life. Annaud, who has often worked with live animals in his films, had to acquire a dozen wolf pups from Chinese zoos because wild wolf populations in China are dwindling. Animal trainers raised and worked with the Eurasian wolves (*Canis lupus lupus*) for two to three years. Annaud devoted several years to filming *Wolf Totem* because he believed "It's more than a movie. It shows that one has to protect nature. And if China protects its nature, the rest of the world will follow." Annaud has a particular interest in wolves. He noted that the Mongols, in conquering and creating their empire, "copied wolves' technique. Observing. Being patient. Always being together." After the filming the wolves were relocated to Canada because they only responded to English.

*Wolf Totem* was filmed under strict environmental protections. Instead of using cars or trucks, which could ruin these fragile grasslands, the crews carried their equipment several hours a day to the mountain top. Film crews laid down cloth to protect grasslands and imported snow from miles away. In the twenty-first century, when films seem more populated by CGI and 3-D-enhanced superheroes with unattainable powers, it is refreshing to see that once again this wild-animal child and environmental story is attracting a huge audience.

Instinctively children understand that as small, often defenseless creatures, they also have a lot to learn from wild animals about survival, escape, and even navigating their own peer group's pecking orders. Children, even those raised in urban jungles, intuitively accept animals as peers. Psychologists tell us that 80 percent of children's dreams center on animals, whereas only 20 percent of adults have animal dreams. This sympathetic identification with other animals in our childhoods—whether it is we who are raised by wolves or we who befriend wolves—offers us other vital ways of knowing ourselves and the wider, often dangerous world.

WHEN WE TELL STORIES about other animals, we are often really talking about ourselves. When we make villains of wolves in our stories, we are often avoiding looking into what Joseph Conrad calls "the heart of darkness" within ourselves. It's telling and disturbing that in a country like America, whose citizens own more guns than in any other country (88.8 percent), it is endangered species like wolves that are also so often in the crosshairs.

In reading about American gun violence, it is revealing to notice the language the media uses. Media coverage of the 2016 Orlando massacre, for instance, incessantly referred to the murderer as a "lone wolf." Even in our language we associate wolves with our own primitive violence. Not only does comparing a man who opens fire with a military-grade automatic weapon on a helpless crowd of people to a lone wolf betray our blatant prejudice against this most maligned animal; it also is not based in any biological fact. A real lone wolf has deeply diminished powers to hunt or kill. A solitary wolf must live off smaller ground prey like squirrels and rabbits. Without family for protection and alliance, the wolf endures the most endangered time of his life and will survive only half as long as the eight- to ten-year life span of wolves in the wild.

Such respected news media as the *New York Times* are guilty of this pejorative language, as when it wrote, "The self-declared Islamic State underscored once again its favored weapon in its war on the West: lone wolves." The *Christian Science Monitor* ran a headline describing a split screen showing an ISIS fighter set to behead a prisoner and a wolf's head with the slogan: "The West has lone muscles; Islam has lone wolves." Every time I hear this misnomer, I cringe. I noticed that in BBC radio and other foreign reporting on the Orlando murderer, the phrase most used was "lone actor."

Tellingly, American gun violence is the most widespread where wildlife recovery on public lands is fiercely opposed and where lethal management of wolves is usually the first, not the last option.

The states most resistant to gun control are also the states where we have a long history of hunting wildlife. Four of the high gun-death states are Wyoming (number one), Alaska (four), Montana (six), and New Mexico (nine)—all states with a penchant for wolf killing. The top three states for gun-related suicides are Montana, Alaska, and Wyoming—again, states that favor wolf hunting.

How we tell stories about ourselves and other species profoundly affects our ecology and our treatment of other predators. As with the "lone wolf" stand-in for a human murderer, our very language and stories can positively or negatively affect our wildlife policies. There's an old adage: "thrown to the wolves." The reality is that it's wolves who are "thrown to the people." And those people have firearms—over 300 million guns. With all these easily accessible firearms, Americans routinely and almost daily not only exterminate wolves and other wildlife but also kill our own.

In such a dangerously violent and gun-toting country, our children being trained and raised by wild animals in their stories might actually be a survival skill they sorely and sadly need. The savage jungle is now in our schools, where kids can be gunned down as brutally as any endangered species. We would all do well to apprentice ourselves to the keen senses of other animals: the stealthy camouflage ability to blend and hide, the sharp hearing and night vision to see in such darkness, the hypervigilance in public spaces that once were safe. Feral children are, most of all, survivors, especially when abandoned by their human village. Why not be adopted, taught, and raised by wolves so we can survive such a terrifying wilderness of *human* nature?

 WHENEVER I TEACH wildlife conservation and ecology in schools I always ask the children to adopt and apprentice themselves to their favorite animal—and then try to learn that animal's real "superpowers." Kids are shape-shifters, easily morphing from human to animal points of view. In their new world animals still talk, adopt humans, and train us. Kids return instinctively to their imagined animal allies. Their identification with and ease of inhabiting another species portends some hope for our own species' survival. To a child nature is not just "out there"—the green world is still *in* their dreams and imaginations. That instinctive identification with other animals can shape our ecology as much as science.

In my wildlife ecology classes both boys and girls often choose the wolf. They tell stories in which their heroes are raised by a wolf family. But their stories are not always what we expect. One middle-school girl, Sarah, whose best friend had recently been killed right in front of her by a drive-by shooter, told her tragic story to my class on the first day. Sadly, the kids showed no shock at her friend's murder. After all, "Weapons-Free Zone" signs adorned their middle-school hallways and metal detectors blocked the entrance of their library—and this was even before the Sandy Hook massacre and other US school shootings. After Sarah told her story I had no choice but to change my lesson plan for the week. I let the children lead the way.

It was to the animals, *not* superheroes, the kids turned to get justice for Sarah's loss and to solve the murder of her friend. Each child chose to become an animal in an imagined landscape of the Amazon jungle. Every day for a week we gathered to develop a group narrative in which the child-animals tracked the murderer. We made animal masks with wide, night eyes and grew imaginary claws; we raced at recess with the breathtaking speed of big cats.

All through the group storytelling I watched Sarah, whose expression changed from flatly detached to suddenly alive with purpose. She claimed the sleek power of a jaguar, prowling around, urging us on to find her friend's murderer, who the children decided must be a drug lord. The group finally found him hiding deep in the jungle and took action: Fish, with her "truth-telling Soul Mirror," capsized the killer's canoe and forced him to confess his crime. Then all the wild children growled and screamed out their demand for his apology. Just as the killer was crying out that he was *sorry, so sorry*, Fish leapt out of the black water and devoured him, body and soul. Then all the young animals cawed and roared and howled out in triumph. Behind their masks shone eyes as dark and satisfied as any wild animal after a kill. For animals have their own ethics. As do children.

The child's imagination is a primal force, as strong as lobbying efforts and boycotts and the Endangered Species Act. When children claim another species as not only an imaginary friend but also as the animal within them, they are shaping a cultural ecology. They are restoring something we've forgotten. In our adult environmental wars the emphasis has been on saving species, not *becoming* them.

At the end of our week together many of the kids, like Mowgli, were reluctant to return to simply their human selves. On the bus home they stayed in costume and character. Sarah took her leave of me with only a deep-throated purr and very quick cat-like tap on my arm. Later she wrote me that she was going to become a poet. "I can still see in the dark."

# 12. WOLF MUSIC

We mostly encounter wild wolves not by sight but by sound—that otherworldly yet eerily familiar head-thrown-back, heartfelt howling. It begins with one voice, a wolf solo lingering in rich, lonely mezzo, rising up higher octaves to tremble on falsetto or haunting, tenor half notes. Then an echoing wolf chorus joins in with ultrasonic whines, staccato barks and yelps, yipping counterpoints, cello-like bass moans, and a braided, beautifully dissonant harmony, slow to fade. Listening to wolves sing changes us in ways that we can't fathom but still recognize. When we hear wolves, we know some wild companionship still survives—for we are no longer alone in these dark woods.

Why do wolves howl? And do these complex vocalizations have a purpose? Howling is one way wolves bond, locate, celebrate, and communicate themselves to one another and the world around them. Howling can be a call to community, a signal claiming territory to alert a rival pack not to trespass, a dinner call for other family members to come share a kill. The University of Cambridge led a team of international researchers to study the howling repertoires, or "vocal fingerprints," of wolves in diverse, geographical populations. The scientists discovered that at least twenty-one different dialects and accents could be identified. By studying sonograms and sound-wave patterns of wolf howls, researchers realized that, like whales and birds, wolves were "controlling their singing and subject to cultural influences."

As one of the researchers, Holly Root-Gutteridge of Syracuse University, noted in her fascinating essay "The Songs of the

Wolves," this means that animals "can be used as a model for humans, allowing us a window into an otherwise cryptic part of our own evolution." She explains that animals often vocalize in complex codes distinct to their own species. For example, a prairie dog's alarm calls can encode the color and shape of a threatening predator; humpback whales sing across hundreds of miles to signal not only their location but also to identify their family group. The study asked the question: Is there a shared culture of howl meanings among wolves? They discovered that wolf howls can transmit intent and meaning, like a musical language. This is a sure sign of culture in any species. Root-Gutteridge concludes that wolves are "like music bands with preferred styles of playing: riff-filled like jazz or the pure tones of classical."

Despite the difficulties of following wolves in the wild, scientists in this study have recorded six thousand howls from both wild and captive animals throughout the United States, Europe, India, and Australia. They have found, for example, that red wolves and coyotes have similar howling vocabularies. Now near extinction, red wolves have crossbred with coyotes in their only remaining North Carolina habitat. That "may be one reason why they are so likely to mate with each other," says University of Cambridge's lead scientist, Dr. Arik Kershenbaum. Does this mean wolves are attracted to howls similar to their own?

When studying other animals, scientists search for evidence that is observable and quantifiable, but signs of culture can be more subtle. There are quite a few scientists now who are beginning to discuss the idea that other animals—such as whales, elephants, chimpanzees, and wolves—all have a culture. In *The Culture of Whales and Dolphins*, biologist Hal Whitehead says, "When culture takes hold of a species, everything changes." The late Alaskan wolf scientist Gordon Haber pointed out that wolves, with their strong family bonds and cooperative hunting skills passed down through generations, were "perhaps the most social of all non-human vertebrates," mirroring many of our human traditions. Every wolf group develops "its own unique adaptive behaviors and traditions; taken together, these can be considered a culture." Wolf howling also has meanings we can interpret only through our own use of language and, yes, music. Musicians—those who have spent their lives listening—can help us understand the culture and howling of wild wolves.

In my search for musicians who are listening to wolves, I was delighted to encounter French classical pianist Hélène Grimaud, who in 1996 cofounded the Wolf Conservation Center in New Salem, New York. I asked this gifted musician why we respond so profoundly to a chorus of howling wolves. Is it woven into our ancestral DNA that we once listened for and located wolves on a kill so that we could hungrily follow and survive on eating their scraps? Perhaps our human ears are warily perked to help us understand that we've entered territory shared by other top predators. Is it an attunement in our muscle memory and even our aesthetic sense that allows us to recognize a more ancient culture, another mesmerizing music?

"Wolves are uniquely individual, so why would we assume that the language is not? You can hear it. Every wolf has a distinct howl," Grimaud tells me in her quick, rhythmic French accent. "No two howls are the same. You can easily imagine that there are some wolf dialects that are pack or region specific, which develop from isolation or geographical location. And then it becomes a behavioral and cultural difference as well. How wolves treat their neighbors, for example, or handle family dynamics. So their howling is an expression of those differences."

Grimaud speaks in thoughtful bursts and riffs, as if following some musical score in her mind that is scrawled over with notes on wolf science. Grimaud is an internationally acclaimed musician, often known for practicing complex piano concertos in her head, not just on the keyboard. Her memoir, *Wild Harmonies: A Life of Music and Wolves*, traces her musical development, interwoven with the natural history of wolves, and her own two decades of work with captive ambassador wolves at the Wolf Conservation Center. This not-for-profit education center is one of the best facilities in the eastern United States and a leader in the Species Survival Program. Since 2003 WCC has helped to breed and release Mexican and red wolves into the wild. They are deeply involved in the Northeast Wolf Advisory Coalition, which works with the public and federal, state, and local organizations.

WCC's education and outreach programs draw over fifteen thousand visitors a year, says director Maggie Howell. Their live webcams have a devoted audience. "Unbeknownst to the wolves, they have a huge, global fan base," Maggie explains. "The wolves are creeping into our homes via these web cams." Some of WCC's most popular on-the-ground events are "Howl for Pups of All Ages" and "Howl for Adults," where people can blend their voices with wolves. WCC founder Grimaud has spent years listening to wolves.

"Why do wolves answer our human howls?" I ask Grimaud now.

"Perhaps wolves are generously nondiscriminating," Grimaud says wryly, then adds, "One of the things that makes working with any wild animal so interesting and humbling is that you have to interact with them on their terms. Often they are quite forgiving of our bumbling attempts to connect in a proper and dignified way, in wolf terms. It could just be that the wolves interpret humans howling as an invasive threat from another pack. So the wolves want to advertise that this territory is already occupied."

In the same way that wolves mark territory by scent, they also set sound barriers that other wolves trespass at their own peril. It's intriguing to imagine what an acoustic map of wolf country would sound like—growls, guttural bluffs and rubato boasts, fortissimo barks, possessive, snarling arpeggios, a mournful undertone like a walking bass. Sometimes the sound map would rise to the sonorous pulse and operatic range of howling wolves. Do wolves ever just sing to make complicated music, as we do?

"One of the most intriguing elements of wolf howling is what scientists call social glue," explains Grimaud. "This spreading of good feeling like humans singing around a campfire, feeling closer to one another—it's that same idea: you howl or harmonize and so reaffirm your social bonds with one another. That's not surprising. Any pack animal really depends upon the other to survive."

Certainly humans are social pack animals. We are also profoundly moved by music, especially by making music together. That's why the word "harmony" relates both to music and to relations between people, groups, even colors. When we hear human music, we physically attune to that vibration; when we sing together, we blend our voices, matching thirds and fifths and sometimes deliberate, clashing dissonance. We try to fit and find our part in the greater chorus.

Wolves actually harmonize their voices with ours. "Have you noticed," Grimaud asks, "that when a human—who is less naturally gifted in that wolf language—joins in a howl and his pitch lands on the same note, the wolves will alter their pitch to prolong the harmonization? It's very interesting. If you end up on the same pitch as a wolf, he will scale up or down, modulating his voice with yours."

If you listen to wolves singing, you'll hear that wolves rarely howl alone for long before the whole chorus is cued. That chorus is not just about harmonizing; it's also about survival. There's a phenomenon called the Beau Geste effect, in which howling together makes it impossible to identify a single wolf's voice or how many wolves are in concert. Even a family of two wolves can raise a mighty chorus to disguise their small size and create the illusion of a larger group's voice. In declaring their acoustic territory, the wolf chorus can travel long distances, giving the group the expansive space it needs to survive and thrive.

An interdisciplinary team of Montana State University researchers, including philosophy professor Sara Waller, is studying two thousand howls from thirteen canid species to better understand "how we can learn about the evolution of language." Dr. Waller is studying how animals communicate with one another—and if that influences how humans see them. "Just howls can tell us who is out there," says Waller. She wonders whether ranchers could play recordings of wolf howls to ward off wolves from their livestock. "Because I'm a philosopher," she notes, "I work with the group on the big, broad questions."

These more philosophical questions belong not only to scientists but also to artists and all of us. And wolves and their music have claimed territories not just in the wilderness but also in our human hearts. Throngs of Yellowstone visitors are thrilled to listen to howling wolves. Social media, film documentaries, and nature channels have hugely popular soundtracks of real wolves howling in the wild. Any online search reveals many audio clips, like the PBS NOVA link "What's in a Howl?" with sound sonography and recordings of a "Lonesome Howl," "A Pup Howl," "A Confrontational Howl," and "A Chorus Howl." Listen to these to help you identify the different qualities of wolf song. Hélène Grimaud has even recorded a "Wolf Moonlight Sonata" on YouTube accompanied by wolf howling.

What do highly skilled musicians like Grimaud hear when wolves sing? What beyond any survival strategy are wolves creating in their chorus? Because wolves have a culture, what does their music communicate—if we could listen as fellow artists, with more than our scientific ears? I'm reminded of a *New Yorker* cartoon in which a huge whale is chasing a human on the beach. The human is waving his arms and screaming in terror. The whale wonders, "Is that a song?" We moderns, with such acoustic familiarity to wolves howling, are no longer afraid when we hear their singing. In fact, we often try to meet them on their same musical frequency. Does this mean that animals also seek to blend with or are attracted to *our* music?

"When you practice your piano," I ask Grimaud. "Do the wolves join in your music by howling along?"

During her seasons when Grimaud lived next to the WCC in upstate New York, she didn't notice any exact correlation between the wolves howling and her piano. "Their howling was random, coincidental with my playing," she says with a laugh. "But there was one foster-wolf pup who seemed to react to violin music when she heard my recordings. She'd come out of her den and raise her head and howl along to the violin strings. There definitely seemed to be a relationship there."

Grimaud offers some anecdotal evidence of another animal's musical appreciation. When she was living in Switzerland, every time she played Bach a cow would come close to her window. "As soon as I stopped playing and went over to the window to make contact with the cow, she'd disappear." When Grimaud returned to practicing her piano, the cow would return. "But when I switched to Beethoven," Grimaud says, "she had no interest. Who knows why?"

Researchers have noted that animals do respond to our music. Cows produce 3 percent more milk when listening to calming music like Simon & Garfunkel's solacing "Bridge Over Troubled Water." Dogs in kennels relax, sleep, and seem less stressed when listening to classical music. Monkeys grow calmer and their appetites increase when listening to Metallica's "Of Wolf and Man." Elephants sway their trunks together to violin music, and there is even a Thai Elephant Orchestra that keeps a more stable tempo on drums than humans do. Cats, who seem to have little interest in our music, will relax when left alone for long hours listening to "Music for Cats," compiled by another classical musician. Other experiments on how animals react to human music are fascinating and sometimes hilarious. There is the YouTube sensation, a cockatoo called Snowball, who dances in perfect beat and screeches along to the Backstreet Boys, or a captive sea lion, Ronan, who jives along to the disco beat of "Boogie Wonderland."

"If you were going to compose a concerto for a wolf audience," I ask Grimaud, "would it be a love song, a requiem?"

I am thinking about the elegy a composer might create for the Judas wolves, those solitary survivors of lethal hunts who are repeatedly radio tagged and then targeted again to betray the location of their next family for a kill. Imagine surviving so much loss.

"I've never been asked that question before." Grimaud is silent for a while, then says pensively, "Probably I'd choose music with a sense of longing. That's always what I think when I hear wolves howling. Endless longing."

Who is not acquainted with the tender ache, the gravitational pull of longing? A yearning for something so intimate and yet so often beyond us. Like our reach for other animals, other ways of knowing them, other ways we might meet.

"What if you played a concert for the wolf? What music most embodies for you the wild wolf's spirit and struggle?"

"Rachmaninoff," Grimaud replies without hesitation. She is acclaimed for her impassioned and iconoclastic Rachmaninoff piano Concerto No. 2. This is also one of my very favorite concertos for Rachmaninoff's brave, muscular musical strength and yet moments of sublime longing. We agree that Rachmaninoff's music claims a vast emotional range—from Promethean struggle, like Beethoven, to utterly exhilarating transcendence.

"There is such a quality of being uprooted in Rachmaninoff's music. And, again, that intense longing," Grimaud says. "Perhaps it comes from Rachmaninoff leaving his homeland and so becoming a hybrid—one who belongs everywhere but, at the same time, not anywhere."

This sounds very much like a wolf's life—often uprooted in battles for territory, wolves must disperse to find another homeland, wandering and searching to belong again.

"If you look at the artistic pendulum, Rachmaninoff was a throwback himself, because the musical movement had evolved, and he wasn't part of that," Grimaud continues with a palpable energy. One can hear her decades of musical devotion to these composers whose struggle and spirit she revitalizes and robustly embodies in every performance. "Rachmaninoff refused to compromise," Grimaud says firmly, and she might as well be talking about her own individualistic work. "He stayed true to himself—even though he was nearly an endangered species himself."

Rachmaninoff's music has the "full spectrum of human emotions," adds Grimaud. "and at the same time there is something inconsolable about his work." Grimaud pauses, then rushes on at her quick tempo. "It also has this primal quality . . . in German we call it *urkraft*—this vitality, this primeval power we feel so deep in our vital core. The force that enables you to make it through everything—even in spite of yourself."

Grimaud is talking about the elemental forces in both music and nature that shape us all. Like water, the subject of her latest recording. And like wolves, her lifelong passion. As she speaks I ponder how music, like life, always wants to live on and on, to make more of itself, to sing its own singular song—whether or not anyone else is listening.

I ask Grimaud about her own life, especially her childhood, in which her parents fretted that she might be too feral for most peers, especially highly civilized French girls. In her memoir Grimaud writes that she has "little nostalgia for childhood" and that she felt her own profound longing for a "paradise inside me, buried." Restless, excessively energetic, exuberantly extreme, enthralled by mountains and sea, Grimaud also discovered a "predilection for the tragic." As a child she felt "joy at the outer edge of suffering," a strange ecstasy that "cast a strange—and I would say, intensely satisfying—spell on me." Music and the piano both captured her prodigious energy and freed her to "wash away from the soul the dust of everyday life." In the 1990s Grimaud's encounter with a captive she-wolf expanded her life's repertoire to embrace the *urkraft* of another wild creature. "The wolf was life itself," she writes, "more biting than the frost. Life itself, with an incredible intensity."

"Speaking of tragedy and ecstasy," I ask Grimaud, "do you know the work of the French mystic Simone Weil?"

"Oh, yes," she responds instantly. We talk about this Jewish-Catholic woman, half-saint, who starved herself to death in solidarity with those suffering in World War II by only eating the same limited rations as others in the war-torn era.

"Simone Weil wrote that there are two ways to know truth," I say. "Suffering—and beauty. Maybe that's what we feel about the wild wolves. The beauty that balances their suffering and ours. What many people feel in this world—this broken-hearted, beautiful world."

"I love the way you say it," Grimaud responds warmly. "Maybe that's why wolves generate so many emotions, good or bad, in people. That makes them both controversial and fascinating. Something beyond all the explanations that makes us respond so profoundly to wolves."

Many scientists, we agree, are wary of speaking about the often deeply emotional connections we feel with wolves. They are afraid of being discredited or losing their research grants if they speak out about the very sensory aspects of this bond. The earthy human-wolf bond relations are explored most in our myths and music. A territory beyond science and logic.

We talk about whether the wolf's life is essentially tragic. After all, wolves in the wild rarely live more than ten years. Every day for a wolf is life and death; their deaths are most often violent at our human hands, the teeth of their rivals, or even their family, much like our Greek tragedies. Simone Weil's tragic vision celebrated the poetic beauty of Greek tragedies. In a book on Weil's philosophy, author Alexander Nava explains that Weil regarded tragedy as a truth of our human condition that "refuses to ignore the dark and brutal forces in human experience. And for those who suffer, artistic expressions of tragedy—in poetry, art, or music, e.g., the blues—just possibly makes life endurable and even beautiful."

As Grimaud and I continue to talk about Simone Weil's vision and how it illuminates how we understand the fate of wild wolves, I remember the most tragic day of my own life. A sunny morning in 1981 that still haunts me. I discovered a dear friend, dead by her own hand. Gunshot. I dropped my warm, neatly folded, clean-scented laundry. Falling down on all fours beside her silent body, I felt the chill from her draped window. A dark light. As I waited for the ambulance, all I could do was lift my head and wail, a wretched cry that my neighbor's dogs also joined, their voices blending with mine. A human and canine Greek chorus. We all howled together in dissonant harmony—until drowned out by sirens. Their high, plaintive howls accompanying mine made that moment bearable.

Maybe wolf howling, like our human music, is really a lament, soulful and also sorrowful. As one of my cellist friends says, "Maybe tragedy to us is the most beautiful—because then all things are possible."

LIKE SIMONE WEIL, many other writers have tried to balance a tragic vision with a sense of a dark, divine comedy— every being, animal or human, stumbling along in our brief, surprising fates. Like those picaresque characters in literature. Literary ecologist Joseph Meeker, in his classic *The Comedy of Survival*, writes that in our literary culture the "tragic hero pits man against nature—both his own and Nature itself." He argues that the Greek tragic tradition has led us to the brink of ecological catastrophe—because tragic heroes are bent on transcending the natural order (and thus life itself) to consciously choose their own moral order. This sounds to me a lot like wildlife managers in their endless attempts to control and impose their own moral values on wolves. Maybe it is we who are the tragic actors and the wolves are just trying to survive us.

Hélène Grimaud reminds me, "We really know so little about wolves. There's still so much mystery about wolves and our relationship with them." She pauses, then adds in a musing voice, "I think understanding wolves is all about acquaintance . . . like when I met Alawa, the first wolf to enter my life."

In Algonquin, *Alawa* means "sweet pea." When Grimaud first encountered this she-wolf she felt "a shooting spark, a shock, which ran through my entire body . . . and filled me with gentleness . . . which awakened in me a mysterious singing, the call of an unknown, primeval force. At the same moment the wolf seemed to soften, and she lay down on her side. She offered me her belly."

Such trust is extremely rare for a wolf, especially with a stranger. Once, when the wolf was howling, Grimaud realized, "Alawa isn't howling—she's calling." Alawa was "one of the great presences" of Grimaud's life. Soon more wolves called to Grimaud and inspired her to study wolf behavior and biology with the same intensity she'd given her music. She visited wildlife reserves in America and took a degree in ethology. Grimaud's bond with Alawa endures still in her work with the Wolf Conservation Center, where one of the ambassador wolves is also called Alawa. Like her namesake, this Alawa and her brother, Zephyr, which means "light" or "west wind," help educate people as part of WCC's education programs.

Acquaintance, as Grimaud says, is one vital way to speak with those who resist the wild wolf's return, who even want to deny again their right to exist. This approach is confirmed by the rather counterintuitive polls that show when wild wolves share our territories, there is more hope for coexistence.

"It's all about acquaintance *and* true cohabitation," she says. "In Europe, especially in Spain and Italy, where wolves were never totally eradicated, the farmers have a higher threshold of tolerance. That's because they never lost their knowledge of living around wild wolves. But, you know, in France, when wolves came back from nearby Italy, it was just as bad as in the worst places. After wolves have been removed, people's opposition to them seems to grow even stronger at the idea of wolf reintroduction. Because farmers feel threatened, unfamiliar about how wolves truly function, and unaware of how unfounded their fears are. Everything grows out of proportion in absence. So wolves fare better in places they've never been eradicated. Acquaintance is everything. What people are afraid of, they have no reason to protect."

"People protect what they love," as Jacques Cousteau says. Perhaps the hope for future coexistence is to keep wolf populations thriving in our wilderness and never let them be *disappeared* again. At the Wolf Conservation Center teaching kids about living with wild wolves in our wilderness is crucial. "One child at a time," says Grimaud. "You never know if that child seeing and loving wolves will grow up to be an environmental lawyer or a wolf biologist. One is never too small to have a role to play and spread the message about wolves."

Knowledge about wolves' lives can lead to tolerance and even caring. Beyond wolf politics and pro- or antiwolf arguments, there can be a more harmonious conversation when talking about the sense of a moral order that both humans and wolves share in their complex societies. Grimaud brings up the concept of *ethikos*, the Greek word for habitual excellence and a philosophy centering on morals and responsibility—what is right and wrong.

"Wolves follow the laws of their nature," Grimaud says. "They can seem merciless, but what wolves do makes sense. While so much of what *we* do doesn't make any sense."

Unlike humans, wolves do not kill entire groups of their own kind. One or two kills in a trespassing family or even a few ferocious fights are usually enough to make a wolf's territorial point. Ethologist Marc Bekoff writes about animals' moral intelligence and sense of fair play in *Wild Justice: The Moral Lives of Animals*: "wild canine societies may be even better analogues for early hominid groups—and when we study dogs, wolves and coyotes, we discover behaviors that hint at the roots of human morality." Even Darwin believed that animals "would acquire a moral sense of conscience."

"What might happen if more artists like yourself also devoted their time and talent to other species?" I ask Grimaud.

"Well, nature is the ultimate muse and the source of inspiration for all art forms," Grimaud answers with her characteristic passion.

"And nature doesn't need much of a chance to prove its resiliency. Nature is always there."

We talk about how being with animals is a respite from our own humanity, sometimes even a relief. "At some point," Grimaud says with an audible smile, "we desire to have something in our lives that's *not* just a human relationship."

Grimaud concludes our interview with a poignant story of a group of business people who recently visited the Wolf Conservation Center. When the wolves began their communal singing, "everyone could feel the energy . . . it was so powerful. You could see it in the reaction of the people, even though they were all being official and dignified. But listening to the wolves' howl, you could see softness in them. Once people are touched, that's how they become motivated to make a difference."

"Resonance" may be the best word to explain this effect. "Resonance" is "sound produced by a body vibrating in sympathy with a neighboring source of sound." This natural law of resonance echoes throughout nature, physics, and music. Water, as Grimaud portrays in her latest recording, has tidal resonance—each cascading wave has a ululating length and width that excites the spacious ocean; a tuning fork once struck will set another tuning fork vibrating at the same exact tone; and acoustic resonance matches pitches, amplifying sound at the same frequency. German jazz musician Joachim-Ernst Berendt writes about "the temple of the ear" and explains that "particles of an oxygen atom vibrate in a major key . . . blades of grass sing." If grasslands and microscopic atoms are singing to us, how much more do we resonate with the wild, compelling harmonics of wolf music?

As Grimaud's work reveals, there is fierce intimacy and tender tension in our musical resonance with wolves. Sympathy. A symphony. We may only hope that the howling of the wild wolf is not simply the tragic anthem of our nation. When we listen and join in their gorgeous chorus, we explore a soundscape that is unsettled, wild, and wide open. A territory, a meeting place, maybe even a reunion. *Ensemble.*

*part five*

# WOLVES RETURN

# 13. OR7:
# A WOLF CALLED JOURNEY

A wolf surviving alone is unusual. Without family, he must hunt much smaller prey and search for other wolves who might either accept or kill him as he attempts to belong again. Even more rare is a solitary wolf who travels twelve hundred miles to find new territory. This is the story of OR7, a wolf called "Journey," who became the first wild wolf returning to California in almost one hundred years and captivated our imaginations and respect in his epic trek.

At any given time in wild wolf populations only 20 percent are alone—and not for long. Without a family, there are so many dangers, not the least of which is the fact that in the West 10 percent of wolves are killed by poachers every year. If a wolf alone faces increased risk, why do wolves disperse? Some wolves leave their families to find mates, others are forced out by family politics, and still others grow weary of life as the omega wolf—the lowest-ranking member—and look for higher status with another group. Any of these realities may have prompted OR7 to strike out from his Inmaha family in sparsely populated Wallowa County, Oregon.

OR7 was born in the spring of 2009, his stud name showing that he was the seventh wolf to be radio collared in Oregon. His parents were the successful breeding pair of mother, Sophie (B300), and father, OR4. Wolves mate for life, and these impressive parents raised an unusually large family of sixteen members.

His father, OR4, a powerful alpha male, was considered to be a very tough but good father. OR4 was the largest wolf collared in Oregon, weighing in at 110 to 115 pounds. His howl was as resonant as a canine Pavarotti. Robust and charcoal black, OR4 was so tenacious a survivor that he "escaped kill orders and poachers. He endured at least 4 collarings and he beat the odds," writes Oregon Wild blogger Rob Klavins. "There aren't many ten-year-old wolves out there."

With such a long-lived and mighty patriarch, a son might do well to disappear if he ever wanted to breed and find a mate and found a family of his own. Our human stories—from Greek myths to *Star Wars*—are full of father-son struggles. Perhaps the same tensions drove OR7 to seek out his own destiny. But nobody could fathom just how far OR7 would wander to find his own territory. There was really no need for OR7 to travel over a thousand miles— or even leave Oregon. In 2011 there were only twenty-nine wolves in the state. These were descended from the few wolves migrating down from central Idaho, where wolves were reintroduced in 1995, through the Cascade Mountains and into far northeastern Oregon on the border of Washington and Idaho. But the westward move- ment of wolves mirrors that of our human pioneer migrations. So like Lewis and Clark and the hordes of settlers who followed, the wolves traveled west.

"There were rumors of wolves in the west—a paw print on Mount Hood there, a sighting on Santiam Pass there," writes Zach Urness in his fascinating series, "When the Wolves Return to Western Oregon." When I covered the 1997 Olympic Wolf Summit in Washington for the *Seattle Times* there were already wolves re- populating the Cascade Mountains on their own, venturing down from Canada. The West was much more welcoming to the return of wolves than the Rockies and the Great Lakes. At the Wolf Summit Washington congressman Norm Dicks had declared, "We have the opportunity to correct a historic mistake." Dicks pointed out that the total cost to taxpayers of all previous wolf reintroduction had only been a nickel per person. Wildlife officials in the West paved the way for returning wolves. But not everyone was excited about wild wolves returning on their own.

OR7's family lived in the heart of hostile cattle country. Wallawa County cattle ranches make up a third of the local economy. "There are nearly 30,000 beef cattle and almost 20,000 dairy cows in the county," notes an excellent article, "What One Wolf's Extraordinary

Journey Means for the Future of Wildlife in America." Even though
70 percent of Oregon residents support wolf recovery, those wolves
"known to have ventured across the Snake River beginning in the
late '90s were shipped back, shot, or run over by cars." These cattle
ranchers graze on public lands and have received almost $2 million
in livestock subsidies since 1995. "I think we're at a tipping point on
ranching," says Jon Marvel, who founded the Western Watersheds
Project. "It's sustained by hobbyists, corporations, and politicians
mired in the past. Absent government subsidies, cattle and sheep
ranching in the arid West would have ended long ago." Growing
up in such a ranch-heavy, hostile land, OR4's family of wolves still
somehow thrived. And they also killed some cattle, one each month
during its first two years, and six cattle killed in one month in 2010.

These losses are highly overshadowed by the fact that in Oregon "55,000 of the state's more than 1.3 million cattle die annually
from almost everything except wolves, and that the elements kill
far more cattle than wolves do. Cattle rustlers have stolen 1,200
head a year over the past several years." According to USDA statistics, all predators—such as coyotes, mountains lions, birds of
prey, and even dogs—accounted for a total of 4.3 percent of livestock losses. Yet wolves are much more highly visible scapegoats
than cattle rustlers or domestic dogs, and there was continual tension between ranchers and the Inmaha pack as they shared public
lands. Wildlife officials were killing neighboring wolf families for
attacking livestock, so OR7's family was often in the crosshairs.

In September of 2011, when OR7 was two years old, he left his
family and headed west. His timing was fortunate—days after OR7
exited, Oregon state officials issued an order to kill his father, OR4,
and one of OR7's siblings for preying on livestock. That kill order
was put on hold by a lawsuit from Oregon Wild. But OR7's brother,
OR9, had been illegally shot in 2010 when he was the first of the
family to disperse, and his sister, OR5, would be killed by a trapper on the last day of Oregon's wolf hunt season in 2013. Had OR7
stayed with his family, he might have met the same fate.

Few people have ever actually seen OR7 except in images captured from remote cameras. The most famous photo shows a black
and tawny wolf, ears perked, tail low, as he walks down a mountain

trail. He seems to be directly peering into the camera, his dark eyes focused, muzzle bright with sunlight. We recognize—from deciphering expressions in domestic dogs—that there is no alarm in this wolf's expression. Only intense curiosity, awareness. Does OR7 hear the camera clicking as he strolls by? Is that why he turns to stare straight at anyone watching? The caption reads: "The westernmost wolf in the lower 48 states, a lone pioneer wandering hundreds of miles west of any known wolf pack."

Because OR7 wore a radio collar, researchers could closely follow his travel. Schoolchildren began to track OR7's trek online and on big, multicolor maps in their classrooms. The risks for a wolf alone on such a long trip were daunting. Without his family, OR7 was vulnerable to mountain lions and bears—or even another territorial wolf. A solitary wolf cannot take down a seven-hundred-pound elk. Hunting alone, OR7 would have to find smaller prey to survive. And always the threat of poaching. With his radio collar OR7 literally had a target on his back for illegal hunters—some of whom bragged on social media that they were gunning for him. Somehow OR7 stayed out of sight as he roamed the wilderness searching for a mate.

On his journey OR7 trotted along the Wallowa Mountains, down through Eastern Oregon near Bend and Burns—very near where the last Oregon wolf had been killed in 1946 by a bounty hunter. Still traveling south, OR7 circled Crater Lake and raced past the mighty Klamath Falls at the very southern tip of Oregon. Then OR7 took a sharp turn to the west into the Cascade Mountains. Here he set his first record: the first known wolf in Western Oregon in sixty years. By this point OR7 was becoming a conservation icon, even a canine celebrity. Oregon's *Statesman Journal* called OR7 "A folk hero."

A rare sighting of OR7 in Lake Almanor, Oregon, was reported by an ex-Iditarod racer, Liz Parrish, of Crystalloid Lodge. She said a wild wolf was drawn to the plaintive howling of her sled dogs. When Parrish investigated her sled dogs' chorus of urgent howls, she was shocked to see a wild wolf standing in her driveway. She and OR7 just stared at each other for a long time. Parrish was struck at how "un-dog-like" OR7 was and how much bigger he was than even her muscled sled dogs. Without a camera or cell phone, Parrish couldn't document the sighting. But another rural resident who also spotted OR7 told journalists that "our forest is healthier simply by his presence." There were a few more signs nearby. In one a neighbor went to feed his yard dogs who were howling for supper. Suddenly there was an answering howl from the north, full bodied and resonant. Not a dog. A wolf. Was it OR7? Or had other wolves without radio collars followed his trailblazing scents into Oregon? A wild wolf howling in answer to dogs is not a good sign, especially for the wolf. Perhaps OR7 was venturing way too close to people.

By winter OR7 was five hundred miles from his home and family. Everything was against him, especially the season. In his wanderings the two-year-old OR7 had found no mate; now the mountain snow was deepening. The life expectancy for any wolf without his pack is only five years. Even though OR7 was hailed as a "one-wolf eco-tourist attraction" and his search followed by hopeful thousands, he seemed doomed. Some conservationists were hopeful about his chances: "That he appeared hopelessly lost mattered less than that he navigated a patchwork quilt of relatively intact lands coveted as natural migration corridors for recovering predators, from wolverines to lynx and now to wolves."

Three months after he began his trip OR7 crossed the California state line in late December of 2011. This crossing meant nothing to him because wolves have no knowledge of all our closely guarded borders. Of course, OR7 didn't recognize his precedent-setting feat. But it was international news. OR7 was the first wild wolf to roam California since 1924—almost one hundred years since any of his kind claimed this territory. Amaroq Weiss was among many conservationists who greeted OR7's arrival with delight. "California laid a welcome mat for this wolf," she says. "It was wonderful, breathtaking, endearing—kind of like the moment you've been waiting for your whole life—to see a state welcome a wolf. And OR7 deserves it."

Even the USDA's blog ran the headline, "California Welcomes Wild Wolf for First Time in 87 Years." By migrating to the Pacific Coast, OR7 may have saved his own life: he chose a homeland where wolves are federally listed as endangered, protected un-der the Endangered Species Act, and so allowed to thrive. "Being an apex predator in a landscape that hasn't had one for a pretty long time—he's got it pretty good right now," Oregon Wild's Steve Pedery said. California conservation groups immediately asked the Fish and Wildlife Service to also place gray wolves on its state endangered list. California wildlife officials began work on a state wolf-conservation plan.

Amidst the celebrations Oregon Wild called a contest for the pub-lic to name this wayfaring wolf. Their intent: "to make OR7 too fa-mous to kill." After all, some people in northern California weren't overjoyed to see a wild wolf return. In Siskiyou County, later one of OR7's favorite haunts, a supervisor declared that she would like to see all wolves "shot on sight." Two children won the naming contest. Their perfect name for OR7—Journey. He was earning his name. All that winter OR7 kept searching for a mate, vagabonding between northern California and southern Oregon, zigzagging up mountain trails and through thick old-growth forests. Wolf tracks were discovered, and his howls were heard again answering ranch dogs. But there was no hint that OR7 might no longer be alone.

 I IMAGINE OR7's howls might have been the loneliest sound in the world. After all, he'd been without family or mate or even companion for well over a year. OR7 was fol-lowing the archetypal "hero's journey," the pattern outlined by Jo-seph Campbell. OR7's odyssey follows the stages that we recognize: leaving the ordinary world for a solo adventure, facing tests of en-durance and strength, surviving setbacks and life-and-death or-deals that challenge the hero to evolve, finding allies along the way. Eventually the hero must earn a reward and return to share his knowledge with "the ordinary world" he once left. But would OR7 ever really accomplish such a journey? Even with throngs of people rooting for him and identifying with him, the journey was still all up to OR7 to achieve. Joseph Campbell wrote, "You enter the forest at the darkest point where there is no path. . . . If you follow some-one else's way, you are not going to realize your potential."

By the early spring of 2012 OR7 had officially logged his one thousand miles; the *Los Angeles Times* claimed his monumental trek was more like three thousand miles. But the *Times*, like most biologists, still predicted that OR7 was "unlikely to find a mate here." That summer of 2012 OR7 spent his days wandering Mount Lassen's High Sierra mountain meadows on the Plumas National Forest. I like to imagine this first wolf to return to California in my native forest. He strolls through coast Douglas fir or Ponderosa pines, hunting the many lean and fleet deer that also nourished my young muscles, blood, and bones. When I heard news of Journey's return, I wanted to take a road trip back to my birthplace to see if I could be one of the lucky ones to discover even one wolf track, a signpost of his odyssey.

All that summer of 2012, through another rough winter, and into the spring of 2013, OR7 rambled between California and Oregon. The only way we could follow OR7 was his radio collar, and that was due to die out. What would happen if we lost track of this now-beloved wolf? Or if after all this wolf had survived, a hunter poached him? If so, OR7's legacy would die, solitary forever. The biologists decided to simply let the wolf's radio-collar batteries fade and give up following him. But then, in May of 2014, a startling discovery—OR7 was captured on camera for the very first time. And he was not alone! When the wildlife officials stopped to check their remote camera's memory cards, they clearly saw OR7 and another wolf photographed within one hour of each other. Had OR7 at last found his lifelong mate?

The mysterious other wolf was slender, black, and squatted when she urinated. It was mating season, and if there were pups, they would leave their den soon. As the wildlife officials waited hopefully for any sign of pups, they admitted that as OR7's travels grew more erratic, they had "always felt it was a real long shot that a female wolf would find him." Many in Oregon and the West celebrated this reunion and union. Oregon, like California, was much more open to wolves returning than other states were. In fact, both Republican and Democrat gubernatorial candidates supported wolf reintroduction. Even an ex-president of the Oregon Cattlemen's Association, Bill Hoyt, noted that he'd "be inclined to compromise with the environmental lobby on a management strategy that only targets wolves that—unlike OR7—have a history of going after livestock."

Wildlife officials gathered scat and determined from DNA tests that this new female wolf was from a wolf family that OR7 must have encountered from northeastern Oregon. We don't know OR7's mate's heroine journey because she wore no radio collar. It may have been even more dangerous when she dispersed from her original family. All we know is that she chose to follow and bond with Journey. Now the pair traveled together, as the *Los Angeles Times*'s headline wryly declared, "OR7, the Wandering Wolf, Looks for Love in All the Right Places." Like our human comedies, which usually end in marriage ceremonies, OR7's mating was greeted with wild applause—and much hope for wolf pups.

OR7 and his sleek, ebony mate were followed even more closely as they roamed a little north again up into Oregon. Biologists there announced in June of 2014 that three pups were with them. Grainy black-and-white photos showed at least one pup racing past remote cameras. Gray like his father, etched with charcoal highlights like his mother, the pup is moving so fast that you can see the slight blur of motion around furry ears and paws. In another black-and-white image we catch only a side view of the pup, ears forward, unafraid, as he ventures onto a gravel road. One can't help but worry about the pups' visibility in such an open space. But another blurry black-and-white photo shows OR7 gazing out, tail raised, staring right into the camera, so we know the parents are nearby.

One color photo from the Oregonian's proud announcement of OR7s pups and their photo gallery quickly went viral. All but hidden behind dead wood and bright green branches, two of the tiny pups gaze out at their new world. They are side-by-side, in shadow, but even so, curiosity and even perhaps a sense of wonder can be seen in their attentive faces. We recognize that expectant and wide-open expression in any species. Their birth is historic—the first known wolf pups born in the Oregon Cascades since the mid-1940s. There was jubilation among wolf advocates but a cautionary note and reminder from Oregon's congressman Peter DeFazio. "As we celebrate OR7 and his new family, the US Fish and Wildlife

Service is threatening to disregard science and take the gray wolf off the Endangered Species List. If the service delists the gray wolf, states could declare open season on gray wolves like OR7 and his mate, and these new pups."

When OR7 at last found his mate and they began their new family, the news enlivened their popularity with a by now international audience. For three years OR7's journey existed only in our imaginations and as colorful pins tracked on classrooms' or biologists' maps. Suddenly this wolf called Journey and his family were fully revealed for us—who are such a highly visual species—to see and witness and watch, mesmerized. Wolf paparazzi had to be kept clueless as to where the family was defining their territory, lest too much love would lead to their destruction by antiwolf poachers. By now OR7s radio collar, first fitted in 2009, was ready to fade out. These collars are meant to last only three years, and this one had diligently radioed its signal for almost five. Biologists finally decided not to replace the battery in OR7's radio collar that had been broadcasting his position every six hours.

Did it matter so much if we lost track of OR7 and his family? Now the family was called the Rogue River pack because of their den in southern Oregon's Rogue River–Siskiyou National Forest. OR7's family might be much safer without alerting us to his presence. And even if we lost radio contact, OR7 was now fully wandering our imaginations. About the time OR7 found his mate, a quasi-documentary film by Clemens Schenk, *OR7: The Journey*, opened to wide acclaim. Employing a captive wolf as a stand-in for OR7, the film follows his harrowing journey. The film includes insightful interviews with wolf biologists and wolf advocates, like ex-trapper and author Carter Niemeyer and wolf advocate Oliver Starr, the "Kosher Cowboy."

Starr's grandfather owned a ranching empire of fifty-four thousand head of cattle in Colorado. Starr told me that he believes his grandfather "rolls over in his grave every time I use the W word." In Starr's decades studying wolves he's realized, "We've never really seen wolves. They are like a vestige of a civilization that has been shattered." Echoing Alaskan wolf biologist Gordon Haber, Starr credits wolves with their own culture and concludes, "Everything

I see in a wolf's behavior is just like how you'd expect a person to behave."

In the film Starr points out that we are still mostly "appeasing" ranchers in our wolf-management policies. "I come from a family with a cattle background, but agriculture has had an incredibly dominant position in decision making, particularly in the Western states." Ranchers need to learn to coexist, Starr advises, as wolves now return west. If the practices of a rancher are the reason his animals are easy prey, those practices need to change. If a particular wolf is preying repeatedly on livestock, Starr would see—only as a last resort—nonlethal removal. But, he concludes, "Generally speaking I've seen the shoot-first-try-something-else-never approach. These guys are used to calling in Wildlife Services and getting a helicopter to come in and take out a whole pack," Starr pointed out. This kind of lethal solution doesn't work. It actually makes things worse in the long run because the surviving wolf family is destabilized and fragmented, so wolves increase their attacks on livestock. "We've been killing coyotes for a hundred years plus," Starr says. "There are more coyotes now than ever before. We don't solve the problem by messing with nature."

Another voice in this fascinating film is writer George Wuerthner, who emphasizes that grazing on public lands is a privilege, not a right. "None of us have a right to damage public lands and resources that everybody else enjoys. If you're going to graze on public land, you assume a certain amount of risk, including any losses that might result from predators."

*OR7: The Journey* was a hit both in theaters and online. But it was not the only film to follow and find inspiration in OR7s story. A 2016 film, *Wolf OR-7: Expedition*, chronicles a team of six adventurers who retrace OR7's trail and "follow in the footsteps of a wolf." Supported by a Kickstarter campaign and several grants, the team is repeating OR7's trek by bicycle and on foot. "To be following in the tracks of this particular wolf as closely as we can," says one of the team members as he trods through snowbanks, "the landscape suddenly became alive in a completely different way." When they stumble upon the set of huge and unmistakable tracks in the snow, a woman, heavy laden with a backpack, exclaims, "My first wolf tracks!"

Rob Klavins of Oregon Wild echoes the hope of the expedition team: "Not all wildlife gets a second chance," Kavins says, "so it's important that we get it right this time." This new documentary film takes as its premise "1,200 miles to explore human and wolf co-existence" and already has a strong fan base on Facebook, Twitter, and at its expedition website, OR7expedition.org. One of the team members, Jay Simpson, will write daily blog posts with photos and with interviews the expedition encounters on their trek. "It is only through walking it that anyone can truly understand that journey," Simpson says. "It's not a thing you can understand on Google Earth."

Along with the films and media coverage, OR7s story also became a children's book, *Journey: Based on the True Story of OR7, the Most Famous Wolf in the West*, by San Francisco librarian Emma Bland Smith and illustrator Robin James. With a timeline of OR7's journey, the book imagines as its main character the child who named OR7. The girl is so inspired by the wild wolf's travels that she follows him with her class and celebrates him as at long last he discovers his mate. The response of many thousands of children to OR7's journey is reflected in the success of this book.

 EVEN WHILE WOLF RECOVERY advocates celebrated OR7's success and his story was reaching a vast and devoted audience, in Oregon things suddenly went backward—bewilderingly fast.

In November 2015 Oregon's Fish and Game Commission voted four-to-two to strip wolves from its state's Endangered Species List. Oregon's more enlightened and sustainable wolf-recovery policies were again falling prey to politics, not science. In an article I wrote at the time, I posted the grainy black-and-white photos of OR7s first pups in the hope that OR7's popularity might influence the Oregon wildlife officials. Oregon had been on the cutting edge of wolf recovery but was regressing to Old West bias, and Oregon's delisting of wolves was not worthy of this usually progressive state. I dearly hoped that perhaps OR7 and his family would migrate back down to California or even up to Washington where wolves were valued and protected, where the New West—for all people and wolves—is still being won. I began to worry that any day I would hear of OR7's family being hunted down. New research data has confirmed that acceptance decreases and poaching flares up again when wolves are delisted.

I was not alone in my disappointment. There was a fierce outcry over Oregon's delisting, not only from wildlife advocates like the Pacific Wolf Coalition but also from scientists who vehemently disagreed with the desilting, asserting that the decision was not based on sound science. University of Wisconsin's Adrian Treves, who has since 2001 conducted the longest-running study of human tolerance for wolves, wrote, "Oregon's delisting misses the mark on scientific evidence." He adds, "I heard from 23 of the 25 scientists opposed to delisting that neither the state nor the commission ever contacted them about their recommendations. Ignoring one scientist might be excusable, but ignoring so many who cited flaws in the commission's evidence is worrisome." Citing the real risks that wolves faced in Oregon, Treves reminds the wildlife commission that they "have legal duties as trustees for wildlife to benefit current and future generations. . . . The health of our wolves reflects the health of our democracy."

Again, as with the federal delisting, science was dismissed and politics prevailed. Oregon's wildlife commission doubled down on its decision, even though it was not supported by the public—twenty-two thousand people wrote letters opposing the delisting, and there is still overwhelming support for wolf recovery in the state. Editorials decried the decision and posted numbers that tell the real story with past statistics: in 2010 there were eighty wolves in all of Oregon and 1.3 million cattle. Total wolf-related livestock kills from 2009 until 2015 were minimal: seventy-six sheep, thirty-six cattle, two goats. Wolves are absent in 90 percent of their historic range in Oregon. They are far from recovered, and this delisting may lead the way to renewed hunting.

With such opposing science and statistics, the reasons why Oregon delisted wolves are disturbing. It is a commentary on the prejudice that continues to condemn wolves, just when they are getting a fragile foothold in their native territory. It also shows the dominance of the $669 million beef industry. Finally, a fact that cannot be repeated too often is that wildlife commissions are significantly funded by hunting and fishing licenses—one-third of the agency's revenue in Oregon. In Oregon several of the commissioners listed hunting or big game as hobbies, and another past board member was chairman of the Oregon Hunter's Association. Until wildlife advocates and nonconsumptive users pay more of their share of wildlife revenue in states, the hunters and ranchers will continue to control the management of wolves and other top predators.

In March of 2016 Oregon wildlife officials had issued yet another kill order for OR7's father, the once-mighty OR4. OR4 was now ten years old, and his age was slowing him down. He had split off from his larger family of eight, possibly because his advancing age led to his overthrow. Also slowing down OR4 was a new mate, OR39, who was so lame that she was called "Limpy." She may have been pregnant. The pair had two young wolves in their small family.

"As wolves grow old or if they are injured, they are unable to hunt traditional wild prey as they have in the past," explained Russ Morgan, the Oregon Department of Wildlife wolf coordinator. This perhaps explained why OR4's family was believed responsible for the death of six sheep or cows over five months. According to the Oregon state management plan, this predation triggered lethal removal. The sheep producer had been doing his part to protect his animals by using nonlethal strategies to ward off wolves, including guard dogs, midnight spotlighting, hazing, and range riders. The cattleman had adopted other protections: pasture rotation, pasturing cows with their yearlings, and range rider patrols for calving cattle. But it was not enough to keep an aging alpha male and his disabled mate with two young wolves, not yet veteran hunters, from surviving on easier prey.

Wolf advocates claimed that the livestock producers weren't required to use colored fence flagging or loud noise boxes known to keep wolves away. "Those things are available, but in this situation they weren't used," said Oregon Wild's Aaran Robertson. "If the agency were more clear on what the requirements were with producers, it would take a lot of the conflict out of this." The kill order came down even when Oregon's wildlife officials' own data shows that in their state wolves are really having no effect on the wild populations of elk, deer, and domestic sheep. This is not science; it is an old blood feud that has flared up again in a state that had once been a model of wolf management.

In his eulogy for OR4 Oregon Wild's Rob Klavins wrote, "He never set paw in Salem or DC, but for better and worse, he had more impact on policy and politics than any animal I know of other than Cecil the Lion." Even *Men's Journal* mourned the loss of OR4. In their photo of OR4 his massive charcoal head and golden eyes still show his powerful presence, even though his ruff is graying and his ears are pocked with green plastic from biologists' tags. Many others eulogized OR4 and his family. The popular wolf blog "Howling for Justice" wrote in its eulogy, "Oregon's Shame," that OR4 and his family "represent every wolf who has ever been senselessly killed for the sacred cow." It grieved for this legendary wolf who had fathered an equally famous son in OR7. Together OR4 and OR7 were the "backbone of wolf recovery in Oregon." In a final and respectful nod to OR4, the blog concluded, "Instead of Oregon treasuring him for the amazing wolf he was, they filled him full of lead as their final tribute."

It is horrific to imagine this master elder of a wolf run down into exhaustion by a helicopter, its loud, metal blades whirring midair, terrifying the yearling pups and parents. Then, the state-sanctioned sniper sights on OR4, his limping mate, and their two pups. Rapid-fire bullets echo in the old forest as the family falls, one by one, their dying bodies close together, as always. "I hope his death raises some serious questions among the public about the way wolves are managed on behalf of special interests," said Amaroq Weiss. OR4 didn't just belong to Oregon—"He belonged to the entire world."

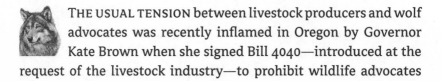 THE USUAL TENSION between livestock producers and wolf advocates was recently inflamed in Oregon by Governor Kate Brown when she signed Bill 4040—introduced at the request of the livestock industry—to prohibit wildlife advocates

from suing Oregon over its wildlife commission's delisting of wolves as an endangered species. Those wildlife advocates, including the Center for Biological Diversity, Cascadia Wildlands, and Oregon Wild, had sued Oregon's wildlife commission for delisting wolves prematurely. Governor Brown's decision declaring her state immune from any further legal action to protect wolves is still highly controversial. Conservationists have challenged Brown's delisting decision as violating the Endangered Species Act and the separation-of-powers clause in Oregon's state constitution. If Oregon's delisting of wild wolves stands, it means that any legal review of wolf protections will be blocked. And it echoes a federal bill now in Congress attempting the same exemption from legal review of any delisting of wolves.

In her 2015 testimony Amaroq Weiss asked, "Have we ever delisted a species with only eighty-some confirmed animals occupying only 5 percent of Oregon's total land mass? Can a species at such paltry numbers residing in such a tiny portion of its suitable habitat withstand the whims of politics and the upheavals of nature? The answer is no. Science says no. This Commission should say no."

With such regressive politics again putting wolves in the cross-hairs, Oregon joins the Rocky Mountain and Great Lakes states in their antiwolf bigotry. Such backward movement doesn't bode well for wolves in Oregon. If the wolf population increases from 110 in 2016, this legislation may make wolf hunts—especially in northeastern Oregon, where most of the wolves live—legal again. The specter of the Old West now shadows every wolf who calls this state home. And yet the wolves, knowing no such dangerous politics or boundaries, continue to migrate West. "I think it's inevitable that other wolves will follow OR7 and that general corridor through the state of Oregon," says Carter Niemeyer, author of *Wolfland*.

Ironically, the same spring that Oregon delisted wild wolves, the state's Supreme Court issued a landmark ruling: domestic dogs were "sentient beings," not mere property. They likened the act of a pet owner who starved her dog, Juno, to the abuse of a human child, and the pet owner was charged with second-degree animal neglect. Wolves in Oregon, as in all of America, are still considered "property" of the government. Will there ever be a time when we give our wild canines the same respect and "sentience" that we bestow upon those dogs we have domesticated to live alongside us?

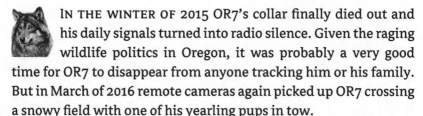 IN THE WINTER OF 2015 OR7's collar finally died out and his daily signals turned into radio silence. Given the raging wildlife politics in Oregon, it was probably a very good time for OR7 to disappear from anyone tracking him or his family. But in March of 2016 remote cameras again picked up OR7 crossing a snowy field with one of his yearling pups in tow.

"He appears well," said USFWS of OR7. And his yearling pups were caught in a time-lapse video romping, wrestling, and playing. The video had almost ten thousand shares.

OR7 had avoided several other attempts to recollar him, and the wildlife officials were planning to try again later in the spring despite the increased danger the collar would bring. Then came the announcement of a second litter of OR7's pups. From their scat these two new pups were declared the progeny of OR7 and his same slender mate. This second generation of OR7's family was greeted enthusiastically by the public and again became front-page news internationally. In other good news, a pair of wolves were spotted just miles away from OR7's family very near the California border. This "Keno pair" may also have a litter, which would mean possible access and genetic diversity when the Rogue pack yearlings decide to leave their family in search of mates.

As OR7 and his generations thrive, there is always the concern that Oregon's delisting of wolves may encourage more antiwolf sentiment. In the late fall of 2016 a three-year-old wolf, OR28, was illegally killed in Oregon's Fremont-Winema National Forest. A new mother with one pup, OR28 was mated with OR3, from the same Inmaha pack that included the formidable father OR4 and the famous traveler OR7. This poaching of Oregon wolves added to the tally of five other wolves, who were poached or "died under mysterious circumstances." Oregon Wild noted that "the state's track record of actually prosecuting wolf poaching cases is pretty abysmal." USFW, the Center for Biological Diversity, and the Humane

Society have offered a combined reward of $20,000 for information leading to the discovery of who killed OR28.

Along with news of OR28's death, there are worries about the safety of OR7. "Is Journey in Trouble?" asked wolf advocate Beckie Elgin, who has long chronicled OR7's life and his Rogue pack family. Citing recent livestock deaths near the Rogue pack's territory, Elgin noted that so far, OR7's family has not been implicated in any livestock deaths. But with a growing family of nine wolves and OR7's increasing age, she says, Journey is "old for a wild wolf and maybe his hunting skills are ebbing." However, OR7's family lives in the western part of Oregon, where the federal Endangered Species Act still protects wolves. Ranchers are increasing their use of fladry and ranch riders "in an effort to keep wolves away."

Many hope that OR7 and his growing family will migrate to much safer territory in California where wolves are still greeted with excitement. A 2015 *Los Angeles Times* editorial exclaims, "Welcome back, gray wolf." The op-ed begins, "Well, hello there, Shasta Pack." Biologists in California were surprised when not long after OR7 crossed its borders to become the first wolf in that state since the last bounty hunt in 1924, another entire family of wolves was discovered. A breeding pair and five pups were caught on remote cameras as they rested in the summer grass. DNA scat tests revealed the matriarch of the Shasta pack, like OR7, had also originated from the Inmaha family; she had also traveled a long way, migrating from northeastern Oregon. So this new mother in California's Shasta pack is OR7's sibling. California's Department of Fish and Wildlife released a YouTube video of the five charcoal-colored pups playing and tussling together against a backdrop of deep woods.

In California wolves are protected as endangered species under both state and federal law. "The return of the northern gray wolf is a welcome sign of nature's ability—and man's—to change and adapt," the *Los Angeles Times* editorial explains as it celebrates the wolves' return, not by reintroduction "into a hostile environment, but by natural expansion into wild territory." The distinction is important. California's wolves cannot be rejected as a federal government overreach into state's rights. The wolves are repopulating on their own. In June of 2016 the California Department of Fish and Wildlife released a black-and-white photo of a possible new wolf roving around Lassen County. Each new wolf to wander into California is critical to the genetic diversity of wolves. California has declared it illegal to shoot any wolves entering its borders. California's Fish and Game Commission is working closely with citizen stakeholders to finalize its wolf-management plan.

Scientists wonder whether perhaps the wolves are establishing their territory in the Golden State because of the glaciers that cover their namesake, Mount Shasta. California, like much of the West, has faced severe drought, and that reduces prey populations like mule deer and elk. But Mount Shasta enjoys generous snowmelt in the spring and early summer, which nourishes the high mountain forests and wild animals. It doesn't seem a coincidence that the wild wolves restoring themselves in the western states have all settled near glaciers with abundant prey—and few people.

Another editorial, "Celebrate the Return of Wolves to California," pointed out that the Shasta pack had chosen "friendly territory" on the border of northern California and Oregon to start their family. It concludes with the telling statistic: "Wild wolves generally fear people and rarely pose a threat to human safety. Still, the U.S. has had two fatalities since 2000. Then again, cows kill 20 people a year." These are the kind of statistics that need to be widely known as wild wolves recover on their own and with our help. As we study the lives of real wolves returning to their native habitat, everything changes. The story is forever revised.

WHEN WE HAVE INVESTED our interest in individual wild animals—say, Cecil the Lion or one of Jane Goodall's well-known chimps—what happens when they are targeted and the whole world mourns their loss? Will state wildlife commissions listen? Will they understand that they are no longer invisible agencies operating, like Wildlife Services, in the shadows? Will they realize the whole world is watching?

Stories of individual animals must now be told. Hearing the story of one child surviving a tsunami or a refugee finding a homeland is what touches us the most. Not stats and population densities, but characters in stories that very much mirror our own daily struggles to survive. An individual, well-loved, even heroic wolf like OR7 with whom we've so deeply identified can never be a statistic again. If we track an animal hero's journey, the death or loss of that animal is not just news—it is a tragedy.

OR7's epic journey drives deep into our American character, like a taproot. What is it about a traveler's tale, an odyssey, that so galvanizes us? Is it because our human history is so migratory, our very DNA a trail of tribulations and triumphs? The immigrant and nomadic lineage of our nation's brief history and the settling of the West is mirrored in OR7's westward migration. The difference is, of course, that OR7 was repopulating territory that is his wolf nation's birthright. Perhaps there were scent traces or dens that had somehow lasted almost a century, even when wolves were just memories. Perhaps the memory was in OR7's DNA, like some biological impulse to return home. If salmon can remember and return to the same creeks and streams of their birth, even after being lost at sea all their lives, and if other migrating animals can retrace their routes using electromagnetic fields in the earth, then why not wolves reclaiming the West that was once all theirs?

In a new century with wolf tales like OR7's, the Old-West story of contented cows grazing on public lands, of cowboys, hunters, and ranchers, is no longer the main event. When a wolf becomes a folk hero, when his journey goes viral, when audiences cheer him on to find a mate and raise pups—that is every bit as compelling a drama as the story cattlemen have long told of round-ups, rustlers, and gunslingers.

When we recognize individual wolves and their wolf nation, we change our own history. Change is painful, and some ranchers and hunters are reverting to violence. Some wildlife commissions are digging deep into past prejudices. But they do so at great cost: the storyline of a rancher killing the well-known and loved wolves who are just beginning to return is bad press. Now certain enlightened ranchers are adapting to a changing story: living with wolves. They join wildlife advocates, becoming heroes of wolf recovery and sustainability.

The Nez Perce tribe, who, like the wolves, have lived in Oregon for millennia, have taken in wild wolves from the original Sawtooth pack on their sovereign native lands. They now offer sanctuary to what they call the Owyhee pack. Their twenty-year-old wolf sanctuary, the Wolf Education and Research Center (WERC), has its tribal offices in Winchester, Idaho, and Portland, Oregon. Their newsletter, *The Sawtooth Legacy*, is required reading in many Oregon schools, and every summer they host an educational two-day Wolf Camp. In their weekly Radio Wild educational podcast series, they have posted an interview with a Nez Perce elder who reminds us: "The wolves have *always* been here."

# 14. SHEEP HIGHWAY: COEXISTING WITH WOLVES

**W**hen a rancher grazed his sheep right on top of an area where wild wolves were denning in 2007—we expected a train wreck," says Suzanne Stone, who works with Defenders of Wildlife and is cofounder of the Wood River Wolf Project.

The Wood River Valley in Idaho's south-central Sawtooth Mountains is summer grazing ground for up to twenty-five thousand sheep. Its "Sheep Super Highway," along which herders move their stock, is legendary. In the summer of 2007 there was a new wolf pack in Blaine County, and the sheep grazing season began just as the wolf pack's pups were growing up and traveling. After the wolves took down several lambs, the pack was slated for removal.

"Blaine County is like our own little Yellowstone Serengeti," Stone explained. "No one wanted to see this sheep rancher lose his livelihood, but no one wanted to lose wolves either. So a lot of people asked state agencies and Defenders of Wildlife to help provide nonlethal defense for sheep."

Idaho, however, has one of the most virulent antiwolf state policies. Its wildlife commission assumed the proposed nonlethal Wood River Wolf Project would fail and the state could simply continue what Idaho has been doing all along—kill wolves.

"This valley is an area where Ed Bangs, head of USFW Northern Rockies' Wolf Program, said wolves would never survive here," Stone noted, "because we have one of the highest concentration of livestock, especially sheep, on public lands anywhere in America." She added that even before wolves returned to Idaho there was livestock predation from coyotes and dogs; together they accounted for 30 percent of sheep losses each year. "But coyote and dog losses do not make the paper or make a big political stir," Stone said. "This has less to do with wolves and more about human fear of what could happen," she explained. After wolves reclaimed the landscape they accounted for only 1 percent of lost livestock. Other livestock losses are from such elements as weather, birthing problems, and disease.

Though few believed that sheep could be safely protected from wolves who had already fed on livestock, wolves were given a second chance. Defenders of Wildlife, wildlife agencies, and sheep ranchers worked together to find common ground and coexistence.

"We're in year nine now of our project," Stone told me, "and we have ten to twenty-five thousand sheep grazing here from the end of May through mid-October. And in all that time since 2007 we've only lost thirty sheep to wolves—total."

That is 90 percent lower than the loss of sheep to wolves in the adjacent grazing land outside of the project's area. And no wolves have had to be killed—at great expense to taxpayers—by wildlife control agents. The Wood River Wolf Project has grown from 150 to 1,000 square miles and is working with all five sheep producers in the grazing corridor known locally as the "Sheep Super Highway," along which move herds, called "bands," of fifteen hundred to two thousand sheep.

"Our project includes some great mentors and people who took risks to try new approaches to age-old conflicts," said Stone, who has traveled all over the world teaching methods of protection pioneered in the project.

The focus is on prevention. Sheep ranchers remove carcasses and bone piles that naturally attract wolves. Scavenging on what is already dead is a lot less work for wolves than hunting. Ranchers who participate are taught to "think like wolves" and not offer them "an easy meal." When farmers throw carcasses into open-pits without any electric fencing or regular monitoring, it naturally attracts wolves. Once those wolves have fed on carcasses, it is a simple next step to hunt live sheep or cows. Burning carcasses in a pit or hauling them away to a rendering facility is advised, whenever possible, instead of leaving them to decay in open fields.

Ranchers apply technology such as telemetry to monitor the wolf family's location and game camera traps that survey the movement of predators, including moose, bears, and cougars as well as wolves. Radio-active alarms and the simple use of "fladry," those nylon fence tags that flap erratically, arouse a wolf's natural wariness of anything unusual in their territory. "Turbofladry" is stringing those red flags along electrified fences that deliver a powerful shock if the wolf tries to trespass into sheep bedgrounds at night. Wolves also keep their distance from noisemakers like starter pistols (using .22 blank bullets), ear-splitting air horns, and—believe it or not—boom boxes. Many wolves are unfamiliar with human music, and it can be jarring, even frightening. Think the Clash or Metallica accosting the sensitive ears of a wolf who can hear sound from six to nine miles away.

Heavy-duty spotlights and Foxlights that project 360 degrees and shine light one kilometer are also quite effective. These computerized, varying spotlights give the illusion that someone is moving around and actually patrolling. These tools are part of the "Band Kits" that the project puts together for shepherds and field volunteers.

Another preventative step is for ranchers, herders, and field techs to build night corrals within a small pasture, protected at night with fladry flags. This is less expensive than fencing or flagging or lighting a very large area. Livestock actually grow accustomed to returning to their corrals at night and enter corrals on their own. Cattle are so used to their routine that one rancher moved his entire herd in less than thirty minutes "using only a whistle, two dogs, and a load of fresh feed."

Some of the fiercest protectors of sheep and other livestock are the domesticated canines whose ancestors once included wolves. Livestock guardian dogs (LGDs) are breeds like Great Pyrenees, Anatolian shepherds, Akbash, and Maremma, who have been engaged in protecting livestock from predators for centuries. In the United States the Great Pyrenees are the most well-known and popular dogs used to guard livestock, whereas border collies are bred to herd the animals. Visit the Facebook page of the Wood River Wolf Project, and there are as many snapshots of Great Pyrenees puppies and guardians as there are sheep. In one photo an adult Great Pyrenees, whose white coat is almost as thick as that of the band of sheep she protects, faces the camera as if to forbid any intruder. In another photo a puppy faces off with the camera, barking aggressively and with a serious expression and deeply furrowed brow, as if to say, "These are *my* sheep. Git!"

These puppies are not raised to bond with humans as our daily companions. Their devotion is reserved for the sheep. At five to six weeks old the barn or outdoor pen is home to these Pyrenees puppies, and the sheep are their extended family. A mother guardian dog trains her pups to bark if a predator is nearby and to patrol the herd. The puppy "needs to be within sight and sound" of his livestock companions, and "pups from working parents usually have excellent early socialization" to the sheep or goats or poultry they protect.

Puppies are trained both by their mother and older guardian dog mentors. But the rancher, although not overly friendly, will hand-feed the puppies. Ranchers move the feed bucket around the perimeter, stopping to let the pups gobble kibbles, before moving on along the fence. This teaches the puppies to patrol the area and be rewarded for their effort. Another training strategy is to put the pup on a long leash while moving around a sheep herd. If the pup goes after a sheep, a quick tug on the lead prevents any damage. Most guardian dogs are not ready to get down to real work until they are two years old.

Just because a guardian dog is raised with sheep doesn't mean there is no connection with people—guardian dogs have always worked with shepherds. However, owners are advised to "minimize the handling and stroking of pups. Do not treat them like pets." They should respond when called and allow handling, "but should not seek attention from people."

LGDs also need protection from predators. Adults have nails embedded in their collars in case they are attacked. They are trained to stay with the herd and not give chase to wolves or other predators. Leaving the safety of the sheep herds, called "bands," can mean injury or death for a guardian dog. Most ranchers work with three or more dogs to defend their sheep. Wolves seem to interpret multiple dogs as another pack and avoid any encounter. But when ranchers employ five or more guardian dogs they are often "more interested in socializing with each other than guarding livestock." Between April and June, when wolves give birth and must protect their dens, guardian dogs are kept away from wolf ranges to avoid wolf-dog conflicts.

Most effective of all in protecting sheep from wolves is a human presence. This includes the range riders who herd livestock and veteran sheepherders from Peru. Wolves are very suspicious of humans and rarely come anywhere near when a range rider is at work. Because wolves hunt mostly at night, the Wood River Wolf Project has set up "sheep camps," often assisted by volunteers. When the sheep are in their bedding grounds, people take night shifts along with their guardian dogs. If they get word from the radio telemetry that wolves are nearby, herders can set up temporary turbofladry and contact project team members if they need assistance. It's very hard and vigilant work to stay up all night using guard dogs and predator deterrents.

In 2012 there was much concern as herders moved their sheep to a watering hole, as they were overnighting the band dangerously near the Pioneer pack's territory. Everyone was keenly aware that right over the border in northeastern Washington State wildlife officials had just killed off all but two members of the Wedge pack for preying upon cattle in Ferry County. Calling the lethal removal a "last resort" and a "sad lesson," a WDFW spokesperson said future wolf culls would be "extremely rare" and that the department "never wants to do this again . . . the social acceptance is just not there." The cost for taxpayers of culling the Wedge pack was $77,000. Conservation Northwest pleaded for more expansive use of nonlethal efforts.

Right across the state line in Idaho the Wood River Wolf Project was just such a strategy. When Peruvian herder Alvarado Baldeon was hired to protect rancher John Peavey's sheep that summer, there had already been a disastrous wolf conflict in early spring— thirty-seven sheep killed by wolves. Of the sheep killed, many were pregnant ewes. In response, federal wildlife officials killed two wolves from the pack believed responsible for the predation.

Peavey was not yet participating in the Wood River Wolf Project. Stone criticized Peavey letting pregnant ewes roam public land without range riders.

"It's like ringing a dinner bell, setting the table, and then shooting the guests when they show up," she said.

Rancher Peavey protested that prowolf advocates didn't realize "the complexities of animal husbandry" or how "pregnant and newly delivered ewes get stressed out when they're bunched together in the tight groups that Defenders of Wildlife advocates for deterring predators." He explained that such bunching creates more stillborn lambs and sometimes nursing lambs can't find their mothers. He also pointed out that sheep ranchers have to deal with predators other than wolves.

When Defenders of Wildlife asked Peavey whether they could sponsor night vigils or sheep camps to help protect his bands, he agreed. Such programs are not cheap. Defenders spend $50,000 to $60,000 each year to fund the Wood River Wolf Project's many non-lethal deterrents. "The goal is to make livestock riskier for wolves to pursue than their natural prey," said Stone.

So when Baldeon spread out his bedroll inside his "campo," or sheep wagon, and settled in for a long, sleepless night with his guardian dogs, the stakes were high for everyone. The summer turned out to be *tranquillo* for Baldeon, even though every night when he howled out into the darkness he was answered by the nearby Pioneer pack. In September, as the sheep were moved deeper into the Pioneer pack's territory, two sheep from Baldeon's flock and seven from another band were killed. Idaho Fish and Game set out wolf traps for the Pioneer pack. The cycle of kill-and-be-killed seemed inevitable.

Additional field volunteers were called in to help Baldeon keep watch—five people now spending the night in shifts with the sheep. A Defenders of Wildlife field manager found wolf scat scattered among the sheep one morning, though no sheep were lost the previous night. No wolves triggered the government's death traps. By October Baldeon and the field technicians marched their fifteen hundred sheep through the Trailing of the Sheep festival. "The sheep were fat and healthy, wearing a season's worth of wool."

THE WOOD RIVER WOLF PROJECT depends upon ranchers' willingness to work closely with USFW, Idaho Department of Fish and Game, the US Forest Service, and conservation groups like Defenders of Wildlife and the Nature Conservancy. There is also support from the national and local Audubon Society, Natural Resources Conservation Service, and LightHawk to sponsor wolf-livestock coexistence workshops for people of all ages. In 2015 the Lava Lake Institute for Science and Conservation joined the Wood River Wolf Project, which also conducts workshops for volunteers.

Field and staff volunteers for the Wood River Wolf Project do more than sitting vigil with sheep. They must be experienced in backcountry hiking and wilderness first aid as well as have some skills in Spanish. The other requirements for field volunteers read like those for a rigorous summer camp: navigating in backcountry without cell service; hiking late at night in the dark; backpacking up to eight miles in rough or mountainous terrain; camping in snow, sleet, and wind; enduring exposure to predators like bears and mountain lions; and, most important of all, being comfortable surrounded by two thousand ewes and lambs, guard dogs, and horses.

Despite these requirements, many volunteers sign up. Some of them help with research, conducting howl surveys of wolf families or monitoring and sorting through the game camera photos. Field assistant Justin Stevenson notes that using telemetry to track signals from radio-collared wolves has been an efficient tool to ward off depredation—"If we can just keep ourselves between the sheep and the wolves." In most instances it hasn't taken much to keep wolves away: "Just human presence is enough." One year Stone chased away wolves near the sheep's bedground by just banging a metal pot with a wooden spoon.

In 2008, the Wood River Wolf Project's leadership role was undertaken by the Lava Lake Institute. Founded in 1999 by a San Francisco couple, Kathleen and Brian Bean, who have ties to the Nature Conservancy, Lava Lake describes itself as "a family of ranchers and environmentalists committed to sustainable ranching," and to "restoring and preserving this land because of its history, its beauty and its biological diversity." The Bean family notes that on its ranch over one hundred species of birds have been sighted "as well as many keystone species such as wolf, black bear, mountain lion, and elk." Lava Lake is remarkable for its dual focus on sheep ranching and conservation.

Their goals are long term for both sheep and wildlands. For two years Lava Lake avoided sheep-wolf conflicts by not grazing sheep on one of their allotments. But when they needed to use their land again so as not to overgraze another range, they were committed to "maintaining a wildlife-friendly reputation."

In the documentary film *Return to the Wild: A Modern Tale of Wolf & Man*, Lava Lake president Mike Stevens says, "We recognize that wolves are an important part of a fully functioning ecosystem." He explained that "we've had zero depredations with the exception of 2005," when they had yet to implement all of the Wood River Wolf Project's recommended nonlethal deterrents. Their communication network in 2005 was also not as sophisticated, so they were not alerted to the presence of a wolf pack. They lost twenty-five sheep over two nights. But instead of instantly demanding that the wolf family be exterminated, Lava Lake bolstered its nonlethal strategies and since then has had no further wolf depredation.

Stevens concluded, "The goal was not just to keep the sheep safe, but to keep the wolves safe too. If those wolves were dead, it would reflect poorly on all the sheep operators in this area."

If more ranchers adapted to the idea that the public support for wolf recovery on public lands is increasing and that wolf-livestock coexistence—not extermination—is the responsibility of both ranchers and wolf advocates, lethal removal might disappear. As Lava Lake's Brian Bean suggested, "If lethal control was unsubsidized on public lands, meaning the rancher had to pay [for it], the phone would be ringing off the hook in terms of people wanting to understand nonlethal methods and how to reduce depredation."

 THE WOOD RIVER WOLF PROJECT'S model of coexistence with wolves was put to the test in the summer of 2016. Once again helicopters right across the border in Washington were searching rugged terrain in the Colville National Forest grazing area—with orders to kill an entire wolf family, the Profanity Peak pack. As with the Wedge pack—some of whom were culled in 2012—and the Huckleberry pack—whose breeding female was shot after her family was suspected of preying upon sheep—there was huge public outcry against these new kill orders. People wondered what "sad lessons," if any, had actually been learned—especially as gray wolves are still an endangered species in Western Washington, where there is profound public support for wolf recovery. Wolves had naturally reestablished themselves in Washington, mostly in the northeast counties of the state. In 2016 there were nineteen confirmed wolf packs (totaling ninety wolves) in Washington. Would killing eleven out of ninety wolves still leave a sustainable population?

"By no stretch of the imagination can killing 12 percent of the state's tiny population of ninety wolves be consistent with wolf recovery," Amaroq Weiss of the Center for Biological Diversity maintained.

Other conservation groups, including Defenders of Wildlife, Conservation Northwest, Wolf Haven International, and the US Humane Society, were caught in the crossfires of this highly controversial culling. These wolf conservation groups had all participated in the twenty-member Wolf Advisory Group (WAG) and had spent two years in difficult but productive dialogues with wildlife scientists, livestock producers, sportsmen, and state and federal wildlife agency reps to set up a protocol for lethal removal—if wolves preyed upon cattle or sheep. After confirmation that the Profanity Peak pack had killed six cattle and notice of three other probable depredations, the Washington Department of Fish and Wildlife (WDFW) was asked, under this WAG agreement, to sanction lethal removal.

"We didn't get the protocol we wanted right off the bat," Suzanne Stone told me about the WAG agreement on lethal removal. "There were compromises. With the Profanity Peak killing in this chronic conflict area, more changes must be made, more consideration for wolves in public lands."

The Diamond M rancher, Len McIrvin, whose livestock loss had also triggered the Wedge pack culling, had used nonlethal deterrents (range riders) and removed livestock carcasses, so the basic requirements for lethal removal seemed to be met. In early August state wildlife officials shot two Profanity Peak wolves from a helicopter. Because it's almost impossible to identify wolves from the air, it was not clear whether they had once again killed the alpha, or breeding, female.

After this was determined, wolf conservation advocates still hoped that the adults remaining in the family would provide food for the weaned pups. The pups had been born in the spring and were now about three to four months old. Many of them did not yet have radio collars. The older wolves, with their radio collars, were easier targets for aerial snipers and trappers. After losing their breeding female and another adult female, the Profanity Peak wolf family retreated to dense, often remote forests, and the lethal removal was halted. Wolf advocates watched anxiously in the hope that the wolf family's remaining nine members would not again be found guilty of any more livestock predation.

But soon more cows were killed or injured—six cattle and possibly five others. WDFW issued an order to exterminate the remaining wolf family. The Profanity Peak pack was originally believed to include six adults and five pups. Because the pups were young and have "greater nutritional needs . . . it's believed that may be the cause for the latest, and fourth livestock attack from this pack during the year." By late August six wolves in the Profanity Peak pack were dead. There were five surviving members, and the culling controversy was big news nationally and internationally.

"Problem is, they first accidentally shot the breeding female," Stone explained. "That will normally cause conflict to worsen rather than to get better." Losing the alpha female often destabilizes the entire family and can actually lead to more depredation by younger, more immature wolves who are not yet trained to be wary of livestock and people.

The highly unpopular kill orders for the entire Profanity Peak pack proved a very difficult situation for those wolf advocates, like Defenders of Wildlife, who had committed to the lethal protocol agreement forged by the Wolf Advisory Group. Jamie Rappaport Clark, the ex-director of the US Fish and Wildlife Service and now president of Defenders, wrote, "This is a point we never wanted to come to. In our vision for wolves, lethal removal would never have to be used. . . . When we lose wolves, it is devastating for those who advocate for their recovery, as we have for decades." Describing gray wolves as America's true "comeback kid," Rappaport noted that ranchers are realizing after twenty years of wolf recovery that "we have to learn to live with them. . . . This might be hard for some wolf advocates to digest, but the reality is that without the cooperation of ranchers, wolves don't have a chance on the landscape."

Wolf advocacy groups who had signed on to the WAG protocol issued a joint statement: "We remain steadfast that our important goals remain the long-term recovery and public acceptance of wolves in our state alongside thriving rural communities. . . . We ask our community and the citizens of Washington State and beyond to engage in respectful and civil dialogue as we work through these challenging events. We believe that ultimately we can create conditions where everyone's values are respected and the needs of wildlife, wildlife advocates, and rural communities are met."

Yet, as so often happens with wolf politics, the conversation was *not* noted for its civility. Facebook pages for the wolf advocacy groups participating in WAG to work together were filled with outrage and threats to withdraw support. As the *Seattle Times* noted, Washington "faces backlash on all sides over wolf killings."

For these longtime wolf advocates—as well as the others on the Wolf Advisory Group now required to support wolf culling in hopes of long-term coexistence—losing the Profanity Peak pack was an excruciating but unavoidable step forward towards long-term coexistence with wolves.

Watching this Profanity Peak pack killing play out so painfully for all involved reminds me of meeting young foresters whose idealism was sorely tested when they were asked to "get the cut out" on the forests they wanted to conserve. The official rationale was always short-term sacrifice for long-term gain—a complex and often personally grueling path with many compromises and moral dilemmas. It takes a toll on those who strive to save wolves only to see these wolf families killed for the "greater good." For surely on the way to coexistence there are not just sacrificial lambs—there are also sacrificial wolves.

THE BACKLASH AND public outrage over the ongoing plans to kill the remaining five members of the Profanity Peak pack were on full display at the September 2016 Wolf Advisory Group meeting in Western Washington. Perhaps it takes a repeated tragedy like targeting an entire wolf family for the third time to ignite public opinion and participation. The WAG meeting was standing room only, with an electric tension in the air. The mediator, Francine Madden, asked everyone to consider whether we would use "words of war or words of peace." In her firm but inclusive mediation style—what she calls "conflict transformation"—she told the contentious crowd, "Peace building is hard to do."

Over a hundred of us witnessed the Wolf Advisory Group as they described their work together to build trust between traditional foes. The meeting began with a prayer by the Montana Blackfoot traditional medicine chief, Jimmy Stgoggard. In his prayer Stgoggard asked the Creator to "bless these farmers and ranchers to help them understand that the *makoyi*, the wolf, is holy to us. . . . We want to teach the children that we can all come together." Then a Native woman moved around the circle of WAG members and sang, a soft rattle accompanying her strong voice. Several of the WAG members, including a few ranchers—one with a knife sheathed at his belt—bowed their heads as the crowd calmed down.

The WAG members each took turns to speak about their two-year struggle to listen and learn from each other. Their stories revealed unexpected humor, courage, and vulnerability. Donny Mortarello of WDFW confessed to feeling unprepared for how troubling the Profanity Peak pack removal was, even for wildlife officials. "We were not expecting it to be so . . . so emotional," he said, his head down and voice muted.

"There was real grief," a brawny wildlife biologist added in a husky voice.

One of the cattlewomen choked on her words. "Cattle producers are not great at change," she admitted. "We haven't had wolves in ninety years, and now they're here, and people are upset that we're not changing fast enough!" She paused, her voice wavering. "But cattle producers using nonlethals is *huge* . . . and using them so quickly is huge. It's hard for us," she punctuated the air with her hand. "And we're doing it! I want to make sure everybody acknowledges that." She broke off, fighting back tears.

In all the polarities of wildlife conflict we rarely see ranchers' real pain at how swiftly the culture is moving them—either along or aside. The US Humane Society representative leaned over as if with the weight of his work, "There has been true compassion and outreach in this group like I've *never* seen before. This is tangible change."

A wildlife conflict supervisor in the WAG praised the range riders. "They put in a ton of time in the field." In the audience he nodded toward two burly men in cowboy hats and battered boots. "Five generations of cattle producers are really stepping up."

One of the rugged range riders, hat in hand, suggested, "If the Forest Service and ranchers can talk right at the beginning of the grazing season, it could really prevent depredations. Let's get this communication going between the Forest Service and USFW!"

Listening to the WAG members, it struck me that most of us carefully curate our information, subscribing to media that reflect back only our own worldview; we rarely have to talk for long with those whose politics or lifestyles are diametrically opposed to ours. To converse respectfully with others who completely disagree with us requires new openness, an elasticity of mind and heart.

Face-to-face, well-moderated discourse—even on an issue like wolves, known for its vitriol—can advance the conversation, and the possibilities, and often change policies. Since WAG began meeting in 2014, three times as many ranchers are adopting non-lethal deterrents in the state. By the time this WAG meeting was held in late fall of 2016, there had been not a single wolf poaching in Washington that year, as compared with hundreds of wolves illegally killed in Idaho, Montana, and Wyoming.

"We still have the best wolf-management policy of any state," Diane Gallegos told me on a break from the intense discussion. "In our first WAG meeting there was so much friction that pro- or anti-wolf WAG members didn't even want to sit next to each other." Now ranchers and conservationists socialize together. Gallegos concluded, "We're listening to each other for a common goal. That's a powerful thing when you have *really* tough work to do together."

What was so different about this working group of traditional adversaries, with so many deeply opposing opinions, was indeed their mutual goodwill. But more striking was their agreement that there was no going backward to an Old-West model. There was only the goal of finding a way forward into coexistence *with* wolves. This is impressive and unusual in state wolf politics. It's also surprising to see a working group that can even tease each other without rancor. Wolf preservation has often been called "the abortion issue of wildlife."

 A LARGER ISSUE at the WAG meeting was that the public has not yet played its full part in the wolf-management policy being hammered out—and that public was now demanding to have its say. The WAG got an earful from people who often feel they have too long been left out of the debate over public wildlife on public lands. Several Native people pointed out that there were no tribal reps on WAG. "Wolves and our people have been erased from public lands," a Native woman said. "Wolves are our kin, our creators. My brother is from the Wolf Clan, and in our stories the wolf is part of our identity."

A Cowlitz tribal leader from Protect the Wolves noted that elder Roger Dobson had just sent a cease-and-desist letter to the state declaring that lethal removal of the Profanity Peak pack violated treaty and religious rights. "This particular rancher is a proven repeat offender of placing his livestock in harm's way for the last three years," Dobson wrote. "It is not the fault of our sacred animals. They did not ask to have their home range invaded by careless livestock owners."

A woman in the crowd, well versed in the history of lethal removal in Washington, read from her copious notes. "Wolf removal is not based on credible science." She paused and looked around the room, which was loudly supporting her. "Coexistence may never be attained with *certain* ranchers." Angry clapping from the crowd. The woman concluded that Diamond M rancher Len McIrvin was no poster child for any use of nonlethal deterrents.

Because wolves had killed livestock on McIrvin's allotment for the second time, many in the crowd were very skeptical of his commitment to coexistence with predators. The *Seattle Times* had just broken a front-page story citing Washington State University researcher Dr. Robert Wielgus, director of the Large Carnivore Lab. The scientist noted that rancher McIrvin "had elected to put his livestock directly on top of their den site; we have pictures of cows swamping it." Wielgus also explained that "the cattle pushed out the wolves' native prey of deer, and with a den full of young to feed."

Using camera monitors and far-ranging telemetry, Wielgus is conducting an ongoing study of wolf-livestock conflicts in Washington. Wielgus questioned why "McIrvin has refused to radiocollar his cattle to help predict and avoid interactions with radio-collared wolves." He concluded that the killing of cows by the Profanity Peak pack was "predictable and avoidable" and that "in Washington, more cattle are killed by logging trucks, fire, and lightning than wolves."

Washington State University then immediately issued an apology and disavowal, calling Wielgus's statements "inaccurate and inappropriate." WSU sided with rancher McIrvin, who had used a grazing permit from the US Forest Service for seventy-three years. Wielgus still maintained that the rancher had "refused to cooperate with us to reduce depredations and has had two wolf packs killed so far. He hates wolves . . . and welcomes conflict . . . because the wolves die in his allotments." Wielgus concluded that where McIrvin grazes, "dead wolves follow. He will be proud of it."

Amidst death threats to both WDFW officials and ranchers—and claims that Wielgus's academic freedom was also being violated—Dr. Wielgus withdrew from the debate, saying, "It's gone too far."

WDFW's Donny Mortarello had publicly defended the wolf culling and countered Wielgus's assertions with details he stressed were really important given the tensions on all sides: "Cattle were released four miles from the den site," Mortarello explained. Because the wolf family's home range is 350 square miles, it was "inevitable that they would cross paths" with cattle. In an interview with the local television station Mortarello concluded that WDFW's commitment to following the WAG's agreed-upon protocol for lethal removal was vital to building trust among all stakeholders and that "nothing less than the future of wolf management is at stake."

 HISTORY AND BAD BLOOD haunts fragile coalitions like the Wolf Advisory Group who are trying to find common ground between often warring factions. In Stevens County, like many places in Northeastern Washington, where a majority of wolves have settled, antiwolf politics have deep roots. It would be risky to wear a prowolf T-shirt there. Stevens County Cattlemen's website headline was "Profanity Wolf Pack Becoming Chronic Killers," with an illustration "Delist the Wolf." An editorial ran in the *Omak-Okanogan County Chronicle* under the headline, "Wolf Kills Step in the Right Direction." The editorial celebrated the fact that WDFW "is finally starting to see that wolves are a problem" and added, "If only the state could listen to ranchers who told them the animals were a bad neighbor all along." The editorial claimed that the fairy tales, including "Little Red Riding Hood," were right and that wolves were "best away from humans or dead." Likening conservationists from the "concrete wilderness" of liberal Seattle to *Jurassic Park* types who, if they had their way, might also unleash a "family of tyrannosaurs . . . to live near humans," the editorial concluded, "Do you really want your grandma getting gobbled up?"

Nancy Soriano of Okanogan County has been monitoring her local government, especially the county commissioners, for years. Her husband runs cattle in the Okanogan yet also supports wolf recovery. "The wolf issue is part of a national, antifederal government agenda," Soriano wrote me. Her county's commissioners, she said, still fiercely resist the Endangered Species Act. "Putting wolves in the crosshairs has been a successful propaganda campaign, which is part of a much larger intention to maximize resource extraction and eliminate environmental protections," Soriano argued. "The goal is transferring public lands ultimately to private ownership. Incumbent commissioners do not have a track record of supporting ranchers. Their policies support the fragmentation of habitat and the subdivision and development of open space, *including* ranches."

This deeper tension between states' rights and the feds was again exposed when Ferry County commissioners, where the Profanity Peak pack lives, passed a resolution to authorize Sheriff Ray Maycumber "to kill the remaining nine members of the wolf pack if state wildlife officials don't resume shooting wolves." Commissioner Mike Blankenship declared, "The sheriff has that power and that obligation as much as he would with a wild dog." He threatened to challenge the state's Endangered Species Protections and their control over wildlife.

Claims of success in seeing the Profanity Peak pack removed may be premature. The more ranchers and commissioners insist upon the very expensive and unpopular—but officially sanctioned—killing of entire wolf packs on public lands, the more the public turns against them. If public animosity toward ranchers increases any more, they may completely lose public support for grazing rights on public lands. Amaroq Weiss responded to Ferry County commissioners' threats to take wolf killing into their own hands, saying, "Thumbing your nose at state law doesn't engender a lot of respect from the rest of the public about your attitudes of living with wildlife. This isn't the 1850s."

Ex-wolf trapper and author Carter Niemeyer commented on the Profanity Peak pack culling: "Public lands have to be managed differently. Those lands belong to all of us, and so do the native wildlife."

New research has shown that the Washington wolf cull, like much of lethal removal, won't actually save livestock. The University of Wisconsin's Carnivore Coexistence Lab published a recent study comparing methods to prevent predators from killing livestock. They found that nonlethal methods, especially livestock guardian dogs and fladry, "had a better track record and none of them led to more livestock losses. But lethal methods did." Nonlethal deterrents were 80 percent more successful at warding off predators, compared to the 28 percent success rate of lethal removal. The researchers recommended that "wildlife agencies suspend campaigns like the one going on in Washington and apply more stringent criteria to future control efforts . . . these recommendations could keep more livestock and wildlife living and save taxpayer money."

Robert Crabtree, chief scientist and founder of Yellowstone Ecological Research Center questions whether shooting predators really saves livestock. Crabtree notes that the science of predator control is flawed and now needs an overhaul. "Lethal control methods need to be subjected to the same gold standard of science as anything else," he said. The federal Wildlife Services, which kills millions of animals each year—3.2 million in 2015 alone—at taxpayer expense has "a big research arm funded for forty or fifty years and they can't seem to do any quality work. Shouldn't someone take a look at what's going on here and evaluate the millions of dollars spent for decades trying to justify lethal control?"

Wolf advocates had held a rally in Washington's state capital of Olympia to protest the Profanity Peak pack killing. The crowd joined in communal howls and waved signs saying, "Real Men Coexist with Wolves," "Welfare Ranchers, Stop Mooching & Destroying Public Land," and "Conserve Wolves, Not Cows." One protester explained, "This is a hail Mary last attempt to get the governor to intervene to stop this wolf slaughter—before there are no wolves left." Other protesters said lethal removal is bad policy and believed that "the state caved to ranching politics." One young protester held a simple sign: "Wolves' Lives Matter." Others chanted, "No public wolves killed on public lands!"

THE VOCIFEROUS CROWD at the Wolf Advisory Group meeting was certainly putting the "public" back in public lands. A silver-haired man with huge glasses read aloud a statement from Predator Defense's Brooks Fahy, noting that McIrvin had only "hired one range rider and two foot patrols to protect four hundred cows on thirty thousand acres of rough landscape. Success would have required an army!"

Again, the crowd applauded. A young man with a notebook full of newspaper clippings shouted out the statistic, "One million cattle and only ninety wolves in Washington state . . . where's the balance?"

There were angry murmurs and fist pumps as dozens of people waved their hands for moderator Madden to call upon them. For a moment it seemed as if everything might get out of hand. But Madden made the wise move of asking everyone to join in suggesting topics for the next WAG meeting in January, which was to revisit lethal removal protocols.

A very elderly woman who could barely stand but whose voice was clear raised one of the most important points of all: "If there is repeat or chronic depredation in one rancher's grazing allotment," she asked, "then why not *deny* a rancher that allotment?" This put the hot-button issue of grazing allotments center stage. Several people stressed that we need national conversations, with the Forest Service getting much more involved, not just rubber-stamping traditional allotments for ranchers. This is a crucial question for the future of wolf recovery, one that Amaroq Weiss has pinpointed: "We can't keep placing wolves in harm's way by repeatedly dumping livestock onto public lands with indefensible terrain, then killing the wolves when conflicts arise. These allotments should be retired by the US Forest Service—or livestock losses should simply be expected, and wolves shouldn't have to pay for it with their lives."

Weiss has hit on a major problem: cattle are often let out to graze loosely on public land allotments that are not at all well suited for grazing, such as the Colville National Forest where the Diamond M rancher was again running his herds. Suzanne Stone echoed this concern. "You have to look at any public land allotment and consider if it is really proper for grazing," she told me.

Stone has walked the land with a lot of Washington ranchers. "There are three times as many Washington ranchers using non-lethals," she noted proudly. "They're doing everything right, with little depredation. But that Profanity Peak pack ranges through four large allotments, some of which are full of downed timber and just little pockets for cattle to graze," Stone explained. "So the cattle have to really spread out to find enough vegetation. It's not like those big, wide-open meadows that you can fit hundreds of cattle in so they can herd together for safety. It's a challenging place for cattle to graze—even *without* predators."

Wolves prefer to hunt wild game that is running away, like elk and deer, and not a close herd. Cattle expert Temple Grandin argues that ranchers need to learn to "rewild" cattle and "rekindle" their herd instinct to "stand their ground" and group together against predators. "Ranching done right improves the environment and wildlife habitat," she wrote.

When cattle are grazed in allotments with sparse forage, heavy undergrowth, and downed trees from fires, they get stressed and easily separated, vulnerable to predators. Cattle grazing near the Profanity Peak den often had to then fend for themselves in a very difficult and rugged terrain. Stone hopes that in response to this highly controversial culling, the Forest Service in northeastern Washington will carefully review grazing allotments to decide whether there are "much better places for livestock than in remote and heavily wooded public lands."

But that's always been the challenge, she adds: "If we start talking about 'get the cattle off public lands' . . . you know, there will be huge political resistance. The livestock industry has deep roots and a lot of power. Generations of ranchers have grown used to grazing their cattle on public lands without much oversight from the public." With growing demands for ranchers to coexist with wolves, "We've got to find a way to bring ranchers along with us on this, not make them feel like this is about kicking them all off public lands."

In conflicts such as these, no stakeholder gets exactly what he wants. It's compromise and endless negotiation. As Stone pointed out, the public must come to understand both sides of wildlife co-existence. "You can't stuff a hamburger in your mouth while you're yelling about the ranchers out there shooting wolves. We vote every time we go to the grocery store for what we believe in."

 AT A QUICK BREAK in the WAG meeting a fisherman took me aside. He owns a cabin in northeastern Washington's wolf country. "Listen," he said, "if I go hiking on public lands and get attacked by a grizzly or mountain lion, the feds or state certainly don't have to compensate me for my medical expenses. My hiking public lands was a risk I took. Well, ranchers who choose to graze on public lands—where the public really wants wolves—must accept livestock loss as just a business expense."

As the public continued with their suggestions for the next WAG meeting, one of the range riders in a buckskin vest confided in me, "There's too much heat in this room, and there have been death threats, even against my family."

There was heat, but there were also now very practical and even ethical arguments made against lethal removal as a wolf-management tool. A Vietnam vet stood up and demanded, "Why hold an entire wolf pack guilty by association? This reminds me of whole Vietnam villages destroyed because a few of the village's soldiers went after us."

A schoolteacher in the crowd took the microphone as if to lecture the WAG members: "What we're trying to say is that public lands now must be managed *first* for wolves, not ranchers. Our beautiful public lands are where wolves, not cattle, belong. Where there is wilderness, there should *always* be wolves."

As the crowd exploded into applause, the WAG members heard just how deeply the public is supporting the return of the wild wolf to the West. In this very room a profound cultural shift was taking place—one that evoked grief and fury and even a hard-won peace. Witnessing this, I remembered the 1993 Wolf Summit speaker who addressed a raucous crowd of Alaskan hunters, hell-bent on aerial wolf culls, predicting that it would be "public perception that most determines the future of wildlife policy." Two decades later we are the future, and the people are loudly demanding that wolf management on our shared lands be now shaped not just by ranchers but by the public as well.

The response to the Profanity Peak pack culling shows us that many voices are now needed to advance the conversation, to change at last this cultural and historical bias against wolves—lawyers to represent wolves, negotiators to broker agreements, and the public to get actively involved. Those who want change can apply to sit on wildlife and county commissions, can financially support nonlethal deterrent programs, and can learn about how complex these wolf politics really are—they are not just simplistic reactions either pro- or antiwolf. "We really have to all keep working together," Stone emphasized. "Lawsuits don't permanently change the culture. It's a victory that doesn't assure real change in people's behavior. It took us generations to get where we are now."

Wildlife politics mirror an increasingly polarized America. The challenge is not just about learning how to coexist with wolves; it is also about figuring out how to coexist with one another.

 BY EARLY OCTOBER the cattle were coming down from their remote and mountainous grazing allotments to more easily patrolled pastures. Conservation Northwest's Mitchell Friedman hoped that "maybe the trauma is over."

Donny Mortarello of WDFW announced to the press, "Removing the two adults that are known to be in the pack and leaving the pups would not be a humane path for us and we wouldn't go down that road. We reassess and look at the conditions every week." There had been no further wolf depredation, and so there was a possibility that no more wolves in the Profanity Peak pack would be killed. In late October WDFW announced that lethal removal of the Profanity Peak pack had been called off—with the promise that in 2017, if wolf depredation occurred again, there would be renewed efforts to kill more wolves. "With the pack reduced in size from twelve members to four, and most livestock off the grazing allotments," said WDFW director Jim Unsworth, "the likelihood of depredations in the near future is low."

The four surviving members of the Profanity Peak pack on their Colville National Forest territory included an adult female and three pups. Many wolf advocates worried that after such a devastating loss and destabilizing of the Profanity Peak family, the remaining adult female would not be able to hunt with and feed such young pups—that they would simply starve. Other conservationists fear that the Ferry County sheriff will make good on his threat, authorized by the county commissioners, to kill all of the surviving Profanity Peak pack, now that the state has stopped its lethal management.

The Profanity Peak pack killings are still a lightning rod for wolf issues in Washington and a central focus of the January 2017 WAG meeting, with much more public participation. The Forest Service has at last signaled that it will get more involved in reconsidering grazing allotments. That is the next crucial step for the future of wolves in America, especially now that the public, not just ranchers or hunters, are participating in wildlife policy. But the public needs to keep the pressure on both state and federal wildlife managers to give the wild wolf equal value on public lands.

Stone concluded our interview by saying that livestock producers are always going to lose some livestock. "But if ranchers don't address what's making their livestock vulnerable to predators in the first place, killing wolves is a temporary fix. New wolves eventually move into the territory and kill more livestock. If the headlines are always 'Wolf Kills Cow, Wolf Gets Killed' and it never moves beyond that, it's not real coexistence—just a never-ending death trap."

Stone wishes that Defenders of Wildlife could expand its program of nonlethal deterrents to many other states, but it doesn't have the funding. She also believes that Wildlife Services itself should seriously commit to more nonlethal strategies for protecting livestock. "Helicopters and aerial shooting are high-ticket items," she says. "That comes from public dollars." What if those public dollars were reserved for ranchers who were *most* successful at coexisting with wolf recovery on public lands?

Stone's comments remind me of the Virginia cattle farmer Elizabeth who said livestock farmers must, first of all, hold themselves accountable for predation and learn nonlethal strategies. Prevention is always better than after-the-loss lethal management. The Lava Lake sheep ranch, which has so successfully protected its livestock through nonlethal deterrents, is an example of an attitudinal shift among ranchers who also hold themselves accountable. "The goal was not to just keep the sheep safe but also to keep the wolves safe too," explained Lava Lake's director. "If those wolves were dead, it would reflect poorly on sheep operators in this area."

The commitment is not an easy one, however. "Living with wolves for a rancher is a headache," admits Douglas Smith of the Yellowstone Wolf Project. He believes there needs to be some form of compensation for livestock loss and notes that in America there are private organizations that do just that. Smith explains that in Sweden the government actually compensates for "allowing reproduction of carnivores in your areas where you raise sheep and cattle. If you can prove that wolves and bears have reproduced, you get paid. So we have to shift some of these costs from individuals to society to change and bear the burden collectively, not individually."

Fernando Najera, a PhD scientist and wildlife veterinarian from Spain who was a lead manager on the Wood River Wolf Project, wrote, "I want to believe that with proper information, people will quit blaming wolves for most livestock losses and stop demonizing them in the media and among agricultural groups. I hope that these people will see that lethal control is more expensive, less effective at protecting livestock, and works against nature, instead of with it, as we do with non-lethal deterrents."

"Coexistence *is* possible," Stone said. Concluding our interview, she reminded me that even in Idaho—which was once ground zero for wolves—this successful project has flourished for two decades. To end the seemingly endless wolf wars, other states could consider the wise practices along the Sheep Super Highway that have allowed both sheep and wolves to survive as well as ranchers and conservationists to cooperate—while sharing lands that belong to us all.

# 15. EL LOBO RETURNS HOME

In the spring of 2015 I visited Wolf Haven International, a wolf sanctuary in Washington State, to witness the first litters of Mexican gray wolf pups born there in seven years. Via live remote cameras I watched as four gangly six-week-old male pups scampered and climbed atop their very patient father, M1066, nicknamed in-house as "Moss." The big-eared and fuzzy pups romped and feigned attacks with tiny sharp teeth, wrestling with each other, then racing into the tall cedar trees. These critically endangered Mexican gray wolves are growing up in the Species Survival Plan (SSP) for possible reintroduction into Arizona, New Mexico, and Mexico. "They're being raised by their parents, just like any wolf pup in the wild," explained Wendy Spender, Wolf Haven's director of animal care. "Their world is so small now," she added. "There is no concept of captivity or even humans for the pups. Just their parents, siblings, and home life."

It's a good and safe life at Wolf Haven, with its eighty-two acres of restored and biologically diverse prairie and oak woodlands, founded in 1982. These prairie lands are quiet buffers for this, the only wolf sanctuary in the world accredited by the Global Federation of Animal Sanctuaries. Here the carbon-rich grassy meadows offset climate change, a lush red and blue riot of native wildflowers like purple camas and golden paintbrush attract honey bees, and the moss-draped trees offer cool shade and refuge to the fifty-two displaced and captive-born wolves. Some have now found their "forever home" here. Of the several Mexican wolf litters born at the sanctuary, two family groups have already been released into the wild (Arizona): the Hawk's Nest pack released in 1998 (part of the initial release) and the Cienaga group released in 2000 still survive today. This wolf family is one of the most genetically valuable in all of America's captive population. By the late seventies wolf populations in the Southwest had crashed to a mere five wolves in Mexico and were all but eliminated in New Mexico and Arizona. Under the Endangered Species Act the federal government must work to recover this critically endangered species.

"All the Mexican wolves living in the wild today come from seven founding animals, composed of three distinct lineages," Spencer notes. "They really need the genetic boost these new pups can give them," she pauses thoughtfully, "if any of them are selected for reintroduction into the wild."

That's a big *if*, especially given the wolf-recovery politics in New Mexico and Arizona, where governors and wildlife commissions passed new rules forbidding any reintroduction of captive-born Mexican wolves. In the Southwest, Mexican wolves are "political footballs," explains Linda Saunders, the director of conservation at Wolf Haven.

But now, as I watched, the six-week-old pups seemed to be playing their own kind of wolf football as one pup streaked across the screen and leapt on his father, M1066, tackling his tall legs. Good naturedly, the father gave up trying to nap in the sun. He stretched, yawned, and play bowed to his offspring. Then all four pups again tried to clamber atop him, only to tumble off when he gave a gentle shrug.

Except for their long-limbed prance and exotic colorings—sable and gray-tinged fur—and their much longer snouts, the little pups could be mistaken for a litter of domestic dogs. But there is something much wilder in their golden eyes—and wariness—even as they play. These pups are hidden from any public view and see humans only for medical exams. If they are the ones chosen for release into the wild, they must remain very cautious of us.

"We're so delighted that this spring *three* litters of Mexican gray wolves were born here," said Diane Gallegos, director of Wolf Haven International. Gallegos is an energetic and articulate spokesperson for wolves, whether it's as a member of the Pacific Wolf Coalition, the cutting-edge Washington Wolf Advisory Group, or even in a Seattle community gathering, a Wolf Salon, with a standing-room-only crowd of Millennials intent on learning more about wolf conservation. Since 2011 Gallegos has led Wolf Haven to become a leader in wolf-recovery efforts internationally. In the office she posted me in front of another remote camera to take a look at a second Mexican gray wolf family led by the breeding pair, F1222 (Hopa) and M1067 (Brother), and their rambunctious pups.

"Oh, look, there's the matriarch," Diane pointed to the screen, where a rather blurry, but still majestic wolf ventures into the remote camera's view.

Like her mate, this mother wolf, Hopa, is lean and almost impossibly long limbed, with an elegant auburn buff on her forehead, intense amber eyes, and a dark mask shading into a long, pale snout. Surveying her three sons, she looks at once dotingly maternal and yet watchful. Certainly she can hear the hidden remote cameras rustle in the leaves above as they shift slightly for better angles in the trees. A first-time mother, Hopa has quite an impressive history already—and she's only four years old.

"She was born at the Endangered Wolf Center in Missouri," the Mexican biologist, Pamela Maciel Cabanas, explained to me in her lilting accent. Like Spencer, Cabanas is an expert at wolf handling and very well versed in international wolf politics. Cabanas works with Wolf Haven's Hispanic Outreach and is a liaison with Mexico's Wolf Species Survival Program.

"In 2013," she told me, "F1222 [Hopa] was transferred to the USFWS's Sevilleta Wolf Management Center at the Sevilleta National Wildlife Refuge in New Mexico for prerelease into the wild. Then, in the summer of 2014, Hopa was transferred to Wolf Haven, where she partnered with Brother, who was born at Wolf Haven in 2007. He is older than she is, but they are well suited and have been devoted parents to their offspring."

This breeding pair was observed in a copulatory tie in the winter of 2015. Excitedly, Wolf Haven staff hoped for pups. Gestation in wolves is usually sixty-three days; by early May Hopa disappeared into her den. Via remote cameras the staff excitedly waited and

watched to see whether the mother had whelped and was not ail-
ing or enduring false pregnancy, common in canids.

Wolves are born blind, and their eyes open after twelve to
fourteen days. With their distinctive brown furry capes and tiny,
flattened ears, neonatal pups live underground their first weeks,
denned up and protected by their mother. She rarely leaves their
cool, musty underworld, like an earthen womb. When Hopa finally emerged from her den in early May of 2015 the Wolf Haven
staff recognized that she was noticeably thinner—a sure sign that
she had, indeed, given birth. For several weeks Hopa left her den
only to eat, drink, or eliminate. After Memorial Day three tiny
pups crawled out of their den, trailing behind her, their snouts
raised high to sniff this new world of air and sheltering trees and
sky.

They were clumsy and shaky as they took their first steps, their
temporarily blue eyes now open, squinting against the sunshine.
After nursing for so long or gobbling the regurgitated bits of food
from their mother's mouth, they now could nibble small bits of
meat. They greeted their father, Brother, for the first time in the
open air. In their next weeks the pups would learn to play and socialize with their family and to follow their parents if frightened by
an unusual sound or scent. For those first four to six weeks of the
pups' life outside their birthing den, none of the Wolf Haven staff
came near. They observed and monitored the family only through
remote cameras.

"Each wolf family is different, just like our human families"
Spencer said. "I can already see patterns of behavior that will eventually contribute to their unique life story—routines, customs that
may eventually be passed on to their wild progeny. Some pups are
more gregarious or curious and wander away from the den or their
siblings. Some are more dominant, others more solitary."

We watched as the father wolf endured his sons and daughter
play by simply rolling over and yawning. He was about sixty to
eighty pounds, and from tail to nose stood a little over four feet.
The slightly smaller mother did a quick patrol of the underbrush,
her ears perked, listening. As if on cue, a communal howl rose up in
the sanctuary, where other wolves added their voices.

We all smiled as the father wolf raised his handsome head to answer a nearby howl with a long, sonorous bass song of his own. Startled, his pups glanced around, rather comically, bewildered at first. Then they lifted their small snouts and let out a series of yip-yip-yips—their very first tentative attempts at howling together with the family.

"Will this be the family chosen to go into the wild?" I asked Diane. I felt utterly privileged to observe these wolf pups without endangering or frightening them. How many people ever get to witness so intimately a wolf family simply going about their daily life?

"We just don't know which or if any of these three Mexican wolf litters will be selected for reintroduction," Diane said quietly. "We can only hope we'll again get the call that our wolves will be the ones chosen to help the wild populations thrive."

Later that spring two of the Mexican wolf pups from one of the other Wolf Haven litters died from parvo, a disease also common to domestic dogs. A Wolf Haven Facebook announcement of the pups' deaths was met with a huge public outpouring of sorrow and support. These wolves are so precious and so essential to their wild cousins' survival that every death is a disaster. That spring of 2015 I framed photos of the six-week-old Mexican gray wolf pups for my writing desk. Every day as I open their photos on my big screen, I gaze at the pups as if my thoughts can also protect them.

In my favorite photo—taken when the pups were crated up for their second medical exam—the frightened twelve-week-old pups huddle together in the fresh straw. Three of the pups flatten themselves in the straw, furry white-gray ears pitched forward. Their close-knit jumble is the very definition of a litter. One pup had climbed atop the others. All gazed directly out at the camera, their now-golden eyes topped by pale white and seemingly worried eyebrows. What dangers loom if they leave this sanctuary for the life of the wild?

 EL LOBO, the Mexican gray wolf subspecies, is one of the most highly endangered of all wolves. Smaller than other North American wolves, these Old-World wolves long ago crossed the Bering Land Bridge to colonize North America. They flourished in the Southwest and Mexico, despite being hunted, trapped, and poisoned for centuries. In 1977 in Mexico there were only five Mexican wolves surviving. These were captured, and three of them were then bred in captivity. In 1998 four more captive individuals from the Species Survival Program were added to the founding population, and some of these Mexican wolves were reintroduced into the wild, but only in the Arizona wilderness. Now, in 2016, there are still only 12 to 17 Mexican wolves roaming all of Mexico, and in America's Southwest the population dropped from 110 wolves in 2014 to only 97 in 2015. Thirteen wolves have died, and only 23 pups survive now in the Southwest. Although there is a new urgency to reintroducing Mexican wolves in the Southwest because of the population decline, there are also political roadblocks to federal recovery efforts, especially from New Mexico and Arizona wildlife commissions.

Wolf Haven has kept readers alerted to the swiftly tilting politics of Mexican and gray wolf recovery in their quarterly *Wolf Tracks* articles. The sanctuary also posts popular videos of Mexican pups now thriving in the sanctuary on their website and Facebook page. Will one of the three Wolf Haven Mexican wolf families be chosen for reintroduction? For a time prospects looked dim. In the fall of 2015 the New Mexico Game and Fish Commission denied permit requests from the US Fish and Wildlife Service for any new release of Mexican wolves raised in captivity. This was a surprising blow not only to a struggling wild population and to Wolf Haven but also to Ted Turner's Ladder Ranch—a prerelease wolf-recovery facility that has been vital to Mexican gray wolf recovery since 1997.

Ranchers opposed the release of any more wolves into New Mexico, citing that in 2015 there were thirty-six confirmed wolf kills on their livestock. The USFWS had asked for release permits for up to ten pups (to cross-foster with wild populations) and one pair of adults and their offspring. Cross-fostering is a survival strategy of moving captive-born pups when they are less than ten days old to wild dens in the hope that the wild wolf mother will also nurse and raise the captive-born pups alongside her own. Cross-fostering has also worked in the wild when pups are transferred from one wild den to another.

This is a very difficult technique because it depends upon so many variables—excellent weather for transport, discovering the exact location of the wild wolves' den, and the wild mother's acceptance and ability to nurture nonbiological pups. In 2015 the first-ever captive-to-wild cross-fostering for Mexican wolves was attempted. Two captive-born sister pups, Rachel and Isabella, at Minnesota's Endangered Wolf Center were transported to Arizona with the hope of finding a wolf mother in the wild. But biologists on the ground failed to find the wild den, and Rachel and Isabella were returned to the Endangered Wolf Center and to their mother, Sibi, a very nurturing matriarch. Though cross-fostering is risky, it is an important element in helping this critically endangered species.

There are fifty-two facilities in the United States participating in the Mexican wolf Species Survival Program, with a current captive population of 270 wolves. These SSP programs await word from the federal SSP program for any chance of reintroduction to join the ninety-seven wild Mexican wolves surviving in the United States. When Arizona, which has a slightly larger wild population of Mexican wolves, denied any federal permits for the release of captive-born wolves, the situation looked really grim for reintroducing the three families of Mexican wolves at Wolf Haven. This was especially troubling because Wolf Haven International has had two family groups successfully released previously (1998 and 2000). Some of the very first Mexican wolves released back into the Southwest and still surviving came from Wolf Haven.

Because of New Mexico's permit denial, the window for any 2015 release passed, and everything was on hold again for all captive-born Mexican wolves. But then the USFWS announced that it would simply go ahead with plans to release more Mexican wolves, over the objections of the New Mexico Game and Fish Department. The majority of the state's residents welcomed this decision to proceed with release, and a strong *Santa Fe New Mexican* op-ed, "Releasing Wolves the Right Thing to Do," echoed this prorelease sentiment: "Good for the government. Managing the well-being of wolves in the wild cannot be left to individual states. Wolves don't recognize boundaries, either between states or countries." The editorial concluded, "It is clear that many people want wolves to die out. But the occasional loss of livestock is no reason to destroy one of God's creatures. . . . By moving ahead despite state opposition, the U.S. Fish and Wildlife Service is giving these wolves a new lease on life. And that's as it should be."

Everyone waited anxiously to see if New Mexico would relent and, as its major newspaper advised, "do the right thing." The state did not agree. But it did move a little. In February 2016 the state's game commission again granted Ted Turner's Ladder Ranch its historical prerelease permits to hold wolves at the Ladder Ranch until they could be moved to Mexico.

I happily heard the good news from Wolf Haven that one of the Mexican wolf families—Hopa and Brother, with their three yearling pups—were chosen for release into the wild. The family had already been identified for release into the wild in Mexico back in July of 2015. These were some of the six-week-old pups I'd first seen last spring. Now, at last, they were going to their native Southwest. New Mexico's game commission's unanimous decision to renew the Ladder Ranch's permit to prepare Mexican wolves for wild release came as a surprise, as just one month earlier they had denied it. But it was no surprise to Mike Phillips, executive director of the Turner Endangered Species fund. Phillips noted that "the commissioners indicated they saw a way forward. We acted on that hope." The fact that the wolf family was to be released in Mexico, not New Mexico or Arizona, might have been why the commission reversed its earlier permit denial. "It's the beginning of us moving back to where we were," Phillips added.

Mexico began its wolf reintroduction program in 2011, and in 2014, the first litter of Mexican gray wolves was born in the wild there in thirty years. "This first litter represents an important step in the recovery program," Mexico's game commission said. "These will be individuals that have never had contact with human beings, as wolves bred in captivity do."

The Wolf Haven family had had very limited contact with human beings, but what would the effect be of their journey by highway, by plane, and then overland from New Mexico to Mexico? Everyone at the sanctuary began the protocol for release with a sense of excitement and urgency. The date for the spring 2016 transport was imminent.

AT WOLF HAVEN the forest is afloat in cool mists like a Chinese silkscreen. And the wolves are already howling—the ancient communal harmonies of high-pitched yips, eerie whines, and haunting keens that I never want to end. How can a wolf's howl sound both elegiac and triumphant? The woven wolf music is so intricate and multilayered, with unexpected baritone riffs and ultrasonic descants. Their voices improvise and counterpoint, like animal jazz. A song sometimes tender, sometimes fierce, always mesmerizing.

"You never get tired of it, do you?" whispers Diane Gallegos, as she greets me at the sanctuary. We are all being respectfully quiet so as not to disturb the many wolves who have already sensed that something is up. "When we hear the wolves howling here in the sanctuary, no matter how many times a day, we just stop and listen," adds Gallegos.

It's a sound that so few people ever get to hear, especially in the wild, which is where these Mexican gray wolves are now at last headed. The wolf family will be transported by plane to Phoenix, then driven in a van all night to Ted Turner's Ladder Ranch in New Mexico, near the Gila National Forest, the sixth-largest national forest in the United States. The Gila Wilderness was the first designated wilderness reservation, in 1924. The transport and journey to New Mexico will be difficult; if it goes off without incident, the Mexican wolf family will spend the next three months in the ranch's large canyon enclosure, acclimating to the high desert and arid climate of their ancestors.

"Quickly," Diane tells me and the photographer, Annie Marie Musselman. "You don't want to miss this!"

Annie heads into the sanctuary, heavy burdened with cameras, and I go into the office, where I will watch the wolves as I have before, via live remote cameras. Very few of the staff are allowed to assist with the delicate and skilled work of capturing the five members of this Mexican wolf family. Dr. Jerry Brown, the Wolf Haven vet of thirty years; Pamela Maciel, the Mexican wolf biologist; and Wendy Spencer are among the other animal care staff in the careful operation. All are highly trained in what's called a "catch-up" and final medical exam of the wolves.

One might imagine catching wolves to be a risky and fearsome job. Images of menacing growls, gnashing fangs, all the Discovery channel documentaries of vicious wolves attacking prey come to mind. But this catch-up is more like a well-choreographed dance or mime. Everyone in the enclosure is silent. When absolutely necessary, only Wendy speaks *sotto voce*.

The father wolf, Brother, and his yearling pups were born at Wolf Haven, and this is the first time any of them will ever leave their sanctuary. When he sees the crates, one yearling jumps atop the reinforced plastic kennel and uses it like a launching pad to leap into space and crash down on the forest floor. The pups have often played a kind of how-many-wolves-fit-on-the-roof-of-their-wooden-den-box. Answer: all five, including the parents. But this is a morning unlike any other in the pups' lives. The close-knit family takes its cue from the matriarch, Hopa.

"She's calm, but really terrified," Gallegos tells me. "She's poised like the family matriarch that she is, but she's also shaking." Gallegos is still whispering, even though we are in the office. Any stereotype of ferocious wolf attacks fades when we witness their fear. It's a reminder that wild wolves are instinctively very wary of humans and spend most of their time in the wild trying to avoid or escape our attention.

Quietly Gallegos explains what's happening on the screen with six people, each carrying a lightweight, four-foot-long aluminum pole with a padded Y at the end. "With each wolf, they'll slide that Y-pole and gently put pressure on the neck and haunches. We don't use the traditional catch poll with its lasso or rope. That can injure the wolves as they race away and then swing from their necks on the catch pole. Instead, we were trained by Dr. Mark Johnson, the wildlife vet for the Yellowstone wolves, to use this efficient but light pressure so as not to stress the animal."

Dr. Johnson visits Wolf Haven yearly for wildlife-handling classes offered to wildlife agency personal and other federal, state, and tribal wildlife professionals. Others who take the class are zoo and sanctuary employees and volunteers, animal control officers, and university students. Dr. Johnson's philosophy is visionary and compassionate. "There is no room for ego when handling animals," he writes. When catching-up a feral dog or a captive wolf, he asks wildlife handlers to use this as an opportunity to "explore our connection with all things and to explore who we are as a person. This is a profound opportunity . . . exhilarating, sacred, and sad."

It is a profound experience, even to watch over remote cameras, as the highly trained wildlife handlers stand in a silent line waiting to catch-up the next wolf, a yearling. None of the staff seem nervous or tense even though they are inside a wild wolf enclosure.

"No, the people are not frightened," Gallegos nods. "They've all been well trained. It's the wolves who are afraid." We watch the action a few more minutes before she adds, "The wolves are now hunkered down, frozen in fear. But we keep it really calm, and animals get used to seeing us at least every year when we do the medical exams and vaccinations." Gallegos pauses and adds, "Like Lorenzo, the very first animal catch-up that I was involved in. As soon as we walked in with our Y-poles, the wolf ran into the sub-enclosure, and it was done. Because he recognized, 'Oh, I know what I need to do here.'"

"The catch-up is very low stress. It's quick." Gallegos explains. "It's like the techniques used in agriculture when a shepherd shears sheep. If you can make it a positive experience for that ram, then the next time you do it, the animals are not stressed out."

"Like Temple Grandin inventing those hug boxes for cows," I nod.

Grandin, a high-functioning autistic author and inventor, revolutionized the cattle industry by designing more humane wooden chutes that gently squeeze cattle into long, narrow corrals. The chutes actually calm the cows, much in the same way Grandin learned to soothe her own autistic anxiety by inventing a hug box for herself. Grandin's groundbreaking research has radically changed animal science, and her animal welfare strategies now set the standard for the cattle industry. Grandin's many books explain how animals think in pictures, like herself and many other autistic people. What pictures must now be fleeting through these wolves' minds as they await catch-up?

Gazing into the grainy remote camera screens, it looks like everyone is silently moving underwater. Throughout the wolf family's enclosure and the prerelease area the staff has hung huge sheets of canvas. These brown sheets easily herd the wolf family together, much the way ranchers use fladry on their fences to ward off wild wolves. For some unknown reason, wolves will avoid those flapping red flags or the canvas drapes.

The wildlife staff handle each animal one at a time, and usually only one or two people restrain the animal. Whether it's some instinctive memory of being carried by the scruff of the neck by a trusted mother or the experience of being captured once a year for medical exams, the wolves are gently directed toward the safety of their crates, which become instant dens.

The three yearlings and their father, Brother, are all quickly crated. Not a howl, not a moan or a whine. The wolves are as mute as the people. Dr. Brown is quickly giving each wolf in the family a check-up. All looks good to go, he nods.

"It's fast and efficient," Gallegos murmurs as we watch. "Because they're going to endure so much after this. Such a long trip."

"Are they tranquilized?"

"No," she replies firmly, "they can't be. We don't usually tranquilize our animals unless we absolutely have to. To fly in a plane tranquilized could be really dangerous. You don't want them in cargo, unmonitored, choking. You want them to stay awake. It's a two-hour flight and good, smooth weather, so we hope it will all go well."

Still in the sanctuary, the mother wolf, Hopa, has denned up. She is the last to be shepherded into her crate. I watch, transfixed, as Spencer almost tenderly reaches into the den with her Y-pole. The mother wolf instantly hunkers down at the touch of the Y-pole on her neck. Quickly, as someone else rests the Y-pole on the mother wolf's haunches, Wendy secures a blue head cover over her face for safety. Covering their eyes and head always quietens wild animals, like horses or animals injured on the road. Something about not

being able to see immediately reassures the animal. Safely muz-
zled, Hopa is lifted into the comfort of her own crate. All five of the
family are now ready to go to the airport. The whole catch-up of the
wolf family has taken just one hour. Smiling and relieved, the Wolf
Haven staff emerge from the sanctuary, followed by Wendy driving
the van. Inside, the wolves, each in their own crate, are utterly still.

Annie's photos and videos are all we see now on the screen. The
most striking portrait of all is the mother wolf, an image I'll never
forget: crouched at the very back of her crate, as if to bury herself
in the blonde straw, she gazes out, her ears perked to fathom each
voice or strange sound; her golden eyes wide, wary, preternatu-
rally focused; her distinctive rust- and black-colored fur dense and
beautiful. But her dripping black nose betrays her terror. Her flanks
are trembling. But she doesn't move or thrash or try to escape. She
looks hypervigilant but eerily calm at the same time. After all, she
has a family to protect from whatever strange journey is being
asked of her—nothing less than leading her pups and her mate into
the complete unknown. The recovery and resurrection of an entire
species await her. When I study this matriarch's face I read both
fear and courage. I'm reminded of the adage that, in humans, the
bravest of us are those who actually feel fear and yet still perform
some perilous feat.

This wolf family must now travel to New Mexico and beyond
into unfamiliar wilderness that has always been hostile to wolves.
They may lack the skills to survive in wild, rugged terrain with not
a lot of prey. If they kill livestock, Mexican ranchers might regress
to their history of hunting wolves. It is difficult to think of Hopa,
and her mate, Brother, and their yearling pups being so vulnerable
to hostile forces as they return to repopulate their native territory.
But it is vital if their species is to again take a foothold in Mexico
and the American Southwest. As I stand a little distance from the
white van that now holds the fate of this wolf family in their five
crates, I can't help but feel both exuberant and anxious.

The amiable Wolf Haven vet, Dr. Brown, notes that all the wolves
are healthy. "They all handled it pretty good," he says, "not a lot of
jumping around and craziness." He has drawn blood from the matriarch to discover if she is perhaps pregnant.

Pamela Maciel, reports, "Now the wolves are very calm, because they are so afraid. Terrified. Trembling. It's like they just completely freeze."

I don't ask anyone whether they are sad to see this wolf family leave their haven. It's obvious from their faces.

There are still two other Mexican wolf families left in Wolf Haven's sanctuary. They too are part of the Species Survival Plan and await possible release, perhaps even as early as next year. "It's so exciting," says one of the Wolf Haven staff. "They will at last be wild and back where they belong."

I stand a little distance from the van that will carry this wolf family to the airport. Inside my jacket I reach for the wolf necklace that has accompanied me on all my wolf research trips. The silver is cool, but the wolf teeth are warm and sharp against my fingers. These are Mexican wolf teeth. After a century they seem almost alive again.

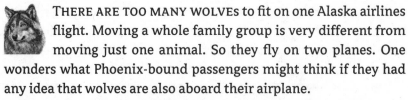 THERE ARE TOO MANY WOLVES to fit on one Alaska airlines flight. Moving a whole family group is very different from moving just one animal. So they fly on two planes. One wonders what Phoenix-bound passengers might think if they had any idea that wolves are also aboard their airplane.

"Typically we drive," Gallegos explains. "But when it's this long a trip—twenty-eight hours—it's better for the animals to fly."

Wendy sends a Facebook photo from the Alaska Airlines cargo area where one large metal cart now holds all five of the crates with the wolf family. In the photo Wendy looks both happy and yet also alert as she poses with an airlines employee. So far, so good.

Imagine what it must be like for these animals who have always known only the quiet and calm life of family and sanctuary to suddenly hear the rumble of SUV tires along a busy freeway, the scream of jets at the airport, the sensory overload of what must seem like multitudes of people jabbering, and the terrifying roar of a jet engine and perhaps even a little turbulence as they fly midair. What does the grease and jet fuel smell like to them? Can they even begin to make sense of the scent of so many passengers? In the cargo hold, which is unregulated and always icy cold, the only thing familiar now is family, the scent and sound of one another in nearby crates.

For the next twenty-four hours those of us who know the importance of this Mexican wolf transport, including the thousands following it on the Wolf Haven Facebook page, will anxiously await word of the wolf family's journey. Radio silence. Then the next day an email from Spencer: "Transport went as smoothly as we could have hoped for (though, no doubt, the wolves were terrified)."

When they opened the crates at 4 A.M. at Ladder Ranch after the all-night transport the father, Brother, and the pups were too afraid to emerge. But the mother, Hopa, raced right out of her crate and into her new life. Normally Spencer would have let the other wolves emerge on their own. But after twenty-eight hours she needed to make sure Brother and the three yearlings were unharmed by the journey and could move easily. "They seemed okay," she wrote, "if a bit stiff. We had to take the top off the crates and literally gently dump them out."

The next morning Spencer and Chris Wiese, who manages the wolf-release program at Turner's Ladder Ranch, drove to the blind to better observe the wolf family. Hidden, Spencer and Wiese could watch the wolf family explore this new canyon land of mountains, prickly sagebrush, hot springs, and wide, semidesert mesas. Once back in the wild, these Mexican wolves may travel forty miles a day at about thirty-five miles an hour. They can swim as much as fifty miles. With such an expanse of territory to reclaim, the wolves can roam together in their trademark single-file line, moving in what's called a "harmonic gait." The back paws fall exactly where the front paws have already landed, giving their movement a "rhythmic job that conserves energy."

"We saw them eating, drinking, chasing ravens, and even snoozing. They looked very much at home—much more so than in the Evergreens of Washington. It was like they had been here their entire lives," Spencer told me happily. While Spencer and Wiese observed the wolf family in their new habitat, several golden eagles circled above. "We should all feel so proud and honored to be a part of something so much bigger than ourselves."

NEWS OF CROSS-FOSTERING SUCCESS soon buoyed hopes for the recovery of Mexican gray wolves in America's Southwest: in May of 2016 the USFWS placed two captive-born, nine-day-old wolves—nicknamed Lindbergh and Vida—into a wild den in New Mexico. The wild mother wolf had her own litter of five pups and adopted the two newborns to raise as her own. Missouri's Endangered Wolf Center calls cross-fostering "a unique and innovative tool" to increase genetic diversity and help grow this sadly dwindled population.

New Mexico immediately announced its plan to sue USFWS to stop the federal plan to release a single family of captive-born wolves and halt any more cross-fostering of wolf puppies in the wild. The Department of Fish and Game asked a federal judge for a temporary restraining order requiring that the feds get state permission for any more wolf releases. In June of 2016 a federal judge granted the injunction. However, the state's request to remove the cross-fostered wolf pups was denied. Many scientists and wolf advocates fear that New Mexico's resistance to continued wolf recovery is a delaying legal tactic that will simply run out the clock on this highly endangered species that has already declined by 12 percent. Scientists point out that in the eighteen years since reintroduction in the Southwest the federal government has shot fourteen wolves and captured dozens more, twenty-one of which were accidentally killed in capture or counting.

Tensions between New Mexico's state wildlife authorities and the federal government increased. In May 2016 a male wolf, M1396, in the Gila National Forest was captured in a steel leg trap and moved to a captive pen for the rest of his life. This wild wolf had been widely celebrated by Albuquerque schoolchildren. A sixth-grader had named him "Guardian" because "wolves need a guardian to keep them safe and help their population rise." Guardian was native to the Fox Mountain pack, one of nineteen wolf families whose territory ranges from southwestern New Mexico to southeastern Arizona. Guardian mated with a Luna pack female, and together they were raising pups. But after reports of livestock loss, the feds decided to remove Guardian from his family and pups.

This decision was greeted with dismay. A mate is very dependent upon male help in feeding and nurturing pups in their infancy. Removing the male not only risks losing the female and her new pups; it may actually increase the risk of livestock predation because without a male, the female can rarely hunt elk or deer, their usual food source. "It's devastating to the pack to lose an alpha," says Regina Mossotti, director of animal care and conservation at the Endangered Wolf Center in Missouri. "It's like it would be to your family. Imagine if you lost your mom or dad at a young age."

The struggle between state and federal wildlife agencies over the Mexican wolf recovery continues. The Center for Biological Diversity urges that New Mexico should "extricate itself from the state politics driven by the livestock industry, stop removing wolves from the wild, release five more family packs into the Gila as scientists recommend, and write a recovery plan that will ensure the Mexican gray wolf contributes to the natural balance in the Southwest and Mexico, forever." Even though the law demands that the USFWS fulfill the Endangered Species Act and wolf recovery has huge public support in the Southwest, the states still continue to resist. In late fall of 2016 an Arizona judge issued a court order requiring USFW to finally update a decades-old recovery plan for the endangered Mexican gray wolf by November 2017. With only about one hundred wild wolves in Arizona and New Mexico, this move toward increasing wolf populations in the Southwest is essential to recovering the Mexican gray wolf in the United States. "Without court enforcement, the plan would have kept being right around the corner until the Mexican gray wolf went extinct," said the Center for Biological Diversity. This court order dismissed protests from ranchers and other antiwolf factions in favor of moving ahead with wolf reintroduction.

But the root cause of much antiwolf bias remains. Wildlife commissions reflect the preferences of their members. A recent Humane Society study of eighteen states' game commissions revealed that 73 percent were "dominated by avid hunters, clearly unrepresentative of the state's public they speak for, but in line with their funding sources." New Mexico's Department of Game and Fish receives $20 million each year from licenses bought by hunters, trappers, and anglers. Not much has changed since 1986 when Ted Williams wrote his famous essay, long before wolf reintroduction: "Wolves do not purchase hunting licenses. . . . That, in brief, is what is wrong with wildlife management in America." But we are on the cusp of a cultural change in wolf recovery. As Sharman Apt Russell writes in *The Physics of Beauty*, "All Americans would feel better if we could agree to share our public land with one hundred Mexican wolves, a fraction of the wildness that once was here."

At New Mexico's Ladder Ranch Hopa and Brother and their young yearlings continue to thrive—and await release. Meanwhile extraordinary news came from Dr. Brown at Wolf Haven. Hopa was indeed pregnant when she endured the long transport from Washington State to New Mexico. In an email photo attachment sent by the Ladder Ranch, five dark-brown puppies huddle together in the straw of their den. Hopa and Brother's family has now grown to eleven. At Ladder Ranch Hopa, Brother, and their nine offspring are growing strong as they roam and hunt in their new territory of crisp sagebrush and arroyos.

In the late fall of 2016 Mexico's National Commission of Natural Protected Areas announced the third litter of wild-born pups had been sighted in the state of Chihuahua. This is the third year running that the breeding pair, M1215 and F1033, have produced pups, bringing the endangered Mexican wolf population in Mexico to twenty-one animals. And in October 2016 a wolf family from a Mexican captive-bred facility released a wolf family into the wild. Early in 2017 Hopa, Brother, and family will begin another long journey to Mexico's Rancho la Mesa refuge before finally being released into the wild. There is hope that Brother and Hopa's family will be less threatened by poachers because they will be released on semiprivate land in Mexico.

AS I READ WENDY'S UPDATES on Hopa and Brother, I often gaze at photos of this wolf family. These Mexican wolves are the small but strong-willed survivors who first captured Edward Seton's admiration and respect in his "Old Lobo" stories. Hopa's powerful life force also echoes the "fierce, green fire" that once changed the heart of Aldo Leopold. The nearby Gila National Forest includes the Aldo Leopold Wilderness.

This wolf family is returning to a country where wolves were all but extinct for three decades, where wolf biologist Cristina Eisenberg's Mexican grandfather ordered her father to kill wolves, but he chose to allow them to live on his own ranch land. Maybe Mexico will now lead the way in restoring this first wolf that crossed continents to claim North America.

In December 2016, Hopa, Brother, and their now nine offspring were at last released into the wild in Mexico. This successful release was the largest of its kind in either Mexican or American history. That snow-swept evening when the eleven crates were finally opened, the wolf family sprang out into the wilderness and freedom—fulfilling their long journey and giving hope for wolf recovery around the world. Wendy and Pamela from Wolf Haven helped release the wolves into a country that warmly welcomes El Lobo home. The next morning, Wendy sent me an email that said it all in one word: "La Liberacion!"

# EPILOGUE: SPEAKING FOR WOLVES

Telescopes trained eagerly, we search the grassy waves of Yellowstone's Lamar Valley, hoping to see wild wolves. It is the National Park Service's hundred-year anniversary. I'm hoping to catch up again with longtime wolf researcher Rick McIntyre—whom I interviewed in 1995 when wolves were first reintroduced. I've also returned to Yellowstone to cover the grassroots Speak for Wolves 2016 conference on wolf recovery, which includes tribal biologists, wolf advocates, and the public.

On a small bluff above Slough Creek Campground about fifteen of us brace ourselves, backs against a ferocious summer windstorm. Suddenly a dust devil snatches up many hats. A few scopes on their spindly tripods fly off like metal praying mantises. Determined, we stand our ground, huddling a little closer together for safety. Our small group of strangers, fast becoming friends, swap wolf gossip.

"Heard one of the Junction Butte sisters was out hunting here before dawn this morning," a lively birder in a brightly woven wool cap informs us.

As she riffs on the complex family tree of the Junction Butte family, the knowledgeable wolf watcher reminds me that in Yellowstone the scientific names for wolves, unlike in other wolf studies, use the number first and the letter last. These so-called stud names help scientists keep track of and update the wolf families' changing populations.

On the bluff several other wolf watchers explain to us the history of this Junction Butte family that we hope to see. A group of adult sisters from the Mollies pack met up with a group of brothers from the Black Tail pack and formed the Junction Butte pack. The last founding surviving sister of the powerful Mollies pack, 970F, was the most recent alpha female, but she died this spring. Her two adult daughters, the three-year-old sisters 960F and 907F, are the mothers of the two litters of Junction Butte pups. Along with two brothers, they formed the Junction Butte pack. In unusual solidarity, the sisters now share a den. They chose the exact same ancestral den that Yellowstone's most famous wolf, the much-loved 06, first dug. Between them the Junction Butte sisters birthed and are communally raising nine pups—five blacks and four grays. One of the pups has disappeared, believed dead.

"Anyone seen the pups?" my friend and photographer Vanessa asks as she joins us on the bluff.

Wolf watchers are especially alert for the thrill of again sighting any of these surviving pups. Born in mid-April, the pups were weaned at about five to nine weeks old. They still depend upon regurgitated food from other family members who will teach them to feed on the carcasses of elk or deer come autumn.

Katie Lynch, who is on the board of the Wolf Recovery Foundation, recalls that first day wolf watchers caught sight of F969's pups: "A round of applause and cheers erupted from the group as what looked like a furry black caterpillar toddled into view on the den porch." It was easy to tell the two litters of wolf pups apart because "the younger pups were far wobblier on their short legs and had short, straight, stick tails, while the older pups were steadier on their longer legs and had longer, curvy tails." Lynch details the Junction Butte family dynamics: one male yearling from last year's litter is especially devoted to this year's pups; he protects and plays with them in his role as doting uncle. Often he allows the growing pups to "crawl all over him." There are five other yearlings—survivors of last year's twelve pups—who also take turns babysitting so these new ones don't wander away or fall prey to grizzlies.

When a bear approached the Junction Butte's den, Lynch notes, wolves surrounded the bear, then nipped at his butt to run him off. Another black bear venturing too near this precious den was treed by wolves who attacked "like a bunch of hounds."

"Look up there . . . across the creek at the Diagonal Forest," the birder now directs us. We search a slanting stand of cottonwoods. "That's where the JB's den is."

This woman has the authority of a veteran wolf watcher and the equipment of an elder—high-powered scope and folding chair, against which rests a skillfully carved wooden cane. She's quickly established herself as the alpha female of our little human pack.

Long-term wolf studies at the Yellowstone Center for Research have shown that wolves organize into matrilineal groups. The project leader of the Center, Douglas W. Smith, notes that it is generally the alpha female—now called the dominant breeder—"who really runs the show." There is some concern now that, with two mothers and multilitters in the Junction Buttes pack, there may be reduced survival for the pups because of competition for food. Mother wolves depend most on prime-age wolves (two to five years old) rather than just yearlings or older "helper wolves." Prime-age wolves are better at hunting and foraging for the whole family.

On the Lamar Valley bluff, our alpha female explains to us, "Life is tough, even for these Yellowstone wolves." Her face is weathered from the wind and wrinkled from long days in high-elevation sunlight—a life of watching wildlife. When she's not spotting wolves, she's following bald eagles, prairie peregrine, mountain bluebirds, or Sandhill cranes, just a few of the abundant bird species in Yellowstone. She shakes her silver head, "Even protected here in the park from human hunters, no guarantees these wolves will survive."

Another wolf watcher, a man in his midforties sporting a camera with a huge telephoto lens, explains that many of the wolf families here still suffer badly from mange—a painfully debilitating infection from burrowing mites. Mange was first actually introduced deliberately to Montana in the early 1900s by a Montana state wildlife veterinarian with the goal of eradicating predators, including wolves and coyotes. Two years after reintroduction into Yellowstone, wolves showed signs of mange, which causes incessant scratching and extreme fur loss. Sometimes mange-infected wolves will freeze to death in winter. Entire wolf families have been decimated by mange, including the Druid pack in 2010. At its peak of 37 family members in 2001, the Druids were the largest pack ever recorded. The latest wolf census in Yellowstone Park itself is 99 wolves in ten packs; the greater Yellowstone wolf population is 510 wolves. But mange is still a problem. Wolves with mange and fur loss must travel and hunt less at night—their preferred time—because of the cold. In 2016 the Lamar Canyon pack was hit hard by mange; researchers believe the disease may have caused the death of the family's six pups.

While we wait for any sign of the Junction Buttes, the photographer shows us snapshots of limping wolves, their legs and fur ravaged by this dangerous canid disease.

"You all up here looking for wolves?" two rangy young men approach and kindly offer their scope to scan the valley.

The young men are wildlife biologists from Georgia who traveled west for a survivalist course. In their well-worn jeans, backward baseball caps, indestructible hiking boots, and windproof jackets, they look well prepared to survive anything. As they stand together behind me, they are a shield from the violent wind that threatens to blow us all off the bluff.

We are all anxiously awaiting the arrival of Rick McIntyre. If anyone can spot wolves in the Lamar Valley, it's McIntyre. When I first met McIntyre here twenty-one years ago he was a tall and wiry researcher whose blazing red hair betrayed his Scottish heritage. I've kept track of his decades of wolf research and am excited to meet this veteran wolf watcher again. His forty years studying wolves have earned him the name "Wolf Man." This is his twenty-third summer observing Yellowstone wolves. He is a historian of their genealogies and family stories. McIntyre is also a wonderful raconteur who makes facts come alive with every new sighting.

On my crackling cell McIntyre told me, "There's a good chance you'll get to see the descendants of the original wild wolves you first watched here so many years ago. Remember the Crystal Creek pack?"

Of course I remember the first wild wolves I ever saw in my life. The Crystal Creeks are Yellowstone's longest-term pack; they eventually became the mighty Mollies, the pack that the founding sisters dispersed from to form the Junction Buttes. Twenty years of science in Yellowstone has given researchers—and us all—the invaluable gift of long-term wolf genealogies. Or, as researchers call such in-depth wolf histories, the "story of their genes." Now, on this late summer evening, I dearly hope I will again witness the new generations of the founder Crystal Creek family.

"No wolves where we come from," one of the Georgia biologists says with obvious regret. "We mostly study snakes—diamondback rattlers and water moccasins." On his cell phone he shows me a brief video of a water moccasin coiling around a metal pole in a fern-choked swamp. "They're easy and really fun to catch," he says with a bravado that is charmingly modest.

"Check out that bison yearling at twelve o'clock," his biologist companion says with real awe. "That boy better not wander too far from his buddies."

"Oh," says our alpha female, "I've seen wolves wandering around bison herds for hours. Big guys pay no mind. Bison even take naps with wolves just a hundred yards away!"

"Right," someone adds with obvious admiration. "Only the Mollies are really powerful enough to take down a bison. And if any wolf goes after a bison, it's at big risk."

I scan the creek, and about thirty-five lumbering hummocks of bison are grazing about a mile away. On my first day in the park I was caught in a traffic jam in west Yellowstone that I assumed was from the crush of tourists. But after an hour of stop-and-go traffic I came to a dead halt for a gigantic bison standing in the middle of the two-lane road. Shaking his shaggy, half-shed fur, he snorted and stood stolidly, pawing the yellow line. No one moved, but a lot of cameras clicked. At last a park wildlife official arrived with a bull horn blasting, "Go on, now! Git!" Slowly he herded the buffalo to amble across the road.

The bison herd in the Lamar Valley is also in no hurry, even though someone says she sees a dark spec dash through the resting buffalo. "Hey, look across the creek, right there . . . at two o'clock!" the young woman cries out. "Is that a wolf?"

All telescopes swing like batons to the Diagonal Forest. A palpable thrill runs through our small gathering. "Nope, it's just a baby bison goofing around," our alpha female finally gives her own short snort, dismissing the sighting. She explains to several Japanese visitors joining us that the Junction Buttes, like all wolves, rarely hunt bison. Elk and deer are their preferred prey. "Wolves usually take down the young and the vulnerable," she says, "*not* the prime-age elk or deer who have the best bet at breeding."

She goes on to explain that after twenty years of wolves keeping the elk population in check, the elk herds have actually grown much stronger because the wolves culled the weakest among them: "Survival of the fittest." She concludes that these stronger elk herds have actually made it more difficult for wolves to hunt them successfully—and that has led to a decline in Yellowstone wolf populations.

I'm struck at how well versed many of my companions are in wolf biology. Back in 1995 those of us who watched the fourteen Canadian wolves—who were the first wolves to repopulate Yellowstone after a seventy-year absence—were as unfamiliar with seeing wild wolves as the wolves themselves were in exploring their new territory. Everything was so new, and there were so many unknowns: Would the wolves survive in this unknown terrain? What would be their effect on prey, like elk and deer? As author Tom Reed notes, "If Yellowstone and its wildlife were like some gigantic machine, elk would be its fuel." Would wolves change or help restore the complex ecosystem? And of course, how would we tolerate living alongside this controversial fellow predator?

But now in 2016, witnessing wolves with so many well-informed wolf watchers is like doing field science with citizen naturalists. Many of these veteran wolf watchers gather daily data and photos to share with Yellowstone researchers. McIntyre has written that these longtime and respectful wolf watchers have become "role models of proper behavior regarding watching and photographing wildlife"—how not to block the road when a wolf needs to cross and how to stay one hundred yards from wolves and not interfere with the wolves' "natural behavior." McIntyre credits these veteran wolf watchers with adding more to the scientific data than "would have been possible with limited staffing. A large number of critically important behavior sequences that have been published in Wolf Project peer-reviewed scientific papers originated with the watchers."

Such long-term study, says Douglas Smith, has "allowed us to look into the lives of wolves like no other study has been able to do." Research into the wolves' role in the ecosystem and "how wolves work in the absence of human exploitation" is Yellowstone's "most important lasting contribution," says wolf biologist Rolf Peterson.

As we all watch and wait for any sight of wolves, the two Georgia biologists talk about the only *Canis lupus* left in their whole southern region, the critically endangered red wolves. Just this summer ground-breaking news about wolf genetics, especially in red wolves, has introduced new science and new arguments about America's wolves. A DNA study from Princeton University offers genetic evidence that there is really only one wolf species in North America—the gray wolf. The red wolf and eastern wolf species, the study claims, are actually hybrids from interbreeding between gray wolves and coyotes. When so many wolves, especially in America's East and South, were eradicated, the surviving gray wolves couldn't find mates, so they interbred with coyotes. This interbreeding began in the 1920s and has resulted in the genomes of several eastern wolves in Algonquin Provincial Park in Ontario that are half gray wolf and half coyote. Red wolves, this new genome study reveals, are 75 percent coyote and only 25 percent gray wolf.

Some conservationists believe this new genome study is not definitive and needs more research. In any case, there are implications for policy. If the eastern and red wolves are not really their own distinct species, then the USFWS must "rethink its plan to delist the gray wolf as an endangered species . . . and to consider instead expanding its protection to hybrid species, which currently fall outside of the realm of government protection." As Linda Y. Rutledge, an expert on eastern wolves, concludes, because eastern and red wolves still carry the DNA of an endangered species, they deserve protection. Even if they are not pure wolves, Rutledge says, these hybrid eastern and red wolves still play an important role as top predators in eastern forests. "If it can kill deer in eastern landscapes, it's worth saving."

As the Georgia biologists and I continue to talk about the plight of red wolves, a nine-year-old girl pipes up. "My school adopted red wolves."

Her elementary school is a proud sponsor of the Red Wolf Coalition and has just watched the award-winning *Red Wolf Revival* documentary on red wolf recovery in North Carolina, their only remaining habitat.

"There are only fifty red wolves left in the wild," the girl informs me with authority. "We're going to save them."

After a week of Yellowstone wolf watching, this nine-year-old is also so well schooled in the family history of the Junction Butte pack that she calls them by name: the Junction Butte sisters, F907 and F969, are simply "the JB girls." The girl scribbles her field notes in a battered sketchpad for her school project.

At last the squall passes over the Lamar Valley, and we can all stand up straight again. Tripods and scopes become steady. Generous, dark clouds swoop over the hills, shielding us from still-intense evening sun. We wait for wolves.

"TO UNDERSTAND AN ECOSYSTEM, one also must know its human history," wrote the longtime African Serengeti researcher R. E. Sinclair. Yellowstone's human history is well documented: the scene of ruthless fur trade and predator control in the park from 1872 to 1926, fire, and, in the 1990s, finally rewilding of bears and wolves. Yellowstone's success has inspired a European rewilding movement to increase wolf populations in Spain and Italy as well as in Scotland, where sheep are overgrazing. Author George Monbiot's book, *FERAL: Rewilding the Land, the Sea, and Human Life*, notes that in Scotland "people are less hostile to the reintroduction of the wolf than one might have imagined. . . . Even sheep farmers, surprisingly were split: antagonistic on balance, but not universally so." This modern tolerance from sheep herders might vindicate Rick McIntyre's Scottish ancestors, who were once forced to become wolf trappers before they too were also removed from their land.

After twenty years of studying Yellowstone wolves, our human history with them has also radically changed. Wolves have come back, says Douglas Smith, "because of a change in human behavior, not because their habitat has increased." Fifty years ago, he notes, "everyone hated wolves. Now half the population hates wolves. We are progressing. It's getting better. We are arriving at the idea that we can live with them." Some wolves now reintroducing

themselves in the West, like OR7, are descendants from these famous Yellowstone founder families.

Yellowstone is now a very different scene from when I first witnessed the reintroduction of wild wolves here in 1995. The once-
sleepy streets of West Yellowstone are wide awake, even late at
night. The Wolf and Grizzly Center welcomes thirteen hundred
visitors every day during the high summer tourist season. The restoration of Yellowstone's wild wolves is so lucrative for tourism
that local gift shops are full of wolf T-shirts, baseball hats, books,
jewelry, rugs, and other wolf memorabilia. Walking the crowded
streets of West Yellowstone, one might wonder whether wolves
were our national totem, our First People.

At the Speak for Wolves conference Blackfoot elder Jimmy St.
Goddard's remarked, "It's time for mankind to realize that they
are not the only sacred beings on earth." When I interviewed him,
St. Goddard told me that in his tribe, speaking out for wolves "is
a spiritual fight." Several other Native men spoke at the conference, including Rain Bear Stands Last and David Bearshield, one
of the Guardians of Our Ancestors Legacy (GOAL), which is one of
the largest tribal organizations in North America. GOAL is working
against the current plan to delist grizzly bears. They fear that delisting the grizzly is scientifically unsound and will only encourage
trophy hunting, which 99 percent of Americans oppose.

"In earlier centuries of Manifest Destiny," Rain told me, "Americans carried a killing gene: if they did not understand a wild animal,
they killed it." His Native tradition gives him an alternative view of
wildlife management. He has suggested moving endangered wildlife to tribal lands and letting tribes partner with the federal government to protect top predators. "We do not want to see what has
happened to the wolf happen with the grizzly bear," he said.

David Bearshield added, "Tribal societies have always observed
wolf packs and learned their societal concepts. For example, it's not
just a female wolf who raises pups; it's also a family responsibility.
Wolves also taught tribal peoples about hunting and tracking. Our
tribal scouts were called 'wolves.' These scouts would signal when
buffalo or relatives or enemies were close."

Rain Bear Stands Last recounted a Cheyenne wolf story told to him by his uncle, GOAL founder and Sun Dance Priest, Don Shoulderblade. In June 1876, prior to the Battle of Little Big Horn, a blind elder named Thorny Timber, Old Brave Wolf, who had the gift of speaking the language of wolves, asked his daughter to take him to the river where Custer would make his last stand. Wolves spoke to the elder and told him they had been following Custer's soldiers from Black Dust River all the way to Little Big Horn, or what the Lakota call Greasy Grass River. Wolves warned Old Brave Wolf that the next time the sun was at the center, "soldiers will be upon you." Because of the wolves' warning, the Cheyenne military society kept their war ponies near their lodgings. Forewarned by the wolf clan, their tribal warriors were prepared and the first to get into the fight.

BACK ON THE LAMAR VALLEY BLUFF I can't help but notice how many of us are wearing wolf hats and shirts as if to identify ourselves as wolf clan. Evening shadows the valley and darkens green hills. We watch with an alert anticipation—and the wolf stories continue.

Our resident alpha elder tells us that long-term Yellowstone research has showed new and surprising nuances in wolf family dynamics, especially among young wolves. There are now many examples of young wolves protecting each other, even at the risk of their own lives. This summer Kira Cassidy of the Yellowstone Wolf Project wrote the story of Triangle, a young male wolf born to the last litter of the Druid Peak pack. Smaller than both his brothers and one of his sisters, Triangle came to his sister's defense when several members of the Hoodoo pack attacked her. "Instead of running to safety," reports Cassidy, "Triangle jumped into the melee twice, bit one of the Hoodoo wolves and distracted the opposition long enough for his sister to escape." After his heroic efforts Triangle was himself bitten on the back but somehow managed to flee his attackers along with his sister.

Cassidy points out that in Yellowstone 68 percent of natural wolf deaths are a result of interpack fights. In the thirty-four attacks that researchers have witnessed, other wolves tried to rescue their pack mate at least six times. Why such self-sacrifice? Cassidy confirms what we have only recently had the scientific data to acknowledge: wolves are capable of much empathy and loyalty to each other, stating, "The family is a crucial part of a wolf's life."

Rick McIntyre now pulls up below the trail in his muddy car, side panels painted with murals of a soaring eagle over a Yellowstone valley. He unfolds his long limbs from the car and immediately sets up his well-worn telescope and tripod. McIntyre is the very definition of calm and patience. Everyone encircles him eagerly.

"Let me just look a little," McIntyre says, his voice as calm as an air traffic controller in the midst of our enthusiastic crowd. Settling on his metal stool, McIntyre sweeps the valley with his scope, hesitating, then scanning intently along the creek.

"You know," our elder wolf watcher laughs and easily yields her solitary alpha status to share it with McIntyre. "Wolves have probably been here the whole damn time. Sometimes it's only Rick can spot them."

Rick McIntyre has been spotting and teaching the public about wolves ever since they arrived in Yellowstone. He's given over two thousand presentations and will be writing books about their stories. McIntyre's field notes and daily, long-term observations of Yellowstone wolves make him a trusted witness to wolf behavior. He's seen wolves—like one of his favorites, M21—take care of a sick wolf and, after defeating other rival wolves in battle, never kill a defeated opponent. This loyal caretaking, he said, might "help explain why dogs tend to devote extra attention to a sick or depressed person."

McIntyre also has a recent theory that dogs, who, recent research has shown, have detected cancer in our species, have inherited this expert sensory skill from wolves. This skill "developed evolutionarily as a way to help wolves survive in the wild," McIntyre notes. "Their descendants, the modern dog, can use it to aid human beings."

We all gather around McIntyre as if around a warm fire. His telescope is never still.

"I've heard you haven't missed a day of wolf watching for twenty years," I tease McIntyre as he searches the long and lush Lamar Valley.

A faint smile, but McIntyre keeps his head down, eyes scanning with his scope. "More like fifteen," he corrects me.

McIntyre explains that he uses telemetry to track the wolves by radio collar and has seen wolves on 95 percent of his days watching wildlife in Yellowstone. Even though he's seen generations of wolf families, McIntyre says he's always excited to get up at first light and watch for them. When asked in his Yellowstone Staff Report profile interview if he ever wanted just to sleep in some dawns and forego wolf watching, McIntyre says, "No. I would feel like I might miss something important . . . like a parent missing his or her child's big sporting event or music recital. I need to be there."

Now McIntyre is practicing what he does so well—explaining the real lives of wolves to those of us who usually see them only on television nature shows. In the field with wild wolves, some of whom now have celebrity status, McIntyre has explained, it is like being a "tour guide in 1964 London, pointing out some guys walking down the street who happen to be the Beatles."

Balanced on his folding stool, McIntyre suddenly leans forward and says softly, "Quickly now . . . take a look."

Instantly we line up to peer through his telescope. Among the children there is a little shoving to get to the scope, but McIntyre tolerantly offers them each a turn.

"He's really knows how to manage wildlife," my friend Vanessa grins as we watch McIntyre make sure everyone, especially the children, gets a chance to see a wolf.

"Do you see the yearling?" McIntyre asks as I crouch to get a better view through the cold scope.

At first I see only rolling green and the lazy gathering of bison. Then suddenly a black flash weaves through brown buffalo. She comes into focus: a sleek and long-legged young wolf trotting toward two grazing bison. The bison are so huge that they dwarf the yearling wolf, who now feints and leaps near the bison. The yearling looks like she is playing. Or is she practicing for some future hunt?

After enduring a few more somewhat comic maneuvers from the yearling, both bison suddenly raise and shake their shaggy heads. Each takes only one step forward to threaten the wolf—and the yearling quickly skitters backward to safety.

It is a scene that is so vivid that we all murmur in astonishment. Everyone around me who is witnessing through a telescope the yearling practice-play at hunting the nonchalant bison narrates the events for those who have only binoculars or naked eyes. It is like hearing a story being created by oral tradition.

"She has two twin sisters," McIntyre explains, then asks a girl who is jumping up and down waiting her turn at the telescope. "Do you have any sisters?

The girl nods excitedly and says, "These are my sisters and they are also twins!"

McIntyre nods. "This yearling female has two sisters that are her same age and also three brothers. She helps out with the little pups, so they're about three months old. She's fifteen months old. She's the big sister to eight pups. She has a big family. Her mother has died, but she has two older sisters—"

"How do you know all this?" the little girl demands.

"Because he watches wolves every single day," our alpha female says firmly.

McIntyre continues his narration, like a voice-over on a documentary. "F970, the grandmother, died in the spring . . . she used to be the alpha female. She is the mother of these two new mothers sharing the same den. There's also a grandfather and father wolf. Father wolf is black . . . the two mothers are gray."

It's a dizzying amount of wolf genealogy to take in, and yet I see people scribbling in notebooks. These are regular people, not wildlife biologists, writing down family histories that are not just their own.

A new visitor joins us and greets McIntyre. "Once awhile back we saw the Druids family. Are these wolves descended from the Druid wolves?"

"Yes," McIntyre nods. "They're descended from the very famous Druid wolves M21 and F42."

I'm thrilled to witness wolves descended from the steady and long-suffering M21 and the "Cinderella" wolf who survived her sister's relentless attacks (with the help of her own sister wolves) and then mated with M21 to become the enduring alpha female of the Druids (see Chapter 5). It's like stepping into a living history, still evolving. M21's death at the old age of nine affected McIntyre as deeply as the loss of a good friend. "He wandered off and curled up under a tree," McIntyre said, "looking like he had just gone to sleep."

Older wolves in any pack are "the most influential factor on whether or not a pack defeated an opponent." Because Yellowstone has low human-caused mortality among wolves, scientists have been able to study more "complex social organizations within wolf packs, including very different roles for old individuals." These older wolves may actually be the "social glue" that helps the pack thrive. Their experience and knowledge, as in any culture, are passed down to help the younger generations survive.

"So these two young mothers, the sisters," I ask McIntyre, "how are they doing with all these new pups?"

"Well, they're going to have to work out who is the alpha," McIntyre explains. "In the past they've not gotten along. The father of these pups is M890, and he's very popular with the female wolves. We have a theory—M890 was born with black fur. He's middle-aged. And of course," McIntyre adds drily, "this won't happen to anyone here, but M890 started to turn gray. We think there's a connection between him and this other gray male, who also seems to be popular with all the females—like George Clooney."

Suddenly McIntyre straightens on his camping stool and asks for his scope back. He makes some adjustments in its range and then announces with quiet satisfaction, "We have a pup. Look now past that river of grass and near the dead tree." He gives the children the first turns at the telescope. "Look for anything that's small, black, and moving. Much smaller than you might expect."

An audible sigh of excitement rises as we all search for one of the new Junction Buttes wolf pups. It's what our alpha woman calls "the Holy Grail" of Yellowstone wolf watching—actually witnessing a new life. When it's my turn to watch the gray-black pup, I am amazed at how little he is silhouetted against a dark boulder, how long legged as he all but prances into the meadow.

"He's all alone," a woman says with some alarm. "Where are the other wolves?"

"Not far," a veteran wolf watcher reassures us. "Never far."

YEAR AFTER YEAR thousands more visitors will travel here to Yellowstone to experience what Douglas Smith calls "wildness in a modern age." After over twenty years of research, after millions of people from around the world have witnessed wild wolves, after all the endless listing and delisting based on politics, not science—what has changed? *Everything.*

Most of all, we have changed. "Wolves are back because people wanted it," says Smith. "We want to put real facts and real answers back in place of myths and tall tales of what people think wolves are like." Future scientific studies will include looking at how wolf interactions might be tempered by biological kinship or escalated by wolves who are unrelated. Yellowstone scientists are patiently piecing together the many puzzles of generational wolf relationships. "That's in the future, and it is remarkable work," he concludes. "Rarely done."

Even though there are still many political struggles, the Yellowstone wolves have given us an insider's view of wolf societies that we've never had before. Because these wolves have been protected in the park for so long, scientists have been able to establish a "natural baseline" for wolf biology that has "led to greater insights into how nature works." This knowledge changes our wildlife management and our policies.

"We have to get beyond the endless cycle of listing, delisting, hunting or killing and then relisting," said Brett Haverstick, who organized the Speak for Wolves Conference. "We need alternatives to just bringing lawsuits for wolf recovery." Haverstick argues that we need a Carnivore Conservation Act, federal legislation that would permanently protect carnivores like gray wolves, cougars, coyotes, grizzly bears, and black bears. These species, he says, would then no longer be under the jurisdiction of state fish and game departments. "Hunting, trapping, snaring, and baiting would be off the table," he says and adds, "The best available science does not support 'managing' these species."

The same week I was in Yellowstone the Republican House again passed another rider to strip wolves of protection in Wyoming and the Great Lakes region. But in a nod to wolf advocates, the Montana Fish and Wildlife Commission rejected a proposal to triple the wolf hunting quotas in areas around Yellowstone from two to six. Commissioner Gary Wolfe said, "I think we are putting pressure on those wolves." This vote was noted nationally because the wildlife commission was finally more balanced by some "nonconsumptive" users of wildlife.

When a pendulum swings out and back, it never returns to its exact starting place. Wolf recovery moves forward, seemingly advances, then just as quickly regresses. But small advances grow bigger with each forward swing—and that's where change takes place. Wolf recovery is a long game.

Yellowstone wolves are now well woven into the fabric of our human story—perhaps very much as wolves first were when our ancestors were more intimate with, and dependent upon, wilderness and wild animals. "Wildness needs wolves," wrote Durward L. Allen in his study of the vital role of wolves in a wild community. More than ever, we need wilderness and wolves.

In Yellowstone and throughout this country as well as in our science and stories, the wolf nation must thrive if we are to make the world wild and whole again.

# ORGANIZATIONS WORKING TO PRESERVE WILD WOLVES

Center for Biological Diversity
San Francisco, California
www.biologicaldiversity.org

Defenders of Wildlife
www.defenders.org

Endangered Wolf Center
endangeredwolfcenter.org

Howling for Justice
https://howlingforjustice.wordpress.com

Humane Society of the United States
Washington, DC
http://hsus.org

Living with Wolves
Sun Valley, Idaho
www.livingwithwolves.org

Lobos of the Southwest
http://mexicanwolves.org

Mexican Wolf Recovery Program
www.fws.gov/southwest/es/
    mexicanwolf

National Wolfwatcher Coalition
http://wolfwatcher.org

Natural Resources Defense Council
www.nrdc.org

Oregon Wild
http://www.oregonwild.org

Pacific Wild
http://pacificwild.org

Red Wolf Coalition
redwolves.com

Rick Lamplugh's blog
http://ricklamplugh.blogspot.com

Speak for Wolves blog
www.speakforwolves.org

US Department of Fish and Wildlife
www.fws.gov

Wolf Advisory Group
http://wdfw.wa.gov/about/advisory/
    wag/

Wolf Conservation Center
Salem, New York
http://nywolf.org

Wolf Education and Conservation
    Center
Winchester, Idaho
http://wolfcenter.org

Wolf Haven International
Tenino, Washington
http://wolfhaven.org

Wolves and Writing
https://wolvesandwriting.com

Wolves in Yellowstone
www.nps.gov/yell/learn/nature/
    wolves.htm

Wood River Wolf Project
Idaho
www.facebook.com/
    woodriverwolfproject

Yellowstone Reports
www.yellowstonereports.com

# NOTES

## CHAPTER 1. AN HISTORIC RAGE

3   Search the Internet for "war against the wolf": "We Didn't Domesticate Dogs. They Domesticated Us," White Wolf Pack, www.whitewolfpack.com/2013/03/we-didnt-domesticate-dogs-they.html.

4   "From the men's cave comes the howling of wolves: Linda Hogan, "The Caves," in Dwellings: A Spiritual History of the Living World (New York: W. W. Norton, 2007), 18, 35.

4   "What the colonists tried to do in their local area: Rick McIntyre, War Against the Wolf (Stillwater, MN: Voyageur Press, 1995), 12–14, 24.

4   Early hunter-gatherer cultures coexisted: Rick McIntyre, A Society of Wolves (Stillwater, MN: Voyageur Press, 1993), 18.

4   "there may have been a faithful Fido: Scott Neuman, "Who Let the Dogs In? We Did, About 30,000 Years Ago," NPR, May 22, 2015, www.npr.org/sections/thetwo-way/2015/05/22/408784216/who-let-the-dogs-in-we-did-about-30-000-years-ago.

4–5   But genetic studies reported: Virginia Morell, "From Wolf to Dog," Scientific American, June 16, 2015, 31–32.

5   McIntyre tells the story of visiting an Alaskan Inupiat: McIntyre, War Against the Wolf, 12–14.

6   "the U.S. Forest Service acquiesced to the stockowners: Bruce Hampton and Henry Holt, The Great American Wolf (New York: Henry Holt and Company, 1997).

6   A 1907 Department of Agriculture bulletin: McIntyre, War Against the Wolf, 149.

8   More recently the USDA reported: Emerson Urry, "'Secret' Federal Agency Admits Killing 3.2 Million Wild Animals in U.S. Last Year Alone," Enviro News, June 27, 2016.

8   On its website Wildlife Services' official mission: "Agriculture's Misnamed Agency," New York Times, July 17, 2013.

9   In the United States hunters are mostly male: USFW census report 2011: US Department of the Interior, US Fish and Wildlife Service, US Department of Commerce, "2011 National Survey of Fishing, Hunting, and Wildlife-Associated Recreation" (US Census Bureau, February 2014).

9   Contrast this agency's "take" with the fact: US Fish and Wildlife Service, "Birding in the United States: A Demographic and Economic Analysis" (Arlington, VA: US Fish and Wildlife Service, December 2013).

9   An award-winning investigative documentary: Predator Defense quotes from film: Exposed. See also "Meet the Whistle-Blowers," Predator Defense, www.predatordefense.org/exposed/index.htm#whistle.

10   These often-hidden toxins: Christopher Ketcham, "The Rogue Agency: A USDA Program That Tortures Dogs and Kills Endangered Species," Harper's, March 2016; "The USDA's War on Wildlife," Predator Defense, www.predatordefense.org/USDA.htm.

11   Since the 1914 federal appropriation, the war against: John A. Shivik, The Predator Paradox (Boston: Beacon Press, 2014), 12.

11   This 2011 federal deslisting not based: Virginia Morell, "U.S. Plan to Lift Wolf Protections in Doubt After Experts Question Science," Science Insider, February 8, 2014.

11   Wolf trapper turned wolf advocate, Carter Niemeyer: Carter Niemeyer, Wolfer (Boise, ID: Bottlefly Press, 2012), 280, 284, 287.

12   *A 2011 report from the Department of Agriculture:* "Coexisting with Large Carnivores," Endangered Wolf Center, 2011.

13   *Wolf parents pass down hunting skills:* "Fair Chase Ethics," Boone and Crockett Club, www.boone-crockett.org/huntingEthics/ethics_overview.asp?area=huntingEthics.

## CHAPTER 2. "WHO SPEAKS FOR WOLF?"

15   *One of the most far-sighted and still ecologically:* Paula Underwood, *Who Speaks for Wolf: A Native American Learning Story* (San Anselmo, CA: Learning Way, 1991). Note: All spelling, phrasing, and capitalizations are from the original poem.

16   *Writing in his journal, Thoreau mourned:* Henry David Thoreau, *The Journals of Henry David Thoreau* (New York: Dover Publications, [1906] 1962); reprinted in McIntyre, *War Against the Wolf*, 51–52.

17   *His best-selling animal stories:* Ernest Thompson Seton, "Lobo, the King of Currumpaw," in *Wild Animals I Have Known* (New York: Charles Scribner's Sons, 1898), Project Gutenberg, www.gutenberg.org/files/3031/3031-h/3031-h.htm.

18   *Lobo's cries were "sadder than I could possibly":* Steve Gooder, "A Man, a Wolf and a Whole New World," *Telegraph*, March 29, 2008.

19   *Lobo's death profoundly changed Seton:* Seton, "Lobo: King of the Currumpaw."

19   *In his "Note to the Reader":* Ibid. (Italics in original source).

20   *Aldo Leopold, the visionary father:* "Aldo Leopold," www.wilderness.net/NWPS/Leopold.

20   *Nevertheless, Leopold wrote in an unpublished foreword:* Aldo Leopold, *A Sand County Almanac* (Oxford: Oxford University Press, 1949), 205.

20   *So intense was the young Leopold's zeal:* Aldo Leopold, "The Game Situation in the Southwest," *Bulletin of the American Game Protective Association* (April 2, 1920): 6.

20–21  *Leopold concluded that the Biological Survey:* Aldo Leopold, "The Game Situation in the Southwest," *Bulletin of the American Game Protective Association* (April 2, 1920): 7.

21   *An essay, "The Historical Sense of Being:* Qi Feng Lin, "The Historical Sense of Being in the Writings of Aldo Leopold," *Minding Nature* (December 2011).

21   *In the unpublished foreword to* Sand County Almanac: Aldo Leopold, unpublished foreword to *Sand County Almanac*, reprinted in McIntyre, *War Against the Wolf*, 324. More quotes from this unpublished foreword can be found online at "Aldo Leopold Quotes," Green Fire, www.aldoleopold.org/greenfire/quotes.shtml#CSCA11.

21   *he wrote, "my sin against the wolves:* Leopold, unpublished foreword, 289, 322.

21   *Leopold's epiphany was vivid, heartbreaking:* Aldo Leopold, "Thinking Like a Mountain," *A Sand County Almanac* (1949), reprinted in Tom Lynch, *El Lobo: Readings on the Mexican Gray Wolf* (Salt Lake City: University of Utah Press, 2005), 84–86.

22   *The wounded wolf looks up at Leopold:* "Aldo Leopold Quotes," Green Fire. "There are two things that interest me: the relation of people to each other, and the relation of people to land" (Wherefore Wildlife Ecology?, unpublished manuscripts, AL 51).

23   *When humans destroy wild wolves, it is because we "have not learned to think like a mountain:* Leopold, "Thinking Like a Mountain."

23   *Leopold's story of this dying wolf:* James J. Kennedy, "Understanding Professional Career Evolution—An Example of Aldo Leopold," *Wildlife Society Bulletin* 12 (1984): 215–216.

23   *This new and more communal way:* Draft foreword to *A Sand County Almanac*, 1947/1987, CSCA 282, "Aldo Leopold Quotes," Green Fire; Leopold, Wilderness.net.

23   *One of the most important lines Leopold ever wrote:* Aldo Leopold, "On a Monument to the Pigeon," *A Sand County Almanac* (1947).

23   *Leopold's legacy of ecology . . . pragmatic conservation of Gifford Pinchot:* Julie Dunlap, "Educating for the Long Run: Pinchot and Leopold on Connecting with the Future," The Aldo Leopold Foundation, August 11, 2015.

23   *Leopold was Pinchot's pupil:* Kennedy, "Understanding Professional Career Evolution."

24 *Controversy about how to best manage:* Dunlap, "Educating for the Long Run."

24 *Pinchot was the progressive but "ever practical:* Steve Grant, "Gifford Pinchot: Bridging Two Eras of National Conservation," ConnecticutHistory.org, http://connecticuthistory .org/gifford-pinchot-bridging-two-eras-of-national-conservation; "Gifford Pinchot: America's First Forester," Wilderness.net, www.wilderness.net/nwps/Pinchot.

## CHAPTER 3. WOLF TEETH ON AN AIRPLANE WING

29 *Alaska's Governor Hickel proposed to exploit:* Timothy Egan, "Alaska to Kill Wolves to Inflate Game Herds," *New York Times*, November 19, 1992.

30 *After retiring from eight years as chief of the US Forest Service:* R. Max Peterson and Gerald W. Williams, *The Forest Service: Fighting for Public Lands* (Westport, CT: Greenwood Press, 2007), 286.

30 *In this position he often advocated before Congress:* Testimony of Max Peterson Before the Senate Environment and Public Works Committee, March 18, 1999, www.epw .senate.gov/107th/pet_3-18.htm.

30 *"You can't just let nature run wild!":* Timothy Egan, "Everyone Is Always On Nature's Side; People Just Can't Agree on What's Natural and What's Not," *New York Times*, December 19, 1998.

32 *"These animals are being managed for the benefit of man:* Egan, "Alaska to Kill Wolves to Inflate Game Herds."

32 *Enthusiastically echoing this hunter agenda:* Ibid.

32–33 *He predicted that aerial shooting would kill 300 to 400:* Kimberly L. Bruckner, "Alaskan Wolf Plan Packs Plenty of Controversy," Working paper, University of Colorado, February 1994, www.colorado.edu/conflict/full_text_search/AllCRCDocs/94-63.htm.

33 *"They'd come in the spring:* Marla Williams, "Wolves: To Kill or Conserve?—Alaska's Dilemma Is Who Decides—And Who Benefits," *Seattle Times*, January 24, 1993.

34 *In a later interview for her book,* Shadow Mountain: Gavin J. Grant, "Renée Askins" (interview), IndieBound/Booksense, www.indiebound.org/author-interviews/askins renee; Renée Askins, *Shadow Mountain: A Memoir of Wolves, a Woman, and the Wild* (New York: Anchor Books, 2002).

34 *"The story of this conflict is the story":* "Readings," *Harpers*, April 1995.

36 *Monogamous, loyal to their families:* Gordon Haber and Marybeth Holleman, *Among Wolves* (Fairbanks: University of Alaska Press, 2013), 9.

36 *"The problem is," he explained:* Bill Sherwonit, "Gordon Haber's Final Days," *Alaska Dispatch News*, September 27, 2015.

37 *A new democratic governor, Tony Knowles:* Sherwonit, "Gordon Haber's Final Days."

37 *In typical impatient style, Haber told the* New York Times: Egan, "Alaska to Kill Wolves to Inflate Game Herds."

38 *Haber's inside information:* Haber and Holleman, *Among Wolves*, 204–205.

38 *In 1991 Frost finally pled guilty:* Timothy Egan, "Protecting Prey of Humans Sets 2 Against a Vast World," *New York Times*, May 2, 1994.

38 *Wolves did not kill more than they could eat:* Haber and Holleman, *Among Wolves*, 221–223.

## CHAPTER 4. A TAXIDERMIST'S DREAM

*Online photo collections of Alaska caribou herds:* Caribou Herd in Snow, Master file, www .masterfile.com/em/search/#id=&color=&colour_key=0&format=hvsp&imgtype =IPV&releases=&keyImage=&keyword=caribou+herd+in+snow&license=ALL&mode =search&sort=alice&aspectRatio=mediumAspect.

40 *His words reminded me of a chilling fact:* Elizabeth Marshall Thomas, *The Hidden Life of Deer* (New York: HarperCollins, 2009), 166–168.

41   *the managers' traditional bias:* Haber and Holleman, *Among Wolves,* 106.

42   *I'd just learned at this summit from an ex-Game Board member:* Vic Ballenberghe, US Forest Service employee and ex-Alaska BOG member report to Defenders of Wildlife Conference, Seattle, WA, 1998.

42   *"You'd think she believed wolves had souls":* Brenda Peterson, *Build Me an Ark: A Life with Animals* (New York: Norton, 2001), 184, 191; Egan, "Alaska to Kill Wolves to Inflate Game Herds."

43   *As the US Humane Society recently noted:* "State Wildlife Management: The Pervasive Influence of Hunters, Hunting Culture, and Money," *Howling for Justice,* March 22, 2010.

44   *The very last afternoon of the Wolf Summit:* Peggy Shumaker, "Caribou," in *Wings Moist from the Other World* (Pittsburgh, PA: University of Pittsburgh Press, 1994); Shumaker, "The Story of Light," Underground Rivers, www.poetryfoundation.org/poem /237596.

45   *The year after the Wolf Summit Haber said:* Susan Reed, "The Killing Fields," *People,* March 21, 1994.

45   *A brief ban on aerial wolf hunting voted in:* Shannyn Moore, "Wolf in Governor's Clothing . . . ," Shannyn Moore: Just a Girl from Homer, September 23, 2008.

46   *Under Governor Sarah Palin wolves were shot:* Karin Brulliard, "Feds to Alaska: Stop Killing Bears and Wolves on Our Land," *Washington Post,* August 4, 2016.

46   *Over twelve hundred wolves were still killed:* Associated Press, "Alaska Puts $150 Bounty on Wolves," Environment on *NBC News,* March 22, 2007, www.nbcnews.com/id/177 35990/#.VnBgdYS7lTZ.

46   *"State wildlife managers have failed to provide:* "Alaska's Predator Control Programs," Defenders of Wildlife, www.defenders.org/sites/default/files/publications/alaskas _predator_control_programs.pdf.

46   *In the summer of 2016 the Obama administration's:* Paul Bedard, "Feds Reclaim Control of Alaska Gamelands, Ban Bear, Wolf Hunts by Air," *Washington Examiner,* August 3, 2016.

46   *In 2015 the Denali Park wolves—once so admired:* Emily Schwing, "Wolf Population Declining in Denali National Park," *Alaska Public Media,* June 4, 2014.

46–47 *This is "the lowest number since wildlife:* Melissa Cronin, "7 Boneheaded Things Sarah Palin Has Done to Animals," *The Dodo,* February 19, 2015.

47   *The National Park Service biologist who had studied:* Krista Langlois, "Wolf Wars: Alaska's Republican Governors Find Vicious Ways to Kill Predators and Mark Their Territory with the Feds," *Slate,* October 31, 2014.

47   *In the summer of 2016 the watchdog group:* "Hunting Compounds Record Low Denali Wolf Survival," PEER news release, May 7, 2015, www.peer.org/news/news-releases /hunting-compounds-record-low-denali-wolf-survival.html.

48   *Even then the winter-kill of wolves goes on:* "Alaska Confirms Massive Decline in Rare Wolves, Still Plans to Hunt Them," *Howling for Justice,* December 4, 2015.

48   *Along with so many of Alaska's wolves:* Haber and Holleman, *Among Wolves,* 106; Bill Sherwonit, "Gordon Haber's Final Days."

48   *Two longtime Alaska residents heard:* Haber and Holleman, *Among Wolves,* 106.

49   *"The pack's decline was fast and drastic:* Elise Schmelzer, "The Last Wolf Family of Alaska's Denali National Park Has Vanished," *Star Tribune,* August 10, 2016.

49   *National Park Service has proposed a ban:* "National Park Service Proposed Permanent Ban on Predator Hunting Practices in Alaska's Preserves," KUAC TV 9/FM 89.9, September 8, 2014, http://fm.kuac.org/post/national-park-service-proposes-permanent -ban-predator-hunting-practices-alaskas-preserves.

49   *A new governor, independent Bill Walker:* Council of Tlingit and Haida Indian Tribes of Alaska, "Gov. Walker Adopted into Kaagwaantaan Clan," April 21, 2015, http://gov .alaska.gov/Walker/press-room/full-press-release.html?pr=7136.

50  *"The most astonishing fact to one:* Patricia Nelson Limerick, *The Legacy of Conquest: The Unbroken Past of the American West* (W. W. Norton and Company, 1987).

CHAPTER 5. YELLOWSTONE: "A WOLF'S PARADISE"

*"Rick McIntyre wolf biologist" recent images:* Wolf Mcintyre Wolf Biologist, Google search, www.google.com/search?q=wolf+mcintyre+wolf+biologist&biw=1407&bih=728 &site=webhp&source=lnms&tbm=isch&sa=X&ved=0ahUKEwiuiLWonPXOAhUY6 GMKHRBVA8EQ_AUIBigB.

*Photos of F5 and chart of original Yellowstone wolves in 1995:* Michael K. Phillips, Douglas W. Smith, and Teri O'Neill, *The Wolves of Yellowstone* (Stillwater, MN: Voyageur Press, 1996), 46–47.

55  *"They were cavorting, playing:* "Wolves Leave Pens at Yellowstone and Appear to Celebrate," *New York Times*, March 27, 1995.

55  *She raised her magnificent head:* Phillips, Smith, and O'Neill, *The Wolves of Yellowstone.*

55  *Usually wolves simply run coyotes off:* "Who Eats Who?" National Park Service, www .nps.gov/glac/learn/education/upload/Who%20eats%20who%20chart.pdf.

56  *"The Yellowstone landscape those first animals stumbled:* Douglas W. Smith and Gary Ferguson, *Decade of the Wolf: Returning the Wild to Yellowstone* (Guilford, CT: Lyons Press, 2005).

56  *He would become as well known:* Josh Dean, "Pack Man," *Outside*, November 11, 2010.

56  *Outside magazine would call him "Pack Man":* Carl Safina, *Beyond Words: What Animals Think and Feel* (New York: Henry Holt and Company, 2015).

56  *In his preface, "Witness to Ecological Murder":* McIntyre, *War Against the Wolf*, 13.

57  *"I have concluded that it is OK to have feelings:* Diane Boyd, "Living with Wolves," in *Intimate Nature: The Bond Between Women and Animals*, ed. Linda Hogan, Deena Metzger, and Brenda Peterson (New York: Fawcett, 1999), 96.

58  *Because usually only the breeding male and female:* Sarah Marshall-Pescini, Ingo Besserdich, Corinna Kratz, and Friederike Range, "Exploring Differences in Dogs' and Wolves' Preference for Risk in a Foraging Task," *Frontiers in Psychology* 7 (August 2016): 1241.

59  *Number 10 was the largest and most confident of all:* Smith and Ferguson, *Decade of the Wolf.*

60  *"That's a wolf, Dusty," he says:* Thomas McNamee, "The Killing of Wolf Number 10," *Outside*, May 2, 1997.

63  *Stevens noted that wolves "are as various:* William K. Stevens, "Wolf's Howl Heralds Change for Old Haunts," *New York Times*, January 31, 1995.

63  *He would later tell a reporter, "Certain wolves:* Carl Safina, "What Do Animals Think?," excerpt from *Beyond Words*, *The Week*, September 18, 2015.

63  *Longtime and respected wolf advocates such as Laurie Lyman:* Laurie Lyman, Yellowstone Reports blog, www.yellowstonereports.com.

64  *In fact, the author of the wildly popular* Game of Thrones: Earthjustice, *The Weekly Howl*, print version, June 21, 2015.

64  *In Yellowstone the Druids, another group of the original:* "In the Valley of the Wolves: The Druid Wolf Pack Story," *Nature*, PBS, June 4, 2008, www.pbs.org/wnet/nature/in -the-valley-of-the-wolves-the-druid-wolf-pack-story/209.

65  *But as Number 40, the once-mighty and malicious matriarch:* Smith and Ferguson, *Decade of the Wolf*, 86.

66  *The true alpha male demonstrates:* Carl Safina, "Tapping Your Inner Wolf," *New York Times*, June 5, 2015.

67  *When biologist Douglas Smith told regular wolf watchers:* Greg Gordon, "The Passing of a Yellowstone Cinderella," *High Country News*, February 16, 2004.

## CHAPTER 6. TROPHIC CASCADES: A NOT-SO-SIMPLE STORY

69 *"We think this ecosystem is unraveling:* Sandi Doughton, "Can Wolves Restore an Ecosystem?" *Seattle Times*, January 25, 2009.

69 *But without wolves to control elk populations:* Ibid.

71 *"The whole ecosystem re-sorted itself:* Ibid.

71 *University of Washington ecologist Robert T. Paine:* "Keystone Species Hypothesis," University of Washington, February 3, 2011; R. B. Root. "Robert T. Paine, President: 1979–1980," *Bulletin of the Ecological Society of America* 60, no. 3 (September 1979): 156–157.

71 *Conservation biologist Cristina Eisenberg of Oregon State University:* Cristina Eisenberg, *The Wolf's Tooth* (Washington, DC: Island Press, 2010, 4–5; "Dr. Cristina Eisenberg Wants Wolves in Our Backyards," OSU College of Forestry, www.forestry.oregonstate .edu/dr-cristina-eisenberg-wants-wolves-our-backyards.

71 *This trophic cascade concept has deep roots:* "Predators Keep the World Green, Ecologists Find," *Duke Today*, February 28, 2006.

72 *In* The Wolf's Tooth *Cristina would later write:* Eisenberg, *The Wolf's Tooth*, 163–164.

75 *This kept us in check and enabled a form of equilibrium:* Arwen, "On the Prowl—A Better Understanding of Wolves with Dr. Cristina Eisenberg," *Viral Media Lab*, May 23, 2012.

75 *A few researchers recently argued that wolves are not:* Arthur Middleton, "Is the Wolf a Real American Hero?" *New York Times*, March 9, 2014.

75 *Another article in* Nature *also questions any overly simplistic:* Emma Marris, "Rethinking Predators: Legend of the Wolf," *Nature*, March 7, 2014.

75 *There's a clear threshold for ecosystem recovery:* "Yellowstone Ecosystem Needs Wolves and Willows, Elk and . . . Beavers?" National Science Foundation, www.nsf.gov/ discoveries/disc_images.jsp?cntn_id=126853&org=NSF.

77 *Storms, drought, disease—all of these contribute:* Cristina Eisenberg, "Wolves in a Tangled Bank," *Huffington Post*, December 23, 2014.

78 *Since 2008 Cristina has been experimenting:* "How Fires Benefit Wildlife," Learning Corner, http://familyonbikes.org/educate/lessons/animals_wildfires.htm.

78 *Certainly her successful and well-funded research grants:* "Benefits of Fire," California Department of Fish and Fire Protection, www.fire.ca.gov/communications/down loads/fact_sheets/TheBenefitsofFire.pdf.

78 *Interestingly, even with that many elk, the wolves:* "Controlled Burning," USDA Forest Service. www.fs.usda.gov/detail/dbnf/home/?cid=stelprdb5281464.

79 *We need to talk about returning wolves:* "Wolf Range in North America: Past, Present and Potential," Defenders of Wildlife, www.endangered.org/cms/assets/uploads /2013/07/PlacesForWolves_VisionMAP1page.pdf.

79 *federal protection for red wolves languished:* "North Carolina Landowners Express Support for Recovery of Endangered Red Wolves," Animal Welfare Institute, January 26, 2016.

80 *"Bringing keystones back, because of their far-reaching:* Eisenberg, *The Wolf's Tooth*, 165.

## CHAPTER 7. 06: THE WORLD'S MOST FAMOUS WOLF

*Photos of 06:* "Wolf 06," Shumway Photography, www.shumwayphotography.com/Yellow stone/Wolf-06/n-f58Vq/i-B2qFdr4.

82 *Because the Yellowstone wolves have been so intensely studied:* James C. Halfpenny, *Yellowstone Wolves in the Wild* (Helena, MT: Riverbend Publishing, 2003), 90–91; Mike Link and Kate Crowley, *Following the Pack: The World of Wolf Research* (Darby, PA: Diane Publishing Co., 1994).

83 *Laurie Lyman, a retired teacher who has been documenting:* Laurie Lyman, *Yellowstone Reports*, www.yellowstonereports.com.

84 *By spring she was seen galloping around meadows:* Joe Rosenberg, "06 Female," Snap Judgment NPR, May 23, 2014, http://snapjudgment.org/06-female.

84  *Through word of mouth, social media, and YouTube:* Natalie Bergholz, "06 The Legend," Legend of Lamar Valley, http://legendoflamarvalley.com/06-of-the-lamar-canyon -pack; "06 Female Wolf: The Legend of Lamar Valley," YouTube, November 28, 2014, www.youtube.com/watch?v=6qMw8lA2qCU.

84  *two brothers forsook seven sisters:* "06 to Be Immortalized on Film," *Howling for Justice.*

84  *In one scene in the documentary about 06,* She-Wolf: Bob Landis, "She-Wolf," film, *National Geographic* interview with Laurie Lyman, Rick McIntyre, Doug Smith, 2014, http://tvblogs.nationalgeographic.com/2014/01/19/she-wolf-rise-of-the-alpha-female.

85  *Once McIntyre witnessed 06, weakened after:* Rosenberg, "06 Female."

87  *She was a legend. And some legends don't outlive:* Jeff Hull, "Out of Bounds: The Death of 832F, Yellowstone's Most Famous Wolf," *Outside,* February 13, 2013.

88  *One of the wolf watchers, Dr. Nathan Varley:* Nathan Varley, "Witnessing the Clash: A Newly Collared 06 Leads Her Pack into Battle," Yellowstone Reports, February 11, 2012.

88  *He describes how they leave scent marks:* Rick Lamplugh, "Life and Death Among Yellowstone Wolves," Rick Lamplugh's Blog, November 2, 2015, http://ricklamplugh .blogspot.com/2015/11/life-and-death-among-yellowstones-wolves.html; "100 Wolf Facts," Wild World of Wolves, http://wildworldofwolves.tripod.com/id7.htm.

92  *But as Rick McIntyre poignantly noted:* Rosenberg, "06 Female."

92  *The* New York Times *eulogized 06 as "beloved:* Nate Schweber, "Famous Wolf Is Killed Outside Yellowstone," *New York Times,* December 8, 2012.

93  *Editorials and social media weighed in with the suspicion:* Hull, "Out of Bounds."

93  *That same year the Montana State House of Representatives:* Wolves of the Rockies, Action Alert, May, 2016, http://us5.campaign-archive1.com/?u=c797c2deeb0a61161eed3c9 bd&id=8eb9eee140&e=c174a7773d.

94  *Wolves, one of the most social animals of all, grieve:* Mark Bekoff and Jessica Pierce, *Wild Justice: The Moral Lives of Animals* (Chicago, IL: University of Chicago Press, 2009).

94  *Like our domesticated dogs, wolves' expressions:* Rick Lamplugh, "Wolves and Coyotes Feel Sadness and Grieve Like Humans," *The Dodo,* May 4, 2015.

95  *But a year and a half after he lost 06, her mate:* Pat Shipman, "The Cost of the Wild," *American Scientist,* November–December 2012.

95  *In the Lamar Canyon pack one of 06's formidable daughters:* "Wild Yellowstone: She Wolf," *National Geographic* documentary, http://natgeotv.com/za/wild-yellowstone -she-wolf/videos/the-invaders.

96  *This fame and this intimate alliance with the other:* Hull, "Out of Bounds."

97  *In addition, because wild wolves' lives mirror:* Nick Jans, *A Wolf Called Romeo* (New York: Houghton Mifflin, 2014).

## CHAPTER 8. OLD GROWTH AND YOUNG HOWLS

*Photos of the original eight members of Sawtooth Pack:* "Sawtooth Pack Wolves of the Nez Perce" (Elder Eight photo by Michael Dustin), Tripod, http://wolf-whisper305.tripod .com/id15.html.

98  *"But wolves have been slowly coming back here since 2008":* PDF info from Oregon State, USDA Forest Service, http://andrewsforest.oregonstate.edu/lter/pubs/pdf/ pub3654.pdf.

98  *Only three weeks earlier, in April 2011, the Republican Congress:* Brenda Peterson, "Despite Howling of Humans—Silencing of the Wolves," *Huffington Post,* March 21, 2014.

99  *The rider set a troubling precedent:* Brad Knickerbocker, "Budget Bill Cuts Federal Wolf Protection, Environmentalists Howling," *Christian Science Monitor,* April 16, 2011.

99  *Even the former director of the USFW, Jamie Rappaport Clark:* Peterson, "Wolves Endangered by Political Predators."

99   *This skill at following a human's gaze:* Virginia Morrell, "Wolves Can Follow a Human's Gaze," *Science,* February 23, 2011.

102  *I knew all about forest canopy research from reading:* Jerry F. Franklin, Kermit Cromack Jr., William Denison, Arthur McKee, Chris Maser, James Sedell, Fred Swanson et al., "Ecological Characteristics of Old-Growth Douglas-Fir Forest" (US Department of Agriculture, Forest Service, Pacific Northwest Forest and Range Experiment Station, 1981).

102  *Franklin called his research "a clarification:* Matt Rasmussen, "A Night in an Ancient Douglas-Fir Reveals the Forest Hidden Amid the Treetops," *California Wild,* Spring 2006.

104  *Filmmakers and wolf researchers Jim and Jamie Dutcher:* Jim Dutcher and Jamie Dutcher, *The Hidden Life of Wolves* (Washington, DC: National Geographic, 2013); Jim Dutcher and Richard Ballantine, *The Sawtooth Wolves* (Bearsville, NY: Rufus Publications, 1996).

104  *But those tree-climbing kids had already made plans:* "Owyhee Pack—The Rescue," You Tube, May 4, 2012, https://youtu.be/wZ6HREUWIMo.

104  *He added that the return to wolf hunts to "placate hunters":* Jim Robbins, "Hunting Wolves Out West: More, Less?" *New York Times,* December 16, 2011.

104  *Bloodlust and backlash against wolves:* Michael Babcock, "Montana's Wolf Hunting Season Ends; 166 Killed," Timber Wolf Information Network, www.timberwolf information.org/montanas-wolf-hunting-season-ends-166-killed.

105  *To put this in historical perspective, in the past hundred years:* Statistics from Living with Wolves, www.livingwithwolves.com.

105  *A billboard paid for by Washington Residents Against Wolves:* Matthew Weaver, "Spokane Group Uses Billboards to Take Stand on Wolves," *Capital Press,* January 15, 2015.

106  *And the tab that taxpayers paid for Wildlife Services to destroy:* Wildlife Services, "Tell Congress: Don't Sell Out Wolves, Wildlife," Center for Biological Diversity, June 13, 2016.

108  *Washington State high schooler Story Warren:* Kids4Wolves, Facebook, www.facebook .com/Kids4Wolves.

110  *Sometimes these wolves were collared for research, but sometimes:* "Idaho's Wolves," Kids4Wolves, March 12, 2016.

111  *This Judas wolf strategy is officially called:* "USDA-Collared Judas Wolves Used Over and Over to Lead Killers to Their Families," Timber Wolf Information Network, www .timberwolfinformation.org/usda-collared-judas-wolves-used-over-and-over-to -lead-killers-to-their-families.

111  *One of the most poignant and remarkable of Story's:* Kids4Wolves, "Kids to Secretary Jewell: Follow the Science," YouTube, March 23, 2014, https://youtu.be/WfUUoLY wUe4.

CHAPTER 9. WOLVES AND THE NATIONAL COMMONS

115  *Our whining about the dull farmland allowed my father:* Wilderness and Federal Land map, Virtual Hermit Unleashed, Tumblr, http://67.media.tumblr.com/b2c5193b 470193f2a72073a9d6842ab0/tumblr_najwjyAolo1sgyd3ro1_1280.jpg.

115  *In fact, in a few years he would be part of passing the landmark:* "What Is Wilderness?" Wilderness Act of 1964, Wilderness.net, www.wilderness.net/NWPS/WhatIsWilderness.

115–116  *My father informed us that in the whole world:* Bec Crew, "Half the World's Population Lives on 1% of Its Land," *Science Alert,* January 8, 2016; World Urban Population Density by Country & Area, Demographia, www.demographia.com/db-intlua-area2000.htm; People Per Square Kilometer in U.S., Per Square Mile, http://static.persquaremile .com/wp-content/uploads/2011/05/us-europe-high-speed-rail-and-density.png.

117  *Time and again the national polls tell us that a large majority:* National Survey Results, Public Policy Polling, Center for Biological Diversity, www.biologicaldiversity.org/ campaigns/gray_wolves/pdfs/NationalSurveyResults4.pdf.

117  *In 2013, when the Obama administration proposed permanently:* Noah Greenwood, "New Poll: Americans Love Wolves and Want Them to Stay Protected," *Huffington Post*, July 22, 2013.

117  *Many wildlife scientists vehemently decried:* Scientists' Letter to Secretary Sally Jewell Against Delisting Wolves in U.S., Center for Biological Diversity, www.biological diversity.org/campaigns/gray_wolves/pdfs/scientists_letter_on_delisting_rule.pdf.

117  *In a letter to Secretary of the Interior Sally Jewell scientists argued:* Jim Dutcher, Jamie Dutcher, and Garrick Dutcher, "Don't Forsake the Gray Wolf," *New York Times*, June 7, 2013.

118  *All manner of bounties, hunts, and trapping was allowed:* Garret Ellison, "Endangered or Not? Scientists, Lawmakers Renew Gray Wolf Debate," *Michigan Live*, December 13, 2015.

118  *In Idaho, during the winter of 2016, a virulently antiwolf Governor:* Associated Press, "20 Wolves Killed in Northern Idaho to Boost Elk Population," *Billings Gazette*, February 11, 2016.

118  *By the end of 2015 a federal judge, Beryl Howell, reversed:* Mark Hicks, Associated Press, "Great Lake Wolves Ordered Back to Endangered List," *Detroit News*, December 19, 2014.

118  *He and other congressional Republicans were "plotting:* Timothy Cama, "GOP Plots New Course on Endangered Species Act Reform," *The Hill*, May 17, 2015.

119  *And even though in 2016 only five to six thousand wolves now occupy:* "Restoring the Gray Wolf," Center for Biological Diversity press release, www.biologicaldiversity.org/ campaigns/gray_wolves.

119  *The first voice belongs to Mike:* Brenda Peterson, "Living with Wolves, Losing Our Orcas," *Ampersand*, June 11, 2015.

124  *The bottom line is that western ranchers can also learn:* Brenda Peterson, "Wild Wolves: The Old and the New West," *Huffington Post*, November 16, 2015.

124  *Friedman wants to use dialogue between ranchers and:* Chase Gunnell, "Ranchers in Wolf Country Finding Continued Success with Range Riding," Conservation Northwest, December 18, 2014.

125  *When wolves killed one of his cows in the summer of 2015:* Don Jenkins, "'Stuck' with Wolves, Rancher Says He'll Make the Best of It," *Capital Press, The West's AG Website*, August 5, 2015, www.capitalpress.com/Washington/20150805/stuck-with-wolves -rancher-says-hell-make-the-best-of-it.

125  *In Washington, Oregon, and California, ranchers are learning nonlethal:* Sandi Doughton, "As Wolves Rebound, Range Riders Keep Watch over Livestock," *Seattle Times*, August 2, 2015.

126  *In the summer of 2016 Washington hosted nineteen:* Associated Press, "Washington State Reports New Wolf Pack," Oregon Public Broadcasting, June 16, 2016, www.opb .org/news/article/washington-state-reports-new-wolf-pack.

127  *By the year 2020 "more than half of the nation's children:* Bill Chappell, "For U.S. Children, Minorities Will Be the Majority by 2020, Census Says," NPR, March 4, 2015, www.npr.org/sections/thetwo-way/2015/03/04/390672196/for-u-s-children -minorities-will-be-the-majority-by-2020-census-says.

127  *As the United States grows more diverse and urban:* Ashley Broughton, "Minorities Expected to Be Majority in 2050," CNN, August 13, 2008, www.cnn.com/2008/US /08/13/census.minorities.

127  *In another shift, there are now as many Millennials:* "Millennial Voters: More Liberal, But Will They Turn Out?" *Here & Now*, February 29, 2016; "The Millennial Generation

Is Bigger, More Diverse than Boomers," CNN Money, http://money.cnn.com/inter active/economy/diversity-millennials-boomers; Derek Thompson, "The Liberal Millennial Revolution," *Atlantic*, February 29, 2016.

127  *An interesting note is that while few Millennials label:* "Are Millennials Environmentally Friendly?" *Carbon Xprint*, July 1, 2015.

127  *They support sustainable companies, solar and wind energy:* Morley Winograd and Michael D. Hais, "How Green Are Millennials?" *New Geography*, February 5, 2013.

127  *This so-called Green generation bodes a different future:* "Millennials Drive a New Set of Animal Welfare Expectations," AgWeb, www.agweb.com/article/millennials-drive -a-new-set-of-animal-welfare-expectations-naa-news-release.

127  *As one Millennial writer noted, "Environmentalism and modern:* Molly Tankersley, "Average Is the New Green: How Millennials Are Redefining Environmentalism," *Huffington Post*, August 16, 2014.

127  *A Millennial I interviewed in North Carolina:* Courtney Perry, "In Sickness and in Sleep: Married to a Chronic Sleep Walker," *Huffington Post*, February 17, 2015.

129  *As we talked about this sad decline in red wolves:* Joanna Klein, "Red Wolves Need Emergency Protection, Conservationists Say," *New York Times*, May 31, 2016.

129  *Rancher's influence in politics is also shrinking:* Tay Wiles and Brooke Warren, "Federal-Lands Ranching: A Half-Century of Decline," *High Country News*, June 13, 2016.

130  *That struggle is embodied in the occupation of the Malheur:* Brooke Warren, "Photos: A protest over imprisoned ranchers becomes an occupation of a wildlife refuge," *High Country News*, January 25, 2016.

130  *An irony that the occupiers seemed to miss:* Sara Sidner, "Native Tribe Blasts Oregon Takeover," CNN, January 6, 2016, www.cnn.com/2016/01/06/us/native-tribe-blasts -oregon-takeover.

131  *One of the most vivid reactions to the Malheur:* Dave Seminara, "Angry Birders: Standoff at Oregon Refuge Has Riled a Passionate Group," *New York Times*, January 8, 2016.

131  *The letter also pointed out that "Wildlife photographers:* Norwegian Chef, "Warning from the Birding Community to the Terrorists in Oregon: We're Watching You," *Daily Kos*, January 5, 2016, www.dailykos.com/story/2016/01/05/1466254/-Warning-from-the -Birding-Community-to-the-Terrorists-in-Oregon-We-re-Watching-You.

131–132  *CNN security analyst Juliette Kayyem:* Juliette Kayyem, "Face It, Oregon Building Takeover Is Terrorism," op-ed, CNN, January 3, 2016, www.cnn.com/2016/01/03/ opinions/kayyem-oregon-building-takeover-terrorism.

132  *Oregon locals held town halls demanding:* Patrik Jonsson, "In Oregon, a Counterpoint to Armed Standoff Emerges," *Christian Science Monitor*, January 22, 2016.

132  *Many of the Malheur occupiers mistakenly believed:* Hal Herrin, "The Darkness at the Heart of Malheur," *High Country News*, March 21, 2016.

132  *"The fate of the West has, almost from the very beginning:* "A Wildlife Refuge Is the Perfect Place for This Standoff" (print headline: "Cowboy Nihilism in Oregon"), *Seattle Weekly*, January 5, 2016.

133  *The Malheur occupation, in the tradition:* Jack Healy and Kirk Johnson, "The Larger, but Quieter than Bundy, Push to Take Over Federal Land," *New York Times*, January 10, 2016.

133  *When the Malheur armed takeover was winding down:* Jenny Rowland and Matty Lee-Ashley, "The Koch Brothers Are Now Funding the Bundy Land Seizure Agenda," *Think Progress*, February 11, 2016.

133  *In the federal trial, all of the Malheur Wildlife Refuge occupiers*: National Audubon Society, "Audubon CEO: Public Lands Don't Belong to Those Who Hold Them at Gunpoint," *Audubon*, October 27, 2016.

134  *And in the West some of those states—especially the ones:* "GOP Politicians Planned

and Participated in Key Aspects of Refuge Occupation," KUOW.org/NPR, March 17, 2016, http://kuow.org/post/gop-politicians-planned-and-participated-key-aspects -refuge-occupation.

134  *With press releases that declare "This is a war on rural America":* David DeMille, "Stewart Joins Chaffetz in a Call to Disarm Federal Agencies," *Spectrum,* March 9, 2016.

134  *After the Malheur occupation there were news reports:* Nancy Benac, "Who Are the Koch brothers?" AP on *PBS News Hour,* January 28, 2016, www.pbs.org/newshour/updates /koch-brothers.

## CHAPTER 10. WOLVES AT PLAY

137  *One of these conservation warriors is Amaroq Weiss:* "Meet the Staff," Center for Biological Diversity, http://www.biologicaldiversity.org/about/staff.

138  *Amaroq is here in Washington to attend:* "Wolf Advisory Group," Washington Department of Fish and Wildlife, http://wdfw.wa.gov/about/advisory/wag.

138  *Along with their many successful lawsuits on behalf:* RareEarthtones, Center for Biological Diversity, www.rareearthtones.org/ringtones/preview.html; Endangered Species Condoms, Center for Biological Diversity, http://www.endangeredspeciescondoms .com.

139  *Veterans with PTSD struggling to reunite:* Sidney Stevens, "How Wolves and Warriors Help Each Other Heal," *Mother Nature Network,* January 5, 2016.

140  *Play is essential to evolution and change:* Joseph W. Meeker, *The Comedy of Survival: In Search of an Environmental Ethic* (Tucson: University of Arizona Press, 1997).

140  *New research in* Science Daily: "'Gambling' Wolves Take More Risks than Dogs," *Science Daily: Frontiers in Psychology,* September 1, 2016.

141  *We touch on the lifework of Dr. Stuart L. Brown:* Stuart Brown, "Animals at Play," You Tube, August 22, 2007, https://youtu.be/iHj82otCi7U; Brown, "Play Is More than Just Fun," TED Talk, May 2008.

141  *In his article "Animals at Play," Brown expands:* Stuart Brown, "Animals at Play," *National Geographic,* December 1994.

141  *James C. Halfpenny's* Yellowstone Wolves in the Wild: James C. Halfpenny, *Yellowstone Wolves in the Wild* (Helena, MT: Riverbend Publishing, 2003), 59.

142  *Does play always have to have some evolutionary purpose:* Brenda Peterson, "Apprenticeship to Animal Play," in *Intimate Nature: The Bond Between Women and Animals,* ed. Linda Hogan, Deena Metzger, and Brenda Peterson, 428–437 (New York: Fawcett, 1999).

142  *Laughter as well as play is hardwired into us:* Stefan Lovgren, "Animals Laughed Long Before Humans, Study Says," *National Geographic News,* March 31, 2005.

143  *Smuts notes that "friendship among animals:* Barbara Smuts, "What Are Friends For?" *Humanistic Science,* July 11, 2012.

144  *With the return of the wild wolf we're learning:* Sharon Levy, "Wolf Family Values: Why Wolves Belong Together," *New Scientist,* wolf.nrdpfc.ca.

144  *One summer Curby camped near a wolf den, using her:* Cathy Curby, "A Family of Wolves," US Fish and Wildlife Service, www.fws.gov/refuge/arctic/wolfstory.html.

146  *Balancing the hopes of "hunters who want to take:* Michael Wright, "Commission Rejects Tripling Wolf Hunting Quota Near Yellowstone," *Bozeman Daily Chronicle,* May 12, 2016.

147  *New reports show that wolf sightings in both:* Michelle Ma, "Wolf Hunting Near Denali, Yellowstone Cuts Wolf Sightings in Half," *University of Washington News,* April 28, 2016.

147  *Important new research from scientists:* Adrian Treves, "Open Letter from Scientists and Scholars on Wolf Recovery in the Great Lakes Region and Beyond," ResearchGate, December 2015.

147  *One of the rationales for lethal management of wolves:* Carter Niemeyer, *Wolf Land* (Boise, ID: Bottlefly Press, 2016), 214.

147  *This study found that the exact opposite was true:* Niki Rust, "When You Start Killing Wolves, Something Odd Happens," *BBC Rare Earth*, May 11, 2016, www.bbc.com/earth /story/20160510-why-it-is-a-bad-idea-to-let-people-hunt-wolves?ocid=fbert.

147  *Culling wolves is not the answer:* Guillaume Chapron and Adrian Treves, "Blood Does Not Buy Goodwill: Allowing Culling Increases Poaching of Large Carnivore," Proceedings of the Royal Society Publishing 38, no. 1830 (May 2016), http://rspb.royalsociety publishing.org/content/283/1830/20152939.

148  *The study concludes with the truism:* Judith Davidoff, "Is Hunting Really a Conservation Tool?" *ISTHMUS News*, May 10, 2016.

148  *She prefers the word "conflict transformation":* Matthew Weaver, "Wolf Advisory Group Seeks Common Ground," *Capital Press*, May 21, 2015.

148  *Amaroq showed me the YouTube video:* Amaroq Weiss, "What to Wear at a Wolf Rally?" YouTube, September 18, 2013, www.youtube.com/watch?v=mGJB1y1uw9E.

149  *Amaroq also shared with me a darkly comic video:* Amaroq Weiss, "One Determined Husky Takes on the Planet's Most Pressing Environmental Problems," YouTube, October 31, 2015, https://youtu.be/Qark1Kw_4C4.

149  *just as Senator Inhofe's attacks on endangered species:* Jim Inhofe, Wikipedia, https:// en.wikipedia.org/wiki/Jim_Inhofe.

## CHAPTER 11. RAISED BY WOLVES

151  *Authors, artists, and musicians are creating a rich habitat:* Farley Mowat, *Never Cry Wolf* (Boston: Little, Brown, 1963); Barry Holstun Lopez, *Of Wolves and Men* (New York: Scribner, 1978); Nick Jans, *A Wolf Called Romeo* (Boston: Houghton Mifflin, 2014); Jiang Rong, *Wolf Totem* (New York: Penguin, 2008); Jean Craighead George, *Julie of the Wolves* (New York: Harper and Row, 1972).

151  *It's not just natural history classics:* "List of Fictional Feral Children," Wikipedia. https://en.wikipedia.org/wiki/List_of_fictional_feral_children.

152  *Perhaps the most famous of all the stories of a child raised:* Rudyard Kipling, *The Jungle Book* (London, Oxford University Press, 2008 [original 1894]).

152  *the Indian news sensation in the 1920s of "a pair of sisters:* Jane Yolen, Introduction to *The Jungle Book* (New York: Tor Classics, 1992).

152  *Kipling's own father had written stories:* John Lockwood Kipling, *Beast and Man in India: A Popular Sketch of Indian Animals in Their Relations with People* (London: Kessinger Publishing, 2010).

154  *The timeless appeal and what the* New York Times: Mary Jo Murphy, "Predicting the Staying Power of 'The Jungle Book,'" *New York Times*, April 7, 2016; Brooks Barnes, "'Jungle Book' Captivates Moviegoers and Captures Box Office," *New York Times*, April 17, 2016; *The Jungle Book* (video clip), YouTube, https://youtu.be/GgGOcEgRh7k. Voices in *The Jungle Book* video clip: https://youtu.be/McZyOEekZy4.

154  *A more realistic book, informed to some extent:* George, *Julie of the Wolves*, 24, 140, 170; *Julie's Wolf Pack* sequel: Jean Craighead George, *Julie's Wolf Pack* (New York: Harper Collins Publishers, 1997).

156  *Because of this wolf-human ancestry, the Mongol herdsmen:* Tuguldur Enkhtsetseg, "A Gift of Wolves," *Up Close*, Nature Conservancy, October 6, 2014; Amy Qin, "Q. and A.: Jiang Rong on 'Wolf Totem,' the Novel and Now the Film," *Sinosphere*, February 26, 2015.

156  *The Mongol culture, like their wolves, is endangered:* Amy Qin, "China Looks West to Bring 'Wolf Totem' to Screen," *New York Times*, February 23, 2015.

157  *Amy Qin of the New York Times wrote, "Political dissenters:* Ibid.

157  *The venerable role of the wild animal as psycho-pomp:* Ibid.

158  *And if China protects its nature, the rest:* "Bringing Wolf Totem to the Big Screen," *Writ-*

*ing Studio,* November 15, 2015, http://writingstudio.co.za/bringing-wolf-totem-to -the-big-screen.

158  Wolf Totem *was filmed under strict environmental protections:* Fu Yu, "Environmental Protection While Filming Wolf Totem Worth It: Director," *CRJEnglish News,* December 5, 2014.

159  *Media coverage of the 2016 Orlando massacre:* "Make It Stop," *Boston Globe,* June 16, 2016; Thomas L. Friedman, "Lessons of Hiroshima and Orlando," *New York Times,* June 15, 2016; "On 'Lone Wolves,'" *New York Times,* June 12, 2016.

159  *The* Christian Science Monitor *ran a headline:* Taylor Luck, "Orlando Attack: 'I Am the Lone Wolf That Terrorizes the Infidels,'" *Christian Science Monitor,* June 13, 2016.

159  *Tellingly, American gun violence is the most widespread:* A. J. Willingham, "US Home to Nearly a Third of World's Mass Shootings," CNN, June 16, 2016, www.cnn.com /2016/06/13/health/mass-shootings-in-america-in-charts-and-graphs-trnd/index .html.

160  *The states most resistant to gun control are also:* "Death by Gun: Top 20 States with Highest Rates," *CBS News,* www.cbsnews.com/pictures/death-by-gun-top-20-states -with-highest-rates/21.

160  *Four of the high gun-death states are:* Erica R. Henry, "These States Have the Highest Gun Death Rates in America," *Aljazeera America,* November 3, 2015, http://america .aljazeera.com/watch/shows/america-tonight/articles/2015/11/3/these-states -have-the-highest-gun-death-rates-in-america.html; Alexander Kent, "10 States with the Most Gun Violence," *Wall Street Journal,* June 10, 2015; Gun Violence Archive, www.gunviolencearchive.org.

160  *Feral children are, most of all, survivors:* Michael Newton, *Savage Girls and Wild Boys: A History of Feral Children* (New York: Thomas Dunne Books, 2002), 14, Kindle version.

160  *Whenever I teach wildlife conservation and ecology:* Brenda Peterson, "Animal Allies," *Orion,* Spring 1993, reposted on Brenda Peterson Books, www.brendapetersonbooks .com/display/ShowJournal?moduleId=18475789&registeredAuthorId=2406057 &currentPage=6.

## CHAPTER 12. WOLF MUSIC

163  *The University of Cambridge led a team:* "Wolf Species Have 'Howling Dialects,'" University of Cambridge research, February 8, 2016, www.cam.ac.uk/research/news/ wolf-species-have-howling-dialects.

164  *Root-Gutteridge concludes that wolves:* Holly Root-Gutteridge, "The Songs of Wolves," *Aeon,* https://aeon.co/users/holly-root-gutteridge.

164  *They have found, for example, that red wolves and coyotes:* Sarah Griffiths, "Wolves Have Accents, Too! Canines Can Be Identified Using 21 Different Types of Howling 'Dialects,'" *Daily Mail,* February 8, 2016.

164  *In* The Culture of Whales and Dolphins, *biologist Hal Whitehead:* Hal Whitehead and Luke Rendell, *The Cultural Lives of Whales and Dolphins* (Chicago: University of Chicago Press, 2015), 13.

164  *Every wolf group develops "its own unique:* Haber and Holleman, *Among Wolves,* 249.

165  *In my search for musicians who are listening to wolves:* Wolf Conservation Center, http://nywolf.org.

166  *Her memoir,* Wild Harmonies: A Life of Music and Wolves: Hélène Grimaud, *Wild Harmonies: A Life of Music and Wolves* (New York: Penguin Group, 2003).

167  *In declaring their acoustic territory, the wolf chorus:* Rudy C. Spatz, "Why Do Wolves Howl?" *FACTFIXX,* February 27, 2012.

167  *An interdisciplinary team of Montana State University researchers:* Marshall Swearingen,

"MSU Researcher Helps Untangle the Language of Wolf Howls," *Montana State University News*, March 10, 2016, www.montana.edu/news.

167  *Any online search reveals many audio clips:* Fred H. Harrington, "What's in a Howl?" *PBS NOVA: Wild Wolves*, November 2000, www.pbs.org/wgbh/nova/wolves/howlhtml.

168  *Hélène Grimaud has even recorded a "Wolf Moonlight Sonata":* "Hélène Grimaud ~Wolf Moonlight Sonata," YouTube, November 27, 2012, https://youtu.be/fwf1Db8hbJQ ?list=FLb7GBbol9GPky5MezzgLBUw.

169  *Other experiments on how animals react to human music:* Zen Faulkes, "Can Animals Enjoy Music the Same Way as Humans Can?" *Quora*, August 4, 2014.

169  *We agree that Rachmaninoff's music claims:* "Rachmaninoff Concerto #2 (Hélène Grimaud)," YouTube, July 11, 2015, https://youtu.be/_asl5WvGVQs?list=FLb7GBbol9GP ky5MezzgLBUw.

172  *As Grimaud and I continue to talk about Simone Weil's:* Brenda Peterson, "The Sacredness of Chores," in *Nature and Other Mothers* (New York: HarperCollins, 1992).

172  *Literary ecologist Joseph Meeker, in his classic:* Joseph W. Meeker, *The Comedy of Survival: In Search of an Environmental Ethic* (Tucson: University of Arizona Press, 1997).

172  *He argues that the Greek tragic tradition has led:* Christy Rodgers, "At Play in the Comedy of Survival," *CounterPunch*, April 10, 2015.

173  *When Grimaud first encountered this she-wolf:* Grimaud, *Wild Harmonies*, 1, 21, 26, 58, 205, 216–217.

173  *Once, when the wolf was howling, Grimaud realized:* "Alawa," Wolf Conservation Center, http://nywolf.org/ambassador-wolves/alawa.

174  *Ethologist Marc Bekoff writes about animals' moral:* Marc Bekoff and Jessica Pierce, "The Ethical Dog," *Scientific American*, February 1, 2010.

174  *Even Darwin believed that animals "would acquire:* Tom Fort, "*Wild Justice* by Marc Bekoff and Jessica Pierce and *Made for Each Other* by Meg Daley Olmert: Review," *Telegraph*, May 21, 2009.

175  *"Resonance" is "sound produced by a body:* Resonance, Dictionary.com, http://www.dictionary.com/browse/resonance?s=t.

175  *German jazz musician Joachim-Ernst Berendt writes:* Joachim-Ernst Berendt, *Nada Brahma: The World Is Sound: Music and the Landscape of Consciousness* (Rochester, VT: Destiny Books, 1987).

## CHAPTER 13. OR7: A WOLF CALLED JOURNEY

179  *Without a family, there are so many dangers:* Rob Klavins, "Hiking with Wolves," *Oregon Wild*, October 6, 2010.

179  *His howl was as resonant as a canine Pavarotti:* *Oregon Wild*, SoundCloud, https://sound cloud.com/oregon-wild/wolf-howl-072313.

180  *Robust and charcoal black, OR4 was so tenacious:* Rob Klavins, "A Eulogy for OR4," *Oregon Wild*, March 31, 2016.

180  *"There were rumors of wolves in the west:* Zach Urness, "When the Wolves Return to Western Oregon," *Statesman Journal*, March 14, 2014.

180  *OR7's family lived in the heart of hostile cattle country:* Emma Marris, "Lone Wolf That Took Epic Journey Across West Finds a Mate," *National Geographic*, May 18, 2014.

181  *Even though 70 percent of Oregon residents support:* Joe Donnelly, "What One Wolf's Extraordinary Journey Means for the Future of Wildlife in America," *Take Part*, December 17, 2014.

181  *These losses are highly overshadowed by the fact:* Ibid.

182  *Oregon's* Statesman Journal *called OR7 "A folk hero.":* Zach Urness, "When the Wolves Return to Western Oregon," chapter 1: "A Folk Hero Called OR7," *Statesman Journal*, 2014.

182  *A rare sighting of OR7 in Lake Almanor, Oregon:* "OR7—The Journey Movie Trailer," You Tube, October 26, 2013, www.youtube.com/watch?v=6WbEbNlyGIk.

183  *By migrating to the Pacific Coast, OR7:* Renee Lee, "California Welcomes Wild Wolf for First Time in 87 Years," *USDA Blog,* January 18, 2012, http://blogs.usda.gov/2012/01 /18/california-welcomes-wild-wolf-for-first-time-in-87-years.

184  *"Being an apex predator in a landscape that hasn't:* Bettina Boxall, "Gray Wolf Takes to California, but Is Unlikely to Find a Mate Here," *Los Angeles Times,* January 1, 2013.

184  *In Siskiyou County, later one of OR7's favorite haunts:* "OR7—The Journey Movie Trailer," YouTube.

184  *OR7 was following the archetypal "hero's journey":* "Examples of Each Stage of a Hero's Journey," YourDictionary. http://examples.yourdictionary.com/examples-of-each -stage-of-a-hero-s-journey.html.

184  *Joseph Campbell wrote, "You enter the forest:* Joseph Campbell, "The Hero's Journey Quotes," Goodreads, www.goodreads.com/work/quotes/1644565-the-hero-s-jour ney-joseph-campbell-on-his-life-work-works.

185  *But the* Times, *like most biologists, still predicted:* Maria L. La Ganga, "OR7, the Wandering Wolf, Looks for Love in All the Right Places," *Los Angeles Times,* May 13, 2014.

185  *Even an ex-president of the Oregon Cattlemen's Association:* Marris, "Lone Wolf That Took Epic Journey Across West Finds a Mate."

186  *One color photo from the Oregonian's proud announcement:* Lynne Terry, "OR7: Biologists Confirm Oregon Wolf Has at Least 2 Pups," *Oregonian,* June 4, 2014.

187  *About the time OR7 found his mate, a quasi-documentary film:* "The Wolf OR-7 Expedition—Trailer," YouTube, January 26, 2016, https://youtu.be/qdEObTbzLWw.

188  *It actually makes things worse in the long run:* Courtney Flatt, "How Killing Wolves Might Be Leading to More Livestock Attacks," Northwest Public Radio/EarthFix, February 18, 2015, www.opb.org/news/article/study-killing-wolves-causes-more-live stock-depreda.

188  *A 2016 film,* Wolf OR-7: Expedition, *chronicles:* Wolf OR-7 Expedition, http://or7 expedition.org/category/news; Wolf OR-7 Expedition, Facebook, www.facebook.com /or7expedition.

189  *"It is only through walking it that anyone:* "After First Wolf Resettles Oregon, Group Retracing Trek of Wandering OR-7," *New Mexico News,* March 19, 2014.

189  *Along with the films and media coverage, OR7s story:* Emma Bland Smith, *Journey: Based on the True Story of OR7, the Most Famous Wolf in the West* (Seattle, WA: Little Bigfoot, 2016).

189  *In November 2015 Oregon's Fish and Game Commission:* Kelly House, "Wolf Allies, Foes Prep for Battle as Oregon Reconsiders Endangered Status," *Oregonian,* June 9, 2015.

189  *Oregon's more enlightened and sustainable wolf-recovery policies:* Brenda Peterson, "Wild Wolves: The Old and the New West," *Huffington Post,* November 16, 2015.

189  *Oregon had been on the cutting edge of wolf recovery:* "Getting Territorial Over Delisting—Controversy Ignites Over Move to Permanently Remove Wolf Designation," *Willamette Live,* January 21, 2016.

190  *New research data has confirmed that acceptance decreases:* Adrian Treves, "Wolf Delisting Decision Not Based on the Facts," *Register-Guard,* February 15, 2016.

190  *Oregon's wildlife commission doubled down on its decision:* "Scientists Slam Oregon's 'Fundamentally Flawed' Proposal to Remove Wolf Protections," Center for Biological Diversity, October 29, 2015.

190–191  *It also shows the dominance of the $669 million beef industry:* Kelly House, "Gov. Kate Brown Signs Bill Blocking Legal Review of Gray Wolf Protections," *Oregonian,* March 15, 2016.

191  *In March of 2016 Oregon wildlife officials had issued:* "Depredations Lead to Lethal Con-

trol for Wolves in Wallowa County," ODFW press release, March 31, 2016, http://dfw
.state.or.us/news/2016/03_march/033116.asp.

192 *The kill order came down even when Oregon's wildlife officials:* Kelly House, "State Officials Kill 4 Wolves After Attacks on Livestock," *Oregonian,* March 31, 2016.

192 *In his eulogy for OR4 Oregon Wild's Rob Klavins wrote:* Klavins, "A Eulogy for OR-4."

192 *Even* Men's Journal *mourned the loss of OR4:* Melissa Gaskill, "Eulogy for a Wolf: The
Life and Legacy of OR4, Oregon's Most Celebrated Wild Wolf," *Men's Journal.*

192 *The popular wolf blog "Howling for Justice" wrote:* "Oregon's Shame—OR4 and His Family Aerial Gunned for the Sacred Cow . . ." *Howling for Justice,* April 3, 2016.

192 *Then, the state-sanctioned sniper sights on OR4:* Joe Donnelly, "Oregon Just Killed a
Family of Wolves," *Yahoo News,* April 2, 2016.

192 *OR4 didn't just belong to Oregon:* Gaskill, "Eulogy for a Wolf."

193 *"I think it's inevitable that other wolves will follow:* Carter Niemeyer, *Wolfland* (Boise,
ID: Bottlefly Press, 2016). Niemeyer is also quoted in the documentary film *OR7—The
Journey.*

194 *But in March of 2016 remote cameras again picked up OR7:* Laura Frazier, "OR-7 'Appears
Well' in First Sighting Since Failure of GPS Collar," *Oregonian,* April 6, 2016.

194 *And his yearling pups were caught in a time-lapse video:* Kelly House, "OR-7's Yearling
Pups Caught on Camera; Second Litter Has Been Born," *Oregonian,* July 7, 2015; *The
Oregonian* photo gallery of OR7s pups: Terry, "OR7: Biologists Confirm Oregon Wolf
Has at Least 2 Pups,"

194–195 *USFW, the Center for Biological Diversity, and the Humane Society:* Zach Urness,
"Oregon Wolf Killed by Poacher, $20,000 Reward Offered," *Statesman Journal,* Octo-
ber 19, 2016.

195 *Along with news of OR28's death, there are worries:* Beckie Elgin, "Is Journey in Trouble?," *Wolves and Writing,* October 13, 2016.

195 *California's Department of Fish and Wildlife released:* "Wolf Pup Video RC3 9 August
2015," YouTube, September 4, 2015, https://youtu.be/Nj3pzWYOQ3s.

195 *"The return of the northern gray wolf is a welcome sign:* "Welcome Back, Gray Wolf," *Los
Angeles Times,* August 25, 2015.

196 *Scientists wonder whether perhaps the wolves are establishing:* Ben Orlove, "Did Glaciers
Lure Wolves Back to California?" reprinted from *GlacierHub* in *EarthSky Voices,* August
28, 2015.

196 *It concludes with the telling statistic:* Editorial Board, "Celebrate the Return of Wolves to
California," *Press Democrat,* March 26, 2016.

198 *The Nez Perce tribe, who, like the wolves, have lived:* The Wolf Education and Research
Center (WERC), Nez Perce Tribe, http://wolfcenter.org.

198 *Their newsletter,* The Sawtooth Legacy, *is required reading:* "Howling for 20 Years,"
*Sawtooth Legacy Quarterly* (WERC publication) (Winter 2016).

198 *In their weekly Radio Wild educational podcast series:* Radio Wild, http://wolfcenter
.org/site/learn/radiowild.html.

CHAPTER 14. SHEEP HIGHWAY: COEXISTING WITH WOLVES

200 *"This has less to do with wolves and more about: Return to the Wild: A Modern Tale of Wolf
& Man,* documentary film, April 13, 2009, www.dailymotion.com/video/x8yx4j_re
turn-to-the-wild-a-modern-tale-of_animals, 10:11 Suzanne Stone, 16:00 Doug Smith.

200 *After wolves reclaimed the landscape they accounted:* "The Truth About Wolves and Livestock," Lords of Nature: Life in a Land of Great Predators, http://lordsofnature.org/
documents/TheTruthAboutWolvesandLivestock.pdf.

200 *The Wood River Wolf Project has grown from 150 to 1,000:* The Wood River Wolf Project,
Facebook, www.facebook.com/woodriverwolfproject.

200 *Ranchers apply technology such as telemetry:* "Nonlethal Deterrents," Wood River Project, www.woodriverwolfproject.org/tools.

201 *These tools are part of the "Band Kits" that the project:* "Livestock and Wolves Wood River Wolf Project," Defenders of Wildlife, www.defenders.org/sites/default/files/publications/coexisting-with-wolves-in-idahos-wood-river-valley.pdf.

201 *Livestock guardian dogs (LGDs) are breeds like:* "Our Guide to Training Pyr's," Milk and Honey Farm, www.milkandhoneyfarm.com/dogs/training.html; "Puppies, Livestock Guardian Dogs in Training," YouTube, January 3, 2014, https://youtu.be/8m S8yia_z7M; "Working Livestock Guardian Dogs in Training (4 Months Old)," YouTube, August 6, 2013, https://youtu.be/nK_U89_xKDo; Jamie Penrith, "How to Stop a Dog from Chasing Sheep Using Professional Dog Training," YouTube, March 23, 2013, https://youtu.be/CpdvFaXnvyg.

202 *These puppies are not raised to bond with humans:* Jan Dohner, "I Just Brought Home a Livestock Guardian Dog. Now What?" *Mother Earth News,* August 18, 2016.

203 *Everyone was keenly aware that right over the border:* Nicholas Geranios, "State Learns Sad Lesson with Wedge Pack Wolf Hunt," *Seattle Times,* October 7, 2012.

203 *Calling the lethal removal a "last resort":* Becky Kramer, "Killing Washington Wolf Pack Cost $77,000," *Spokesman-Review, Seattle Times* blogs, November 14, 2012, http://blogs.seattletimes.com/today/2012/11/killing-washington-wolf-pack-cost-77000.

204 *Stone criticized Peavey for letting pregnant ewes:* Becky Kramer, "Wolf Project Shows Promise for Sheep Herds, Wolf Pack," *Spokesman-Review,* December 18, 2012.

204 *By October Baldeon and the field technicians marched:* Ibid.

205 *Field and staff volunteers for the Wood River Wolf Project:* Fernando Najera, "Home on the Range: A Day in the Life of the Wood River Wolf Project, Where Wolves and Livestock Share the Landscape," Defenders of Wildlife, October 28, 2014, www.defendersblog.org/2014/10/home-range; "Overview of the Wood River Wolf Project," Information Guidelines, https://static1.squarespace.com/static/56f46eb48259b5654136fce5/t/57 0ebca027d4bd2e542f8b44/1460583600972/WRWP+Volunteer+Protocol.pdf.

205 *In most instances it hasn't taken much to keep wolves away:* Return to the Wild, documentary film.

205 *The Lava Lake Institute was founded in 1999:* "Conservation Efforts at Lava Lake Ranch," Lava Lake Lamb, www.lavalakelamb.com/lava-lake-story/conservation/#145641926 5805-c5259435-4e30.

206 *But when they needed to use their land again so as not to overgraze:* Kramer, "Wolf Project Shows Promise for Sheep Herds, Wolf Pack."

206 *Stevens concluded, "The goal was not just to keep the sheep safe:* Ibid.

206 *Once again helicopters right across the border in Washington were searching:* Alex Johnson, "Washington to Kill 11 of State's 90 Endangered Gray Wolves for Preying on Cows," *NBC News,* August 23, 2016, www.nbcnews.com/news/us-news/washington -kill-11-state-s-90-endangered-gray-wolves-preying-n636851; press coverage of Profanity Peak pack wolf killings: Kale Williams, "Entire Washington Wolf Pack to be Killed After Attacks on Cattle," *Oregonian/Oregon Live,* August 23, 2016; Rich Landers, "Profanity Peak Wolf Pack to be Exterminated After Cattle Kills," *Spokesman-Review,* August 20, 2016; "Lethal Action to Protect Sheep from Huckleberry Wolf Pack FAQ," WDFW, http://wdfw.wa.gov/conservation/gray_wolf/huckleberry_faq.html; Emily Schwing, "Authorized Wolf Killings Already Underway in Washington State," NPR/ KUOW Seattle, August 25, 2016, http://kuow.org/post/authorized-wolf-killings -already-underway-washington-state; "WDFW to Remove Profanity Peak Wolf Pack," Stevens County Cattlemen, August 5, 2016, https://stevenscountycattlemen.com /2016/08/06/wdfw-to-remove-profanity-pack.

208 *The highly unpopular kill orders for the entire Profanity Peak pack:* Jamie Rappaport

Clark, "Defenders of Wildlife: Protecting and Recovering Wolves," *Huffington Post*, August 26, 2016.

209   *Wolf advocacy groups who had signed on to the WAG protocol:* Daniel Person, "Why Not All Wolf Advocates Oppose Killing the Profanity Peak Pack," *Seattle Weekly*, August 25, 2016.

209   *As the* Seattle Times *noted, Washington "faces backlash:* "Washington State Faces Backlash on All Sides Over Wolf Killings," NPR/KUOW.org, August 26, 2016, http://kuow .org/post/washington-state-faces-backlash-all-sides-over-wolf-killings.

209   *For these longtime wolf advocates—as well as the others:* "Tenino's Wolf Haven Among Groups Promoting Dialogue Over State's Plan to Kill Wolves," *Chronicle*, August 25, 2016.

212   *A Cowlitz tribal leader from Protect the Wolves:* Seerat Chabba, "Proposed Wolf Killings in Washington Spark Outrage Amongst Conservation Groups, Tribes," *International Business Times*, August 26, 2016.

213   *The* Seattle Times *had just broken a front-page story citing:* Lynda Mapes, "Profanity Peak Wolf Pack in State's Gun Sights After Rancher Turns Out Cattle on Den," *Seattle Times*, August 25, 2016.

213   *He concluded that the killing of cows by:* Mapes, "Profanity Peak Wolf Pack in State's Gun Sights After Rancher Turns Out Cattle on Den."

213   *Washington State University then immediately issued:* Robert Strenge, "WSU Statement Clarifying Comments on Wolf Pack," *WSU News*, August 31, 2016.

213   *Amidst death threats to both WDFW officials and ranchers:* Alison Morrow, "Wolf Pack Killing Prompts Death Threats," *King 5 News*, August 30, 2016, www.king5.com/ tech/science/environment/wolf-pack-killing-prompts-death-threats/310874679.

213   *WDFW's Donny Mortarello had publicly defended:* Lynda Mapes, "Claim That Rancher Turned Out Wolves on Den Untrue, WSU Says," *Seattle Times*, August 31, 2016.

213–214  *In an interview with the local television station Mortarello:* Tracy Staedter, "Washington Wolf Cull Won't Save Livestock: Study," *Seeker*, September 9, 2016.

214   *Stevens County Cattlemen's website headline:* Heather Smith Thomas, "Dealing with Wolves," *Progressive Cattleman*, February 24, 2016.

215   *This deeper tension between states' rights and the feds:* Don Jenkins, "Washington County Authorizes Action Against Wolves," *Capital Press*, August 19, 2016

215   *"Thumbing your nose at state law doesn't engender:* "Conservationists Express Outrage That Entire Pack of Wolves, 12 Percent of State Population, to Be Killed for Preying on Livestock on Public Lands," Center for Biological Diversity, August 24, 2016.

215   *"Public lands have to be managed differently:* Carter Niemeyer quoted in Lynda Mapes, "Death Threats, New Conflict Over Killing of Wolves," *Seattle Times*, August 30, 2016.

215   *New research has shown that the Washington wolf cull:* Adrian Treves, "Predator Control Should Not Be a Shot in the Dark," research study by Miha Krofel, Jeannine McManus, Ecological Society of America, http://faculty.nelson.wisc.edu/treves/pubs/Treves_ Krofel_McManus.pdf%20.

216   *Robert Crabtree, chief scientist and founder of Yellowstone:* Ben Goldfarb, "No Proof That Shooting Predators Saves Livestock," *Science*, September 7, 2016.

216   *The federal Wildlife Services, which kills millions:* Darryl Fears, "This Little-Noticed Court Settlement Will Probably Save Millions of Animals," *Washington Post*, October 13, 2016.

216   *Wolf advocates had held a rally in Washington's state capital:* "Wolf Advocates Rally in Olympia," *King 5 News*, September 2, 2016, www.king5.com/news/wolf-advocates -rally-in-olympia/312751813.

216   *Other protesters said lethal removal is bad policy:* "Protesters Rally to Stop Wolf Pack Killing," *King 5 News*, September 2, 2016, www.king5.com/tech/science/environment /protesters-rally-to-stop-wolf-pack-killing/312724982.

218 *Wolves prefer to hunt wild game that is running away:* Temple Grandin, "Experts Say Ranching Done Right Improves the Environment and Wildlife Habitat," *Beef Magazine*, February 26, 2015; Lynda Mapes, "Profanity Peak Wolf Pack in State's Gun Sights after Rancher Turns Out Cattle on Den; 6 Wolves Killed So Far," *Yakima Herald*, August 26, 2016.

218 *Stone hopes that in response to this highly controversial culling:* Beckie Elgin, "Washington vs. Wolves," *Wolves and Writing*, August 25, 2016.

220 *Conservation Northwest's Mitchell Friedman hoped:* Mitch Friedman, "Profanity Gets the Best and Worst of Me," Conservation Northwest, August 31, 2016.

220 *In late October WDFW announced that lethal removal:* "WDFW Stops Killing Wolves from Profanity Peak Wolf Pack," *Northwest Cable News*, October 19, 2016.

221 *What if those public dollars were reserved for ranchers:* Joseph Dussault, "Can Washington State's Wolves and Ranchers Find a Way to Coexist?" *Christian Science Monitor*, August 26, 2016.

CHAPTER 15. EL LOBO RETURNS HOME

223 *In the spring of 2015 I visited Wolf Haven International:* Diane Gallegos, Wendy Spencer, interview with author, April 6, 2016.

223 *the first litters of Mexican gray wolf pups born there in:* Wendy Spencer, "At Long Last, Pups!" *Wolf Tracks*, Fall 2015.

223 *These critically endangered Mexican gray wolves are growing:* "Conservation," Wolf Haven International, http://wolfhaven.org/conservation.

225 *F1222 (Hopa):* Born at the Endangered Wolf Center, Eureka, Missouri, www.endan geredwolfcenter.org.

225 *M1067 (Brother):* Born at Wolf Haven International, Tenino, Washington, Wolf Haven International, http://wolfhaven.org.

227 *We all smiled as the father wolf raised his handsome head:* "Mexican Wolf Dad at Wolf Haven Shows Pups How to Howl," YouTube, June 30, 2015, https://youtu.be/EulEDZqqWfk.

227 *El Lobo, the Mexican gray wolf subspecies:* Tom Lynch, *El Lobo* (Salt Lake City: University of Utah Press, 2005).

228 *Now, in 2016, there are still only 12 to 17 Mexican wolves:* Wendy Spencer, "At Long Last—Pups!," *Wolf Tracks*, Spring 2016, 19.

228 *Ted Turner's Ladder Ranch—a prerelease wolf-recovery facility:* Turner Endangered Species Fund, http://tesf.org/prj-mw.html.

228 *Cross-fostering is a survival strategy of moving captive-born pups:* "Cross-Fostering," *International Wolf Center* magazine, Summer 2015.

229 *The majority of the state's residents welcomed this decision:* "Our View: Releasing Wolves the Right Thing to Do," *Santa Fe New Mexican*, October 17, 2015.

230 *Phillips noted that "the commissioners indicated:* Rebecca Moss, "Ladder Ranch Wolf Program Resumes with State's OK," *Santa Fe New Mexican*, February 26, 2016.

230 *Mexico began its wolf reintroduction program in 2011:* Megan Gannon, "First Litter of Wild Wolf Pups Born in Mexico," *Discovery News, Live Science*, July 22, 2014; "Mexico Reports Litter of Mexican Gray Wolves Born in Wild for First Time in Decades," New Mexico Wilderness Alliance, October 19, 2015; Megan Gannon, "First Litter of Wild Wolf Pups Born in Mexico," *Live Science*, July 21, 2014.

232 *The pups have often played a kind of how-many-wolves:* "Den Box Game (or How Many Wolves Fit on a Roof?)," YouTube, March 1, 2016, https://youtu.be/WgT_89ggjno.

232 *Quietly Gallegos explains what's happening:* Dr. Mark Johnson, Global Wildlife Resources, http://wildliferesources.com/perspectives.

233 *It is a profound experience, even to watch over remote cameras:* "Mexican Wolf Family," YouTube, March 1, 2016, https://youtu.be/EB3QldLeRBA.

233 *Grandin, a high-functioning autistic author and inventor:* Mac McClelland, "This Is What Humane Slaughter Looks Like. Is It Good Enough?" *Modern Farmer,* April 17, 2013.

237 *Once back in the wild, these Mexican wolves may travel forty miles:* Jason Mark, *Satellites in the High Country: Searching for the Wild in the Age of Man* (Washington, DC: Island Press, 2000); Jason Mark, "Can Wolves Bring Back Wilderness: [Excerpt]," *Scientific American,* October 9, 2015.

238 *News of cross-fostering success soon buoyed hopes:* Lauren Villagran, "Two Newborn Wolf Pups Release into a Wild Den," *Albuquerque Journal,* April 29, 2016; Rebecca Moss, "Gray Wolf Pups Released into N.M. Wild," *Santa Fe New Mexican,* April 29, 2016.

238 *Missouri's Endangered Wolf Center calls cross-fostering:* Michael Robinson, "Mexican Gray Wolves Need Rescuing from Politics," *Albuquerque Journal,* June 9, 2016.

238 *New Mexico immediately announced its plan to sue:* Cristina Eisenberg, "El Lobo's Uncertain Future," *Huffington Post,* May 26, 2015. See also "El Lobo's Uncertain Future," Cristina Eisenberg, http://cristinaeisenberg.com/?p=470.

238 *Many scientists and wolf advocates fear that New Mexico's resistance:* Susan Montoya Bryan, "New Mexico Seeks to Stop Feds from Releasing Wolves," *San Antonio Express,* May 13, 2016.

239 *"It's devastating to the pack to lose an alpha":* Regina Mossotti quoted in Elizabeth Miller, "Cornered: Mexican Wolf Management to Appease Livestock Producer May Run Out the Clock on Recovery," *Santa Fe Reporter,* June 15, 2016.

239 *The struggle between state and federal wildlife agencies:* María Inés Taracena, "Court Settlement Forces Fish and Wildlife to Have a Recovery Plan for Mexican Gray Wolves by 2017," *Tucson Weekly,* April 27, 2016.

239 *The Center for Biological Diversity urges that New Mexico:* "Step Aside, New Mexico, It's Time to Release More Wolves," Wolf Conservation Center, April 21, 2016.

239 *and wolf recovery has huge public support in the Southwest:* "One Million Facebook Supporters Rooting for Tiny Southwest Population of Endangered Mexican Gray Wolves," Lobos of the Southwest, press release, June 5, 2015, http://mexicanwolves .org/index.php/news/1461/51/Press-Release-One-Million-Facebook-Supporters -Rooting-for-Tiny-Southwest-Population-of-Endangered-Mexican-Gray-Wolves.

239 *In late fall of 2016 an Arizona judge issued a court order:* Susan Montoya Bryan, "Court Mandates New Recovery Plan for Mexican Grey Wolves," *Brandon Sun,* October 18, 2016.

239 *A recent Humane Society study of eighteen states' game:* Elizabeth Miller, "Cornered," *Santa Fe Reporter,* June 15, 2016.

240 *Not much has changed since 1986 when Ted Williams:* Ted Williams, quoted in Miller, "Cornered."

240 *As Sharman Apt Russell writes in* The Physics of Beauty: Sharman Apt Russell, "The Physics of Beauty," excerpted from *Kill the Cowboy* (Cambridge, MA: Perseus Publishing, 1993, 2001).

240 *In the late fall of 2016 Mexico's National Commission:* "Mexico Wolf Pair Welcomes Third Litter of Wild-Born Pups," *Northern Arizona Gazette,* September 7, 2016.

## EPILOGUE. "SPEAKING FOR WOLVES"

*Video of the Junction Butte wolf family:* "Junction Butte Pack in Yellowstone," YouTube, April 10, 2015, https://youtu.be/cvsO2ZhM_Xo.

*Photos of the Yellowstone wolf families:* "Update on the Junction Butte Pack and lover boy Twin," Running Wolf Nature Photography by Deby Dixon, Facebook, February 20, 2015, www.facebook.com/debydixonphotography/posts/785392398180733.

243 *I've also returned to Yellowstone to cover the grassroots Speak for Wolves:* West Yellowstone, July 2016 and July 2017, www.speakforwolves.org.

244 *Lynch details the Junction Butte family dynamics:* Kathie Lynch, "Yellowstone Wolf Update: June 2016," *Wildlife News*, June 4, 2016; Kathie Lynch, "Yellowstone Wolf Update: December 2015," *Wildlife News*, December 7, 2015.

245 *Long-term wolf studies at the Yellowstone Center for Research:* "Yellowstone Science: Celebrating 20 Years of Wolves," *Yellowstone Science* 24, no. 1 (June 2016), 15: Douglas Smith, "Motherhood and Wolves" (citing McNulty 2001 research), 43; and Smith, "Women in Science," 79 "Five Questions: Three Scientists at the Forefront of Wolf Ecology Answer the Same Questions About Wolf Biology and Management."

245 *Entire wolf families have been decimated by mange:* Brett French, "Mange Changes Yellowstone Wolves' Hunting, Travel and Food Needs," *Billings Gazette*, April 2, 2016.

245 *But mange is still a problem:* Megan Gannon, "Yellowstone Wolves Hit by Disease," *Live Science*, September 10, 2012.

248 *Such long-term study, says Douglas Smith:* "Wolf Expert Doug Smith on the Yellowstone Wolf Project," *Nature*, PBS, available on YouTube, July 19, 2011, https://youtu.be/CZnayct6uZg.

249 *the critically endangered red wolves:* Caroline Hudson, "Red Wolf Film Seeks to Educate NC Residents," *Washington Daily News*, July 8, 2016.

249 *A DNA study from Princeton University offers genetic evidence:* Carl Zimmer, "DNA Study Reveals the One and Only Wolf Species in North America," *New York Times*, July 27, 2016.

249 *Even if they are not pure wolves, Rutledge says, these hybrid:* Susa Wolpert, "Should the Gray Wolf Keep its Endangered Species Protection?" *UCLA Newsroom*, July 27, 2016.

250 *Yellowstone's success has inspired a European rewilding movement:* George Monbiot, *FERAL: Rewilding the Land, the Sea, and Human Life* (Chicago: University of Chicago Press, 2014), 118.

251 *Several other Native men spoke at the conference:* Rain Bear Stands Last and David Bearshield, interview with author, West Yellowstone, July 17, 2016; "Feds Announce Proposed Rule to Delist and Trophy Hunt Grizzly. Oglala Lakota Vice President Tom Poor Bear Responds," GOAL, www.goaltribal.org/feds-announce-proposed-rule-to-delist.

253 *Rick McIntyre has been spotting and teaching the public:* Rick McIntyre, "A Peak Life Experience: Watching Wolves in Yellowstone National Park," National Park Service, Yellowstone, www.nps.gov/yell/learn/ys-24-1-a-peak-experience-watching-wolves-in-yellowstone-national-park.htm.

253 *In the thirty-four attacks that researchers have witnessed:* Leo Leckie, "Gray Wolves Support Each Other in Times of Danger," *Yellowstone Reports*, June 29, 2016.

253 *McIntyre also has a recent theory that dogs:* Dean, "Pack Man."

254 *Now McIntyre is practicing what he does so well:* Rick McIntyre, Yellowstone Staff Profile, November 25, 2008, www.ypf.org/site/News2?page=NewsArticle&id=5137.

256 *M21's death at the old age of nine affected McIntyre:* Dean, "Pack Man."

258 *But in a nod to wolf advocates, the Montana Fish and Wildlife Commission:* Michael Wright, "Commission Rejects Tripling Wolf Hunting Quota Near Yellowstone," *Bozeman Daily Chronicle*, May 12, 2016.

258 *"Wildness needs wolves," wrote Durward L. Allen:* Durward L. Allen, *Wolves of Minong: Their Vital Role in a Wild Community* (Boston: Houghton Mifflin, 1979), cited in "Yellowstone Science: Celebrating 20 Years of Wolves," 11.

# ACKNOWLEDGMENTS

Every book has its believers, those allies who help the author find her way through the seeming wilderness of creation. From the beginning Merloyd Lawrence was the editorial guide for *Wolf Nation*, helping me build a narrative arc. It was at Merloyd's urging that *Wolf Nation* strives to be both historical and yet up to date, combining science with storytelling. Sarah Jane Freymann, my longtime literary agent and coauthor on *Your Life Is a Book,* is my wisest ally in all my writing. I cannot imagine doing a book without her brilliant counsel, her bracing call-and-response. My fiercely talented editorial assistant, Hailey Dowling, kept pace with the revisions and tight deadlines. She is not only my right hand; she is another set of keen eyes and a quick-witted editor, with an impressive literary sensibility. My trusted, longtime editor, the writer and publisher Marlene Blessing, has lent me her guidance and poetic insights for thirty years. It was my great fortune that Kelley Roe Yavorsky line edited and midwifed *Wolf Nation* before birthing her own daughter. My expert researcher, Mike Scstrez, ploughed through many scientific publications to fact check, but he also challenged me on some of my own dearly held opinions. Another of my wolf researchers, Anne Griggs, lent me her wolf library, her years of Yellowstone activism, and her lifelong devotion to canis lupus.

This book is built upon many valiant voices of wolf advocates whose interviews make *Wolf Nation* a chorus, not just a solo: Yellowstone's "Wolf Man," Rick McIntyre, has studied and taught thousands of people about wolves for decades. When I was covering the 1995 wolf reintroduction to Yellowstone, it was Rick who firmly told me, "The wolf needs storytellers." His stories have forever changed the way we understand and value wolves. I am especially thankful for in-depth and remarkable conversations about wolves with Amaroq Weiss of the Center for Biological Diversity; formidable French classical pianist Helene Grimaud, founder of the Wolf Conservation Center, and Maggie Howell, its director; far-sighted wolf biologist Christina Eisenberg;

the knowledgeable Suzanne Stone of the Defenders of Wildlife; and those enduring wolf champions Wendy Spencer, Diane Gallegos, and Kim Young of Wolf Haven International.

Others whose wolf stories and science have profoundly influenced and inspired this book are Wolf Fund advocate and author Renee Askins; the late, great wolf researcher Gordon Haber; Alaska's Vic van Ballenberghe; Yellowstone Wolf Project leader Douglas Smith; the "Living with Wolves" researchers, Jim and Jamie Dutcher; Laurie Lyman of Yellowstone Reports; and Story Warren of Kids4Wolves. Helpmates for this book include the French artist Virginie Baude of Among the Wolves Studio, Brett Haverstick of Speak for Wolves, and the Native wildlife activists David Bearshield, Rain Bear Stands Last—and always the revelations of my longtime coauthor, Linda Hogan, whose essay "Deify the Wolf" should be required reading for all wildlife managers. This book is graced by wildlife artist William Harrison's gorgeous illustrations, Jane Raese's elegant book design, the reassuring expertise of Christine Marra's editorial production, and the hardworking publicist Michael Giarratano. Wolf portraits by wildlife photographers and my often coauthors, Annie Marie Musselman and Robin Lindsey, enliven my study and screen as I write. The intuitive Yeats scholar Anne DeVore has helped me navigate the literary life for decades.

Every author needs muses, and mine are both animal and human: my father, Chief Emeritus of the US Forest Service, first generously called me to meet him and witness Alaska's 1993 Wolf Summit; my mother has filled my home with wolf art; my brother, Dana Mark, with his daughters and family, offers such support and loving kindness; my smart and witty friend Tracey Conway and her Siberian husky, Ella; Vanessa Adams, my traveling editorial assistant and photographer; my chosen sister, the editor and publisher Maureen Michelson; my musical mentor, Dianochka Shvets; my neighbor and time twin, Mindy Exum; and the gifted acupuncturists who keep me healthy and productive, Jim and Carey. The weekly dialogue with my students in our Salish Sea Writers community sustains my own work. I'm always amused and grateful for the felines Loki and Tao, who sit on my lap as I write—and are no longer startled by haunting wolf howls echoing out of my computer. Finally, my deepest gratitude to the wolves who have endured our history yet still claim their birthright in our wild lands.

# INDEX

# ABOUT THE AUTHOR

As a novelist and nature writer, Brenda Peterson's curiosity about and respect for nature radiates through her twenty books, which range from her first memoir, *Build Me an Ark: A Life with Animals*, chosen as a Best Spiritual Book of 2001, to three novels, one of which, *Duck and Cover*, was chosen by *New York Times* as a Notable Book of the Year. Her second memoir, *I Want to Be Left Behind: Finding Rapture Here on Earth*, was selected by the *Christian Science Monitor* as among the Top Ten Best Non-Fiction Books and chosen as an Indie Next and a Great Read.

Her nonfiction books include *Living by Water* and the National Geographic book *Sightings: The Gray Whale's Mysterious Journey*. Peterson's anthology, *Intimate Nature: The Bond Between Women and Animals*, is taught in university courses. Her nonfiction has appeared in numerous national newspapers, journals, and magazines, including the *New York Times, Chicago Tribune, San Francisco Chronicle, Seattle Times, Sierra, Reader's Digest*, and *Christian Science Monitor*. Oprah.com and the Oprah Book Club Newsletter often featured her *Your Life Is a Book: How to Craft and Publish Your Memoir*. Peterson's novels include *Animal Heart, River of Light, Becoming the Enemy, The Drowning World*, and *Tattoo Master*. Children's books include *Leopard and Silkie* and *Seal Pup Rescue*, named an Outstanding Science Book for Students K–12, and the forthcoming *Wild Orca* and *Lobo: A Wolf Family Returns Home*. Her recent best-selling photo-essay book is *Wolf Haven: Sanctuary and the Future of Wolves in North America*.

Peterson lives in Seattle. For the past two decades she has studied and written about animals, especially marine mammals and wolves. Since 1993 Peterson has contributed environmental commentary to NPR and is a frequent contributor for *The Huffington Post*. Read more about Peterson's books on her website, www.BrendaPetersonBooks .com.